KINGS OF CONVERGENCE

KINGS OF
THE FIGHT FOR

CONVERGENCE
CONTROL OF CANADA'S MEDIA

GORDON PITTS

DOUBLEDAY CANADA

TO ELAINE, AS ALWAYS

Doubleday Canada and colophon are trademarks.

National Library of Canada Cataloguing in Publication Data
Pitts, Gordon
Kings of convergence : the fight for control of Canada's media /
Gordon Pitts.

Includes bibliographical references and index.
ISBN 0-385-65836-2

1. Mass media—Canada—Biography. 2. Mass media—Canada.
I. Title.

P92.5.A1P58 2002   302.23'092'271   C2002-902064-6

Jacket design: Bill Douglas
Text design: Carla Kean
Printed and bound in the USA

Published in Canada by
Doubleday Canada, a division of
Random House of Canada Limited

Visit Random House of Canada Limited's website: www.randomhouse.ca

BVG   10 9 8 7 6 5 4 3 2 1

CONTENTS

INTRODUCTION: THE GANG OF FIVE   I

PART 1 THE PLAYERS
1/ The Tao of Ted   15
2/ The Shaw Redemption   35
3/ All about Izzy   53
4/ The Son Also Rises   81
5/ The Full Monty   97

PART 2 THE DEALS
6/ Bells and Whistles   115
7/ Citizen Asper   135
8/ Vidéotron Games   155
9/ Rogers and Me   173
10/ A Corus Line   189

PART 3 THE FUTURE
11/ Okay, Who's Left?   207
12/ Life after Ted?   231
13/ The River Heights Kids   249
14/ JR's Dynasty   271
15/ The Perils of Pierre Karl   287
16/ Content and Discontent   301

CONCLUSION: THE LAST MOGULS   323
ACKNOWLEDGEMENTS   333
INDEX   335

INTRODUCTION THE GANG OF FIVE

IZZY ASPER IS UNDER FIRE, AND HE ISN'T BACKING DOWN an inch. Standing on the stage in a conference room at Vancouver's Bayshore Hotel, the portly, combative chairman of CanWest Global Communications is confronting allegations that he is trampling on the independence of his local newspapers, which constitute by far the largest chain in Canada. The 2002 annual general meeting of CanWest, one of Canada's major communications companies, is unusual for the crush of non-financial journalists in attendance. On this late January day, the mass of reporters are not here to learn about CanWest's profit outlook—they want to hear what Izzy Asper has to say about freedom of the press—notably, freedom from its own proprietors. As new arrivals on the newspaper scene, Izzy and his family—including his sons David and Leonard, who is CanWest's president—have suddenly become hot copy for their apparent willingness to flout Canadian journalistic tradition. According to their critics, the Winnipeg-based Aspers are centralizing editorial opinion and stifling diversity in their major newspapers. But in Izzy's view, it is a matter of rights—the right of the newspaper owner to express his own views, and to run his own newsrooms. "No owner would back off from what we are trying to do—there is nothing to back off from," Izzy snaps, as he answers questions from a union official in the audience. In this battle of words, the Aspers have managed to alienate much of Canada's journalistic community, including a large number of their own employees.

The controversy flared up soon after the Aspers—until then, known mainly for their Global TV network—gained control of the Southam newspaper chain in a spectacular $3.2 billion deal announced in the summer of 2000. The properties they bought from newspaper baron Conrad Black included fourteen major daily newspapers, a number of Internet sites, and 50 percent of Black's beloved *National Post*—which, in a year, they would own entirely. The Aspers, reputed supporters of the Liberal Party, immediately stirred up controversy when David, in an open letter, criticized the press's handling of conflict of interest allegations against Liberal Prime Minister Jean Chrétien. The temperature rose in late 2001, when Southam began issuing centrally produced editorials from Winnipeg, as many as three a week, to run in its papers. It was a radical move in an industry where local papers in a chain were usually left free to chart their own editorial policies. Journalists at the Asper-owned Montreal *Gazette* withdrew bylines, and many signed a petition demanding the policy be revoked. Journalists' associations and academics decried CanWest's micromanaging of the local editorial pages, arguing that this practice struck at the heart of a regional paper's role.

The dispute took on a new complexion when Stephen Kimber, the head of journalism at University of King's College in Halifax, announced that he was resigning as a columnist with the Southam-owned Halifax *Daily News* because, in his view, CanWest was "slicing and dicing" his work and that of other columnists. In Kimber's final column, which was killed by *The Daily News,* he wrote that "the Aspers support the federal Liberal party. They're pro-Israel. They think rich people like themselves deserve tax breaks. They support privatizing health care delivery. And they believe their newspapers, from Victoria to St. John's, should agree with them." The spiking of the Kimber column raised the concern that the Aspers were not just imposing their own editorials, but restricting the diversity of views in their newspapers. There were more reports of columns killed, stories allegedly changed to fit the CanWest agenda, and journalists rising in protest against what they deemed to be corporate censorship and demanding a government inquiry into media concentration.

Izzy, of course, was not the first Canadian newspaper owner with strong views and a compelling need to express them. After all, he had bought his Southam newspapers from Conrad Black, a man whose mission was to bring a conservative ideological perspective to Canadian political life. But before the Aspers, there had never been owners who enjoyed such broad access to Canada's mainstream media—through the ownership of most major newspapers (commanding nearly 35 percent of the country's daily newspaper circulation), its second-largest private television network, and Canada.com, a significant Internet news source. Thirty years ago, when the Davey Commission studied the concentration of mass media, the two largest chains—FP and Southam—together totalled about the same percentage of daily newspaper circulation—but they had no significant holdings in other media.

In Izzy's opinion, the Aspers were not imposing their views, they were encouraging dissent by offering an alternative viewpoint to the Eastern Canadian soft-left consensus. In his view, he and his family were the outsiders, even though they have emerged as the most powerful force in the Canadian media, even though they are insiders with the party in power in Ottawa. The Aspers' paradox—their sense of power and powerlessness—became the most fascinating, and frustrating, issue in Canadian journalism. The debate would spark broader questions: Have the media, as Izzy contends, become fragmented to the extent that CanWest's "dominance" is just a myth propagated by his enemies? Or would a free and independent press be one of the casualties of the tidal wave of convergence and consolidation sweeping the communications industry?

Indeed, the firestorm over the Aspers' growing clout in Canadian media was just a sideshow to the powerful global changes in the first two years of the twenty-first century. The seminal event was the blockbuster US$165 billion merger of AOL and Time Warner, announced in January 2000. The merging parties were two of the United States' best-known companies. America Online—or AOL, as it had become known—was a corporate comet that had blazed out of nowhere to grab a big chunk of the new Internet economy. The other player, Time Warner, had parts that could be traced to the beginning of the century, the company of *Time* magazine legendary co-founder Henry Luce and Daffy Duck.

AOL coveted a guaranteed supply of "content"—entertainment, news, sports and information—to distribute over its powerful Internet portal, as well as access to cable broadband "pipes" to ensure that its portal and web applications would have entry to households and offices. Its stock price had been bid up to stratospheric heights in the crazy stock market of the late 1990s, but chief executive officer Steve Case and his cohorts felt they needed to lock in its high valuation by merging with or taking over a company with more tangible assets.

The ideal candidate was Time Warner, a company born of a merger in 1989 between Time, with its vast traditional media interests, and Warner Communications, the music, TV and movie powerhouse. It had content aplenty, with cartoon libraries and magazine archives and a strong regional cable system, but felt it needed access to the new media and the élan of the Internet. The world woke up on January 10, 2000, to the largest corporate merger ever, but even more significantly, the first giant convergence deal, one that blended print, music and broadcast content, and the potential of cable networks, with the magic of the Internet.

Even before the deal was announced, convergence had become part of the industry's lexicon, although its meaning was vague. Some saw it as mere consolidation, as the industry shrank to fewer and bigger players. Others saw it as some old ideas in new clothing. By owning a raft of different properties, companies had an enhanced ability to cross-promote their big shows or ambitious print articles in other media—or to sell integrated advertising packages that blended different media formats. But the revolutionary concept, embodied by AOL Time Warner, was to integrate "content" assets—a term for everything from entertainment to news and sports—with companies that controlled "the pipes" of cable, satellite, wireless and telecommunications links. The two sides needed each other: The content creators, from *Time* magazine editors to rock 'n' roller Neil Young, needed guaranteed access to as many pipes as possible. The pipe players, whose services were becoming cheaper, much like a commodity, needed must-have content to attract and keep fickle, distracted customers. Hence, the buzz-phrase "content is king." What's more, this content could now be converted to digital form and "repurposed" efficiently across television, print, radio, wireless, and broadband (that catch-all term for high-speed, high-capacity networks). That's what the AOL Time Warner deal was all about, and that dream would soon come to obsess Canada's media owners as well.

The impact of the AOL Time Warner marriage was evident the moment it was announced. Terry Kawaja, an investment banker who advised AOL in the deal, remembers breaking away from final negotiations and flying out to Scottsdale, Arizona, for the media and telecommunications conference held each year by his firm Salomon Smith Barney. When Kawaja and his fellow deal-makers landed in the desert, they were treated as conquering heroes by executives at the conference. "It was like we were coming on our chariots into the Colosseum," the Canadian-born Kawaja says. At past conferences, he had always hoped to grab a moment with Australian-American media titan Rupert Murdoch. But this time, it was Rupert Murdoch rushing up to shake the hand of Terry Kawaja, and saying, "Hey, it's a helluva deal you've got there."

Suddenly, being big was what it was all about. The convergence game was to be played across media and distribution systems by huge and highly capitalized players. The industry had been moving in this direction for some time, and other global players had been positioning themselves: Murdoch's News Corp. combined newspapers, television networks, satellite distribution and even sports teams. Vivendi of France, a former water utility, was buying Canada's Seagram, mainly to get at the liquor giant's Universal movie and music archives. Other ambitious players included Germany's Bertelsmann—an on-line, broadcasting and publishing giant—and two U.S. behemoths: Viacom, the owner of MTV, CBS and other top content assets; and Disney, with its movie studios, theme parks and ABC television network. Tribune Company, owner of the *Chicago Tribune*, was perhaps the most advanced convergence player, exploring journalistic and ad-selling synergies in its newspapers, television stations and Internet sites. And there was giant AT&T, spending hundreds of billions to add cable systems to its telephone capabilities.

"The impact of AOL Time Warner was to up the ante in the media world," Terry Kawaja would say later. The big communications players suddenly realized the challenge of creating new and compelling content. All the new content vehicles being created seemed extremely narrow— the next cable channel might be for "seventeen- to nineteen-year-old curlers from Saskatchewan," Kawaja joked. There were content assets with broader appeal, but to buy them, you'd have to raise the bidding. The media game had become a real estate play, and it seemed they weren't making much new real estate anymore. That set off a feeding frenzy to grab the best properties still available. It was fuelled by a dot-com mentality that, at the height of a stock market boom, caused even conservative companies to consider using their high-flying stock as a takeover currency.

The Canadian players were watching what was happening in New York, Chicago and Paris. In Montreal, there were Jean Monty, the decisive CEO of BCE, the holding company for the country's largest telephone company, and Pierre Karl Péladeau, the unpredictable heir of a huge newspaper and printing empire; in Winnipeg, Izzy Asper, the pugnacious maverick who controlled Global Television, Canada's second-largest private television system; in Toronto, Ted Rogers, the scattered and brilliant cable and wireless baron; and in Calgary, the up-and-coming Shaw family—father JR, son Jim and daughter Heather— ambitious media and cable owners.

In Canada, the shortage of prime media assets was perhaps more notable than in the United States. There were only three national TV networks and one of them was the publicly owned Canadian Broadcasting Corporation. A new generation of specialty TV channels had emerged, but all the analog TV slots were taken up, and Canada's TV universe had not yet moved into the digital age. A few big companies were buying up much of the radio industry, and newspapers were mainly local with a couple of exceptions—*The Globe and Mail* and the fledgling

National Post, which were locked in a scorched-earth circulation war. Aided by a more favourable regulatory climate for cross-media ownership, the sector had gone through dramatic consolidation, as family companies had gobbled up other family companies, until there were only a handful left. It meant that in the overheated stock markets of 2000, any deals would be big and pricey, at least by Canadian standards, but the acquirers would suddenly own strong national multi-media franchises.

In the wave of the AOL Time Warner tsunami, the backrooms of Canada's media industry began to rock. Over the next seven months, the moguls would launch three deals worth more than $11 billion—a drop in the bucket compared with AOL Time Warner, but stunning from the Canadian perspective:

—In February, BCE bid $2.3 billion for the largest private television network, CTV.

—The same month, Ted Rogers went after Le Groupe Vidéotron, the giant Quebec cable company, but lost out later to an eye-popping all-cash $5.4 billion bid by Pierre Karl Péladeau.

—CanWest bought most of Conrad Black's Canadian newspapers for $3.2 billion, the biggest pure media deal in Canadian history.

And it wasn't over. Frustrated at losing Vidéotron, Ted Rogers grabbed the Toronto Blue Jays baseball team in a deal worth only $171 million but essential to his sports-based convergence strategy. Then, six months after announcing its CTV takeover, BCE added *The Globe and Mail* and blended it with CTV and Sympatico to create a new media / old media powerhouse called Bell Globemedia, in partnership with the Thomson family. Corus Entertainment, the new content engine of the Shaw family, had launched itself on a buying spree, adding $1.5 billion worth of broadcasting and production assets.

When the smoke cleared, Canada had five powerful media groups, all of which had made huge—and very different—bets on convergence. But the deals were also significant for who was selling, as well as buying. Conrad Black had torn like a hurricane through the genteel world of Canadian newspapers in the 1990s. Now, just as abruptly, he was departing, and would eventually leave even his prized *National Post* in the hands of the Aspers. The Thomsons, Canada's richest family, were selling off their newspapers, including the once untouchable *Globe and Mail,* and moving more resolutely into electronic publishing, largely in the United States, while retaining a piece of BCE's media complex. Torstar, torn by divided ownership, would stay on the sidelines. Western Canadian telephone giant Telus decided that it would not own consumer-related content but would challenge BCE's telecommunications franchise in Eastern Canada. Everybody was making a bet—and in some cases, the biggest bets consisted of not putting any money on the table.

The new Kings of Convergence were an odd lot in their diversity, but a cross-section of Canada: Ted Rogers, the old-boy WASP; the Shaws, Ontario farmers turned Alberta city slickers; Pierre Karl Péladeau, the son of a separatist sympathizer; Izzy Asper, the child of Jewish immigrants from Ukraine; and Jean Monty, the Jesuit-trained professional manager. And these people knew each other well—too well. They were the best of friends and worst of enemies. Ted Rogers had battled BCE's Bell Canada subsidiary since he first started building cable systems in the 1960s. Inside Rogers's company, BCE was still the "evil empire." Izzy Asper was an implacable foe of BCE's CTV network, which he saw as a personification of the Eastern Canadian elites he despised. CanWest's *National Post* and BCE's *Globe and Mail* were waging a take-no-prisoners newspaper war. It's rare to find an industry riven by such personal animus, where the combatants know each other by first names—as in "Ted" or "Izzy" or "JR" or in Pierre Karl Péladeau's case, "PKP" or just "PK." (Jean Monty was almost always just "Monty.") They battled for market share, for broadcast licences, for advertising and subscriptions and to be top dog in the convergence game. Perhaps such enmity is intensified by close quarters. These companies had flourished in regulated oligopolies or monopolies, largely shielded from foreign competition by the federal government. Now, they were the last moguls, the final stage in a Darwinian evolution that had seen the media herd in Canada reduced to five behemoths.

But as the Big Five continued their consolidation binge, they were already looking ahead to another stage—the expansion of U.S. ownership into this last truly Canadian industry. The media barons were agents, victims and beneficiaries of the onrushing global consolidation. Television programming in Canada was already dominated by U.S. studios and U.S. cultural values, as *Friends, The West Wing* and *Frasier* ruled the nation's sets. Now the doors were expected to open to direct U.S. ownership of the Canadian communications industry.

First to fall would probably be the rules for distributors, which put a 20 percent ceiling on direct foreign ownership—and 33 percent on indirect ownership—of telephone and cable companies. These players, such as Telus, Shaw and Rogers, were lobbying for liberalized foreign ownership, on the grounds that they needed this capital source to modernize their networks and lift their stock prices to levels comparable to the United States. After that, how long before content players would be up for grabs? The American clamour for media to be treated as a commodity, not the soul of a nation's culture, was sure to continue relentlessly at the World Trade Organization. The prospect of higher foreign ownership would be a double-edged sword for Canadian media barons—more competition from well-financed U.S. players, but also the opportunity to sell out to buyers with deep pockets. All this convergence could turn out to be nothing more than a prelude to an irresistible payday for the mainly family companies that dominate Canada's media industry.

Government policy and regulatory decisions had favoured the building of large Canadian-owned media players, large enough to play on the world stage. The outcome of those policies was this powerful Gang of Five. How the future plays out will depend on the will of government and on the dynamics of these five companies. Four of the owners are families that have reached important points in their succession from patriarch to children. On the death of founder Pierre Péladeau, Quebecor has already done the generational transition, for better or worse; the Shaws and the Aspers are passing through the hand-over, and it seems to be going well in both cases. Rogers is a huge question mark—what will happen after Ted? At BCE, a widely held company, there was no family in charge, but professional managers who often act as if the company is their personal property. Even so, Jean Monty was the most vulnerable King of Convergence, and indeed, he was the first to fall on his sword: Under a barrage of criticism for his diversification moves, he resigned in April, 2002, before he could see whether his convergence strategy would ever bear fruit.

Monty will not be the only one whose strategy is questioned in the months and years ahead. It goes with the territory. The year 2000 saw an avalanche of deals that were not inspired by any sure-footed business model—they were bets, informed and calculated bets, on whether certain visions of the future would ever work out. The deals also represented a sharp reversal from the management thinking of the 1990s, when it was assumed that large companies didn't have to buy all the talents they need and store them under the same roof. They could contract, outsource and build alliances. Now these new deals suggested a return to conglomeration, the idea that big and diverse is best. Will these new conglomerates unravel, just as their predecessors had in the past, despite their vaunted "synergies"?

The great leap into convergence was, above all, driven by a need to own the consumer, to hold the unwavering loyalty of millions of Canadian households. Each of the players began with a slender conduit into the house—a telephone wire, in the case of BCE; coaxial cable for Rogers and Shaw; broadcast licences for the Aspers; newspapers and TV signals for Quebecor. The challenge was how to leverage that entry point into an array of indispensable services, to add pieces, as in a puzzle, to create the must-have blend of properties. Nobody was able to put together the whole puzzle. And by the time all the pieces fall into place, will consumers still want that particular offering? More important, will they pay for it? At some point, on-line purveyors can no longer afford to offer free services. The convergence players wanted to line up the brands and the services that could hold a fee-paying audience. And by the time they do, if they ever do, will the technology have already moved on, to customized newspapers, video-on-demand and personal video recorders? So far, the consumer seems more bewildered by than plugged in to the new vision.

The convergence craze was also about fear. All these executives were haunted by the prospect of being painted into a corner, forced to bend to their rivals—or even their allies. They wanted to be in control of their futures, not beholden to anyone. They felt they could not afford to be left behind in the media-buying binge. As I talked to these people, I kept hearing the same message. As Izzy Asper said, "I would have been happy with one TV station but we had to be masters of our own destiny." The great merger game of the early twenty-first century was at once offensive and defensive.

PART 1 THE PLAYERS

1 THE TAO OF TED

TED ROGERS MAY BE A FINE MAN, A GREAT CANADIAN, BUT try telling that to my neighbour. "What's your book about?" she asks me on the street one sunny February day. When I mention media moguls, she asks if Ted Rogers is one of the subjects. The mood suddenly turns dark as she launches into a fifteen-minute diatribe about Rogers Cable, about how she switched to satellite and paid her cable bill but Rogers failed to acknowledge her final payment and wouldn't leave her alone.

One day, I have lunch with a consultant, a New Zealander newly arrived in Canada. I ask him about the adjustment to a new country and he takes me through the process: great new schools, nice new house, and then he grits his teeth and practically spits out the words: "And I had to deal with Rogers." Then follows yet another impassioned outpouring on the service inadequacies of Canada's largest cable company.

When I visit John Tory Jr. in his Toronto office, the president of Rogers Cable is on the phone talking to a doctor in southwestern Ontario, who is complaining about his high-speed cable service. Tory, an old and dear friend of Ted's, appears to be the most level-headed man in the world, a perfect foil to Ted's enthusiasms and rages. By the end of the conversation, the doctor is mollified and clearly impressed that the head of the cable company has taken the time to call. The amiable Tory does a lot of that. Dealing with customer complaints is a big part of his job.

So how does Tory cope with the visceral hatred of Rogers Cable, the company, and, to some extent, Ted Rogers, the man? "My way of dealing with it is we have to change it," Tory says, as if any fool should know that. "We're having some success. It will take time." He says that on this day in 2001, surveys show that more than 85 percent of Rogers Cable clientele are satisfied with their service, and the numbers keep getting better. Tory says any lingering animosity reflects the fact that everybody loves to hate a monopoly. Even though direct-to-home satellite television has undermined Rogers' cable monopoly, people still carry around this ingrained dislike. For some Rogers-haters, that's a carry-over from the negative option billing uproar of the mid-1990s. With the introduction of new cable channels, customers were automatically bumped into new higher-cost packages unless they explicitly informed Rogers Cable that they wanted to opt out of these pricier packages. It was attacked as an outrageously sneaky gambit to get a price increase, and fuelled a noisy public protest that ended up in the House of Commons. The company's retreat was one of the most ignominious in recent Canadian corporate history. But there was no way to really punish Rogers in the pocketbook because cable customers had nowhere else to go in those days.

More recently, Rogers, as well as a number of other cable operators in North America, had to contend with the constant glitches of Excite@Home, the California company that provided the backbone network for its high-speed Internet service. Rogers was tightly connected to @Home's parent company, and was a business ally of AT&T, the largest shareholder of the California company. In the end, the Internet firm went bankrupt and Rogers—as well as other cable companies—was forced to scramble to find another network supplier. Deserved or not, the mess added to the lore of Ted Rogers as a dreamer and innovator who is unable to deliver on customer service. "That's been part of Ted's story," John Tory says. "He's never afraid to go out there and be a pioneer, knowing that when you're a pioneer, you pay a bit of a price because things won't be just perfect the day you launch them, or in three months or in six months or a year."

Why people hate Ted Rogers is, of course, of considerable interest to the tall, orange-and-grey-haired man who inhabits the corner office of the tenth floor of the Rogers Communications building on Toronto's Bloor Street. Ted Rogers often seems a bit baffled by the venom directed towards him. He suspects the vituperation is at least in part because he is so strongly associated with Toronto: the Calgary-based Shaws, who have enjoyed a similar regional cable monopoly as Rogers, escape intense antipathy. But Torontonians themselves have shown antagonism towards Rogers. A better comparison might be drawn with Montreal-based Bell Canada Enterprises—another unloved former entrenched monopoly accused of clinging to its old ways. But even BCE doesn't evoke the same degree of animosity as Rogers. Perhaps that's because BCE lacks a human focus for the animosity. Jean Monty is just the latest hired hand, part of a passing parade, but Ted Rogers really *is* Rogers Communications.

Ted feels that the anti-Rogers sentiment reflects, to some degree, the personalization of business journalism in the modern age. "It's hard now to separate the man from the company, the family from the company." Newspapers and magazines treat business leaders in the same way they used to reserve for sports and entertainment celebrities. "All of a sudden, this grey-suited person who goes to the office every day, minds his own business, is on the front page of the paper. He's got public relations people around telling him to wave his hands a bit at the meetings and show some bloody enthusiasm, now he's a star." But Ted, of course, hardly fits this image of the plodding executive, reluctantly thrust into the public eye. In the end, he agrees, the antagonism is mostly about him and the way he is: "I think it's about my personality because I'm pretty straightforward and blunt."

Indeed, Ted Rogers is a huge public personality, constantly exposed in all his contradictions. Ted can be blunt and bullying, yet quite sensitive and touching. He's also an establishment figure who works like the most insecure small businessman. This dichotomy, this split personality, is Ted's strength, and his cross to bear. Rogers has always lived a double life, growing up in the tony areas of North Toronto, but imbued with the insecure ambition of a Horatio Alger hero. He is the insider as outsider. He has almost lost his empire four or five times but he keeps bouncing back. He is a lawyer, but he has the soul of an engineer. He loves new stuff, mechanical stuff, even though the personal computer has baffled him at times.

He also loves his wife and children intensely but is perhaps the most absent father in creation. He inspires great loyalty in his managers, yet they leave him in droves, exasperated by his addictive meddling. He is, in short, everyone's crazy oddball Uncle Ted: he drives you nuts—he embarrasses you all the time—but you can't ignore him and you can't help but feel a tug of affection. His smart, funny daughter, Melinda, expresses it best: "I would want him to be always the way he is." Then, as if she is astonished to hear herself say it, she adds: "Truthfully, actually."

Ted's background and childhood are a fascinating yarn. The Rogers were old Ontarians, pacifist Quakers who entered Canada just after the American Revolution and settled around Newmarket, north of Toronto. The Rogers family eventually moved into Toronto, where Ted's great-grandfather Samuel made a fortune by selling his fuel supply company to Imperial Oil. Ted's father, also knows as Edward or Ted, was a boy genius, a tinkerer and hobbyist. He dropped out of University of Toronto to fool around with mechanical stuff. He started dabbling in business and in 1925, working out of an old Eaton's warehouse in downtown Toronto, he developed an electric radio to run off standard household current, a vast improvement over the heavy battery types that existed until then. He started a radio manufacturing company, called Rogers Majestic, to manufacture his creations. A bit of a convergence pioneer himself, he needed content to feed into his new-fangled radios. So he moved into broadcasting, starting, among other things, radio station CFRB, whose call letters were a model of cross-promotion—they stand for Canada's First Rogers Batteryless.

But on May 3, 1939, Ted Rogers Sr. drove home from the Rogers Majestic factory at the foot of Bathurst Street to the family home at 405 Glenayr Road. After dinner, as he often did, he retired to the basement to fiddle with his radios. In the late evening, his wife, Velma, awakened to the sound of a cough and moans. She rushed to the bathroom, where she found her husband hunched over the sink, unconscious, surrounded by blood and stricken with an aneurysm. He died three days later. His wife and five-year-old Ted Jr. were left with about $380,000 in property, stock and other assets, but the family had to sell the radio manufacturing company and the broadcasting assets, which meant that Ted had to start out pretty much from scratch.

It is moving how Ted has acknowledged the role of the father he hardly knew in driving him to where he is today. As his sponsored biography of his father relates, Edward Rogers Sr.'s short, purposeful life has both haunted and motivated him. One executive who has worked with both Izzy Asper and Ted Rogers says each is blessed with ordinary grey matter, but with a powerful driving force: for Izzy, it is being Jewish and an outsider; for Ted, it is the father he hardly knew. It's as if Ted has sprung from the Frank Capra movie *It's a Wonderful Life,* about the heroic father, an idealist and a dreamer, who was not a great business-man, but in life and death inspired the worshipful son. There is even a bit of Jimmy Stewart in Ted, the wide-eyed kid who wanted to change the world. But unlike the movie's hero, George Bailey, Ted has a focused aggression that can be frightening. "He has the skin of a rhino and the balls of a hippo," one of his cable industry colleagues once told journalist Matthew Fraser. And Rogers Communications is not the good old savings and loan.

Ted was born sickly, with severely limited vision in his right eye and a host of other complaints that would grow increasingly serious as he moved into adulthood. But he was lucky in the circles he moved in. He had the benefit of rich friends and backers, but also the drive to suc-ceed of someone who is more penurious than those around him. His mother, Velma, a recovering alcoholic, remarried a good man in John Webb Graham, a prominent Toronto lawyer who became Ted's friend and mentor. Ted was able to continue growing up in the same Forest Hill neighbourhood as his friends and future partners. He attended Upper Canada College, where at fourteen he ran wires from a makeshift antenna on a dormitory roof and arranged for his classmates to watch the primitive TV shows beamed in from Buffalo. Classmates remember that the earnest Ted was bullied badly at the private school.

The best thing Ted Rogers ever did was join the Tories—both the party and the family. The Tory party put him close to the Eatons and the Bassetts and he became part of the investment group that formed CFTO, a Toronto television station that was one of Canada's first independent stations and one of the foundations of the CTV television network. The party introduced him to John Diefenbaker, a "progressive conservative" who became one of his heroes, and Joe Clark, to whom Ted has remained steadfastly loyal as Conservative leader. While others in the Toronto business establishment may have dabbled with the Canadian Alliance, Ted has remained true to the party and the leader.

The Tory family was the driving force behind the great law firm Tory Tory Deslauriers & Binnington, where Ted Rogers articled as a young lawyer. More important, he became a lifelong friend of John Tory Sr., who, along with his brother Jim, has been a valued courtier to the Canadian corporate establishment. John Tory Sr. has been instrumental in nurturing two great fortunes—Thomson and Rogers—but there have been others too. Cut through the fabric of establishment Ontario and you will find the Torys everywhere. Now John Tory Jr., the onetime assistant to a former provincial Tory leader, is Ted's able lieutenant and perhaps successor as Rogers Communications CEO.

As a young man in college, Ted was always doing entrepreneurial things, such as running dance bands out of his back pocket. One New Year's Eve at the University of Toronto, he managed ten orchestras at ten different locations, with ten different sound systems. He sold tickets and had photographers take pictures of the dancing couples, but, alas, Ted himself didn't have a date that night, he later told *The Toronto Star.*

But Ted's future course was being set in other parts of the country. Cable television was making inroads in the fifties, as television was gaining a foothold in the nation's living rooms. Ted Rogers was just finishing high school at Upper Canada College when Ed Jarmain's dream was taking shape in London, Ontario. In 1952, Jarmain was running his family's dry cleaning business, but, like Ted, he had a knack for tinkering and was a bit bored with his vocation. Television had made its way to London, but there was no local station yet. Londoners couldn't pick up Toronto signals because of the Niagara escarpment, and U.S. television transmitters in Erie, Pennsylvania, and Detroit were still rudimentary. Jarmain started reading about cable TV and went down to the United States, to Pottsville, Pennsylvania, where a local retailer, with the wonderful name of Marty Malarkey, was gaining fame as one of his country's first cable operators. Malarkey was a television salesman whose customers kept returning their sets because of the poor reception in their mountain-ringed town. So Malarkey built a receiving tower on top of one of the mountains, strung some cable around to his customers' homes and mass-market television was born in the United States.

At the end of his visit to Pottsville, Jarmain asked to take a look at Malarkey's books, and he was mightily impressed. "Once I saw the numbers, I said, 'That's for me,'" recalled Jarmain, in a 2001 interview when he was in his nineties. Jarmain went home, put up a big antenna in his South London backyard, strung around some cable to fifteen local homes—he had to lend most of them TVs—and went into business. He did well and became the pioneer of the Canadian cable industry. He inspired imitators, and across the country there developed a patchwork quilt of family-owned cable operators.

These were money-spinning local monopolies, throwing out cash, and in time using their coaxial cable access to bring more and more channels and services into the home. As the world moved from *Romper Room* and *The Ed Sullivan Show* to *Mary Tyler Moore* and *The Brady Bunch,* Ed Jarmain's company started buying out smaller operations, in partnership with the theatre chain Famous Players, and became a big operator in Ontario, under the corporate name of Canadian Cablesystems. But in the late 1970s, Canadian Cablesystems was taken over and the Jarmain family was relegated to the sidelines. The new owner was an entrepreneur by the name of Ted Rogers, who suddenly emerged as the cable king of Ontario.

Ted had not been content to be a young lawyer at Torys. As an articling student in his mid-twenties, he started the company that became Rogers Communications, the holding company for his various interests. He became involved in CFTO with the help of his partners, the retailing Eaton family, newspaper publisher John Bassett and a deep-voiced television announcer named Joel Aldred. (He later had to sell his CFTO interest because of a regulatory ban on cross-media ownership.) He saw the vast promise of FM radio, with its crystal-clear signals, so in 1960 he bought a fledgling FM station in Toronto called CHFI, for $85,999. At that time only 5 percent of Toronto's homes and cars had FM reception, while AM radio enjoyed 100 percent penetration. "But I believed in the superior sound of the FM technology and felt customers would purchase FM receivers once they had the opportunity to hear the difference," Ted would later recall. "I had FM radios produced by Canadian Westinghouse and sold them at cost to build up potential listeners to CHFI." Even then Ted was a convergence pioneer. Today, of course, FM is king, and AM is struggling to find formats that work; CHFI is the most listened to radio station in Toronto and Ted has a network of more than thirty radio stations across the country.

Ted was also lucky in love. In the early sixties, he was at a party in Nassau in the Bahamas when he met Loretta Anne Robinson, the daughter of the British aristocrat Lord Martonmere, who had been a Member of Parliament for more than three decades in England and was recently governor of Bermuda. Ted asked her out on a date, but her parents turned him down. Instead they invited him to dinner, and, according to a profile by writer Jennifer Wells in *Toronto Life* magazine, Ted spent the first twenty-five minutes in the doorway discussing politics with Loretta's father. Loretta and Ted were married in September, 1963, and her parents bought a fine house on Frybrook Road in Forest Hill for their daughter. Lord Martonmere was concerned about Ted's entrepreneurial instincts, and made sure that he promised never to mortgage the house. Of course, Ted did, over and over. "We've had triple mortgages on our home to meet payrolls," he once said, "and we dared not tell her parents."

The perpetually tanned Loretta is Ted's closest confidante, and sits on the board of the holding company, Rogers Communications. She is not an aggressive participant in board discussions, but she has a strong background influence on her husband. She is also an accomplished oil painter of vividly colourful outdoor scenes, in Canada and the Bahamas, where the Rogerses have a house. The executive floor at Rogers Communications head office contains a hall called Loretta's Walk that is devoted to her work. At first the couple had trouble having children, so they adopted a child, Lisa, who was born in 1968. Then Loretta gave birth to Edward Jr. in 1970; Melinda in 1971; and Martha in 1972.

In 1966, while Ted was on vacation, he had read a book about the emerging cable industry—vacations with Ted are not real holidays. He returned to Toronto and acquired a licence to provide cable TV in one area of the city. Cable had been around for more than a decade, but it was still relatively underdeveloped in most parts of the country. Ted was not on the ground floor, but at least he was an early adopter. He did very well in cable and started to develop the rich cash flows that allowed him to start soaking up other little cable systems. His adviser and ally Phil Lind had noticed that ethnic families weren't watching TV and, as a result, were not buying cable subscriptions. So Rogers became a player in ethnic programming through its own community cable channels and then with Toronto TV station CFMT, and that helped fuel the cable demand. In time, Ted became the country's fifth largest cable supplier, and he was looking for more.

The deal for the Jarmains' Canadian Cablesystems, the country's second largest cable supplier, made Ted's reputation as a fearless deal-maker. In his creeping takeover, for a while Ted shared ownership of about half of Canadian Cablesystems with Brascan, a holding company controlled by brothers Edward and Peter Bronfman, cousins of the liquor-empire Bronfmans. But the Brascan mastermind was Jack Cockwell, a cannily ruthless South African accountant who was the custodian of the brothers' business empire. As partners, Rogers and Brascan had a shotgun clause in their agreement, stipulating that either one could trigger a sale by making a bid for the other's stake. In 1979, Ted sensed that Brascan was going to pull the trigger and buy him out. He was in Nassau at the time, and was talking regularly to his partners in Toronto. After one of those conversations, Ted rushed to the Nassau airport, hopped on a plane and, unknown to Cockwell and the Bronfmans, flew into Toronto to see Richard Thomson, chairman of the Toronto-Dominion Bank. He asked Thomson, if he had to buy out his partners, how much he could bid per share of Canadian Cablesystems. Thomson's answer: go all the way up to $21. Ted flew right back to Nassau that evening and got on the phone with Cockwell the following morning, just as if nothing had happened.

When he got back to Toronto, the Brascan team, as expected, came to his office, and after some niceties, Peter Bronfman observed that it would be tough for the two partners together to take on the entrenched management of Canadian Cablesystems. It should be only one of them, Peter said, and since Ted was in the cable business he should make the choice: Brascan would name a price, Ted could buy or sell at that price, but Ted would have to respond within three days instead of the normal thirty days for a shotgun response.

Ted replied that he would indeed give a quick answer, but he would not agree to a three-day wait—he insisted that he would respond within thirty seconds, as long as, no matter who bought or sold, the deal would close that night. Bronfman uttered the price: $18. Knowing he had the financing locked up, Ted quickly blurted out: "We buy." With his acquisition of the Brascan stake, Rogers was soon able to take over Canadian Cablesystems on his own, gaining an important building block towards a cable empire. Two years later, in 1981, he took a run at another pioneering system, Premier Cablesystems in Vancouver, and was able to acquire it too.

But there were some troubling developments that have afflicted Rogers ever since. His friends like to say that Ted has "a value-creation strategy"—in other words, he builds things, he adds stock market value, but he doesn't really make money—at least, hardly ever. He tends to take on huge debt and hates to issue common equity, which would dilute his own holdings. Although the company rarely makes a cent after taxes and interest, cash flow is usually strong, and bankers, particularly Toronto-Dominion, would generally lend against the cash. But his companies were always very close to the line financially. "One year when we just didn't have sufficient cash to pay all the suppliers, I put all the bills in a hat and after meeting the payroll I'd keep drawing invoices until we ran out of money," Ted recalls. "Can you believe that some creditors didn't appreciate such innovation and would shout at me over the telephone? When I said I was getting a headache and asked them to stop yelling, they sometimes angrily asked me what I would do if they kept yelling. 'Very simple,' I said, 'I won't put your invoice in the hat next week.' Nobody sued—they all got paid with interest. No one in my lifetime has ever lost one cent in receivables or interest on a Rogers account."

Ted also collected bright young managers, including a transfusion of talent from Canadian Cablesystems, such as Colin Watson and Graham Savage. They came because they wanted to work with Ted, who was the most exciting entrepreneur around. He was that rare CEO with a compelling vision. But working for Ted required a special kind of person who could stand up to his barrage of verbal abuse and around-the-clock demands. Not everyone shared Ted's work ethic and those people quickly left the company. But those who stayed revelled in the atmosphere of change and confrontation. For years, Rogers Communications was way ahead of its rivals in vision and ambition, because it thrived on a remarkable tension, a love-hate relationship between its CEO and its senior managers. Ted believed that confrontation was a learning opportunity, which was fine as long as you understood his premise. The plus side was a company with almost no hierarchy that could make a decision on a moment's notice. The negative side was burnout and exhaustion.

Colin Watson, who was the target of some of the most savage personal attacks, remembers one of his colleagues saying to him, "You only know that Ted Rogers is taking you seriously when he's yelling at you." Watson admits that this constant barrage used to scare other people but it was never personal and Ted never carried a grudge. "You'd be yelling at each other, using questionable language and Ted would shake your hand at the end and say, 'That was a great meeting.' You'd walk away shaking your head and thinking, 'I didn't think it was a great meeting.'" Watson says the challenge for Rogers executives was to avoid passing on that behaviour to others, to the people who reported to them.

Other former executives describe life with Ted as being similar to the tension between a battling husband and wife who have lived together too long, or an intense and competitive father-son relationship. "He was a man of extremes, he could love you and hate you," one says. "The only way to survive was to stand up and say what you thought, without fear of being fired. We had some raucous screaming matches either as a group or individually with Ted. He liked the idea of confrontation because out of it you got better decisions and the right decisions."

Ted's executives learned how to cope, often with humour. A senior manager once kicked off a speech at an industry conference with the news that Ted had recently undergone a bypass operation at the Mayo Clinic, and that when the surgeon opened up his chest and looked at his heart, he had exclaimed, "This heart has never been used!" In fact, Ted did care about his people, in his own way. He was extremely close to Bob Francis, his chief financial officer for a decade, and a close and quietly influential confidant. In January, 1986, in the middle of Rogers's hectic growth years, Ted had assembled his management team at his winter place in Lyford Cay, Bahamas, for a planning session. One morning, Francis didn't come down for breakfast, and one of the team found him dead, at fifty-two, of a heart attack in his room. Ted was greatly distressed by Francis's death.

But he could also march into an executive's office after being up all night working, and straight-out tell the executive just how stupid he was for something he had done. And the two of them would get into it, because his most senior managers wouldn't take that kind of abuse from Ted. And he wouldn't take it back. It was a highly charged atmosphere. "He was so far ahead of us in intellectual capability most of the time and worked so much harder than anyone else and that combination was a killer," one former manager says. "He would know more than you did, [he] thought it through more than you did, and no amount of anticipation would help. I don't know why he tolerated us, he was so far ahead of us. Maybe because he didn't know of anyone [else] who was stupid enough to put up with that kind of crap for so long."

But there were rewards: Ted encouraged his people to try things that were new. And as long as the project was interesting, and the person could prove his case, it had his full support. He was also able to make very fast decisions, because he didn't follow the committee approach to decision making. He had a small group of people he consulted, but in the end, his decision was all that was needed. His board rarely tried to overrule him and he could usually wear it down anyway. This allowed him to be incredibly opportunistic. Says one former Rogers aide, "It is amazing a company that size can move as fast as it does. It's also surprising how much micromanaging he does."

Young Jim Shaw, who has been something of a protégé of Ted's, has seen that part up close. If Rogers Cable decided to change the order of its cable channels in Toronto, Shaw says, it would be Ted who would do all the work. "If you said, let's have a dinner for two hundred people, you know who would personally figure out where everybody sits. It would be Ted. I once said to him, 'Ted, you're a psycho.'"

One day Rogers showed Shaw a report that he had compiled on every person who was sick in his company.

"What do you do with it?" Jim Shaw asked.

Ted's reply: "Well, I just like to know it."

According to Shaw, "I've never seen a report like that, nor do I want to. We're talking a major control guy. And listen, I love him to death, I like the guy, and he knows he has this issue: there is no decision at Rogers too small for Ted to make."

Shaw picks up a pencil on his desk, looks at it and, only partly in jest, says, "Oh, look, HP pencils." Ted, he suggests, would then check the grade of pencils off his list of things he had to do for that day. "It's very hard to manage there, but there is one other thing: Ted's just brilliant."

With the help of Graham Savage, his key financial executive, Ted was also inventive when it came to financing the company, which was always debt-leveraged to the hilt. At one point, in the tight-credit era of the early 1980s, when bank financing was not forthcoming, the Rogers team flew to Los Angeles to meet Michael Milken, the controversial king of high-coupon junk bonds at Drexel Burnham Lambert, who was able to quickly raise $300 million for Rogers Communications. Ted had great admiration for Milken, but the junk-bond king ultimately went to prison for breaking securities laws, while still managing to command great loyalty in corporate circles.

Bright managers were particularly drawn by Ted's vision that he was going to be the essential gatekeeper into the Canadian home. It would be coaxial cable at first, but he could see his primacy extending to wireless, and to the telephone. He was a firm believer in convergence when nobody else had even thought about it. His view was that if he could control what went into the house, that would be even better than owning the content. In fact, given regulatory constraints against cable companies owning TV operations, he couldn't really own the entire content. According to a former Rogers Communications manager, Ted's attitude was that content was certainly valuable, "but I am controlling entry. That's fine but I want to control all the entry." He was also a great believer in building vast scale in his cable and wireless systems, not just for efficiency but to be able to influence the future direction of communications. He was one of the first cable operators to emphasize concentration of systems in large urban areas. He sought to unify the quilt-like map of small systems that made up Toronto, Vancouver and other major cities.

That visionary sense was reflected in Rogers's bold move to become a pioneer in cellular telephone, joining up with Montreal entrepreneur Philippe de Gaspé Beaubien and the Belzberg family to found Cantel Wireless in the mid-1980s. According to one executive, Ted based his enthusiasm on "one lousy experiment in the city of Chicago that Ameritech was running. He thought this was going to be fabulous. We said it was crazy, the phones weighed four pounds then, but he said, 'No, cellular is the way to go." Colin Watson, who was president of Rogers Cable, says the decision to go into wireless was strongly opposed by himself, senior manager Phil Lind and by the board, but Ted did it anyway, investing through his own private company. "He was all by himself on that. To his credit, he was right and everybody else was wrong. But what the hell do we know?"

But Ted has also been restrained at times from doing things that might have been disastrous. Watson and Lind resisted going into the British cable television business, which turned out to be the correct decision. Watson adds, "Ted takes advice but ultimately if he believes he's right, he kind of counts his vote as ten to one and all the other votes as one to one."

The one constant through all this has been Phil Lind, a good-looking fellow from Ted's neighbourhood in Toronto. Ted knew Phil's sister, then got to know Phil, even before Lind went off to university and got a graduate degree in sociology. Fresh out of university, he was invited to join Rogers Communications in the early going. It seemed to Lind that what Ted was talking about was a hell of a lot more interesting than sociology. Lind is also a fellow Conservative who feels the intensity of the wins and the losses even more deeply than his friend and boss.

Lind explains that he and Ted have gone on together "because I don't kowtow, yet I get along with him fine. Sure, if he's barking up the wrong tree, I'll tell him that he is." More than that, Lind brings some indispensable qualities to the narrowly focused Rogers, such as an innate ability to network. Ted is a hail-fellow-well-met type, greeting people in his familiar bellow. But he lacks a broader understanding of the world, and of people beyond the corporate elite. "He is sometimes more insular, so I bring a feel of the public, a feel about what's do-able politically and things like that," Lind says. "He just wants to do something—it doesn't matter that politics or people or anything like that are involved, he just wants to do it. I tell him what can be done and what can't be done. I'm more interested in people."

Lind also sees the missed opportunities. He is particularly regretful that Rogers had to sell its U.S. cable operations in 1989 to help fund the company's Canadian expansion, including the move into long-distance telephone service with Unitel. He felt the company had proved it could compete in the United States, which was a rare thing for a Canadian business. "There is a graveyard littered with the bones of Canadians that have gone to the States and a year or two later they slink home with their tails between their legs. Generally it's dismal how Canadians are doing in the U.S. as corporations. I felt we were really a great opportunity to show the flag." But he didn't oppose Ted's decision to sell—"No, he owns the company."

Combined with the Maclean Hunter cable assets bought in the early nineties, it would have had an interesting potential, Lind feels. "I think we could have been number two or number three in the U.S. right now." But he also knows that Rogers would have been stretched to both own the U.S. operation and move into new technology areas, such as wireless and long-distance telephone service. "I think that Ted didn't feel as comfortable in the States—he was more comfortable in this environment here."

That raises another issue about Ted—the lost opportunities. He has accumulated an amazing set of assets, combined with a far-reaching vision, but he was always too heavily burdened with debt to pull it off. Ted is truly Canada's Bill Gates, admired, feared and hated, and he is now a multi-billionaire. But there is a certain sad regret to the Ted story—a sense that it could be much more glorious if he hadn't lived his life so close to the line, if he could have somehow controlled all the various strands in his wildly eclectic vision.

As the 1990s dawned, Ted was continuing to wheel and deal: Rogers was part of a consortium that brought long-distance telephone competition to Canada, an alternative to Bell Canada and its telephone allies. Rogers Communication held a 32 percent interest in Unitel, along with partner Canadian Pacific, which held 48 percent, and the U.S. telecommunications giant AT&T, which owned the rest. This was a difficult chapter in Rogers's life, because he felt he could knock off the old telephone company monopoly in long-distance communications. But in the end, after Rogers had lost $500 million, it got out of Unitel, which became the basis of what is now AT&T Canada. The Rogers organization still feels the deck was stacked against them in terms of the network fees they had to pay the giant phone company.

Ted insists he has few regrets about the Unitel fiasco. In the CRTC hearings to apply for Unitel's licence, he had considered it a "holy war" against BCE, but he does not feel that way anymore. It's un-Canadian to talk about holy wars, he says—such extreme language is more an American trait. "I'm glad we got into the war, that we learned something, I don't think we would have been as successful afterward if we hadn't made the mistakes we did then, that I made then. I should have handled the situation much better."

Rogers does regret his personal relationships with his partners and their role in the failure of Unitel. According to some Rogers executives, relations were impossibly tempestuous between the impatient, aggressive Ted and the more staid, bureaucratic Canadian Pacific. "I got into battles when I should have got into seduction," Ted says. "We're all to blame. I'm to blame in our company and so I learned from that and we've changed. I thought we could run it better than the trio could run it; I still think that." For that matter, he also thinks that CP alone could run it better than a trio of companies could have run it. "I'm not sure it would have made any different with the result. I guess the cards are stacked against it; it certainly looks that way," he says, noting that AT&T Canada is the major long-distance competitor to survive the deregulation wars, and its future in Canada is less than certain. But Ted has never given up on telephone competition and still harbours the hope of taking on Bell and Telus in the local phone game.

In the middle of the Unitel fight, Ted looked for opportunities to strengthen his cable franchise in his strong Ontario market, and spied

Maclean Hunter, a diversified media and cable company based in Toronto that had a collection of wonderful assets—including 700,000 cable subscribers—but was undervalued in the stock market. It had been run by smart, able accountants but it was a conservative company whose disparate assets, on their own, were far more valuable than the conglomerate that contained them. In the late eighties, its CEO was Ron Osborne, a classics scholar from Cambridge University who had taken up accounting and moved to Canada to work for one of the big public accounting firms. Ted announced in early February, 1994, that he would bid for Maclean Hunter, setting off a war of nerves with Osborne, who was determined to stave off the bid, or, failing that, to extract the best possible value for shareholders. Osborne won admirers with his blend of bluster, combativeness and street smarts, but Ted was determined to have MH.

The Maclean Hunter battle was a civil war within the Toronto business establishment. While Ted Rogers was old Toronto, Maclean Hunter was old, old Toronto, the company of the Maclean and Hunter families, *The Financial Post* and *Maclean's* magazine and of legendary editor/philanthropist Floyd Chalmers. As the backer of both Rogers and Maclean Hunter, the Toronto-Dominion Bank was clearly divided. Corporate lawyer Garfield Emerson, a key Rogers adviser, had been close to both companies, and his support of Ted was a bitter pill for the Maclean Hunter brain trust.

But the standoff had its moments of levity. After Ted had announced his intentions, it took weeks for his formal offer to surface. In the middle of the tension, the Toronto social set ran its annual Brazilian Ball, an orgy of fun, frolic and philanthropy. In preparation for the ball, the clever Osborne and his merry pranksters came up with a fancy poster titled "The Phantom of the Offer," by Rogers and Emmerstein, since Gar Emerson was Ted's legal henchman. It was "a tragicomedy in four acts," presented by "King-Fell Productions"—a reference to the investment bankers. At the ball, the Maclean Hunter team paraded the poster past Ted's table, and everyone had a good laugh over it, although some of the smiles were a bit forced.

Eventually Ted laid out his bid, a $3.1 billion offer, which if successful would give him a rich trove of assets, including *Chatelaine*, *The Financial Post*, control of the *Sun* tabloid newspapers, and the crown jewels—extensive cable systems in Canada and the United States. While Ted claimed to like the look of the media assets, it was the cable systems he truly coveted.

But in the heat of battle, the resourceful Osborne was talking to a little-known cable entrepreneur in Calgary by the name of James Shaw Sr., a man who would later change his name to simply JR—no periods—to avoid confusion with his son and successor Jim Shaw Jr. Osborne discussed the possibility of Shaw riding in from the West and saving Maclean Hunter from Ted. It was a scenario that Ted Rogers could not ignore.

2 THE SHAW REDEMPTION

THEY MET IN TORONTO IN FEBRUARY, 1994, TWO SIXTY-year-old men—Ted Rogers, the son of the Eastern establishment and James Robert Shaw, the son of a Southwestern Ontario farmer and now an Alberta entrepreneur. They knew each other as cable TV magnates, but they now found themselves on opposite sides of the table. JR Shaw was the potential white knight to save Maclean Hunter from Ted Rogers. He had been negotiating with MH president Ron Osborne as to how he might play a role in rescuing the dignified old dowager of a media company and end up with a rich lode of Canadian cable subscribers. But he also knew that Ted was a formidable opponent.

The two men were meeting on Ted Rogers's turf, the exclusive, darkly luxurious Toronto Club, to decide: would they be foes or allies in the consolidation of the Canadian cable industry? Ted chose the venue, made the reservations. "So here we are in one of these rooms upstairs— one table, two chairs—I thought I was in Buckingham Palace," JR says today, playing his familiar role of the wide-eyed country boy. He describes himself as "this little guy from Western Canada, who parks his car outside in the wintertime all the time. He doesn't even have a garage to park it in. But here we'd become of such a size that we're the potential white knight for Maclean Hunter, and that was hard for me to fathom."

In JR's view, he wasn't in favour of Maclean Hunter or in favour of Rogers in the takeover fight. All he wanted was what was best for Shaw. So in the wood-panelled opulence of the Toronto Club, Ted brought up the delicate issue: "I hear you're interested in some parts of MH?" JR considered his options: He desperately wanted MH's cable properties in the West, because he yearned to be an industry giant, just like Ted. He was convinced that the best way to go is to cluster your cable properties in big areas, where you can save on networks and overhead costs. The small cable shops were going to be an endangered species, and the Shaws planned to be among the survivors. But if they messed things up for Ted Rogers in his battle for Maclean Hunter, Ted would a tough fellow to live with. "If it's going to end up being an industry where there are three, four or five of us, you need to have the ability to meet and talk and work together, because it's too small an industry," JR was thinking.

Just being there with Ted, as part of this stunning reorganization of the cable industry, was discombobulating for JR. It was a sign that he had finally arrived. He had just come off a deal with another cable baron, David Graham, that had added thousands of subscribers to the Shaw network. In the heat of the talks with Maclean Hunter, Ron Osborne, the smart British-born president of the Toronto company, suggested the Shaws could go out and borrow a billion dollars to buy Maclean Hunter by themselves. The statement bowled over JR, who still saw himself as a little operator from Edmonton.

Meanwhile, he was getting phone calls from the aggressive, over-the-top Ted Rogers, who had caught wind of JR's interest in MH. "Well, gee, Ted's on the phone, and you know how Ted is," JR recalls, his eyes rolling. "I just said, 'I can't talk to Ted right now.' Finally, Ted's executive assistant says, 'Can I tell Mr. Rogers that Mr. Shaw does not want to talk to him?' Well, that wasn't the case, it was a timing situation." JR hadn't made up his mind yet.

So son Jim Jr. called Ted, and told him that his father couldn't talk to him right now, but he'd come down to Toronto the following week and meet with him. That gave the Shaws a little breathing room to talk to Ron Osborne and make up their minds. To make the deal work, they figured MH would have to sell its U.S. cable assets separately, and that process was not progressing quickly. They could see the writing on the wall—if they went up against Ted and lost, they would lose the chance to pick up anything. But if they made peace with Ted, they could end up with some nice properties, because Ted couldn't handle the whole bundle of cable assets. Besides, JR had another big deal up his sleeve. He had been getting feelers from some shareholders of another big Toronto cable outfit, CUC, who wanted to sell out. JR figured that if Ted was going to get big, Shaw Communications had to, as well. "Ted was getting expansionary—you know he takes on the big ones, he doesn't gobble up very many little ones. He loves the big ones and going after them."

But what clinched his decision was his family's reaction. The night before he flew to Toronto and the Toronto Club, JR had dinner with his two older children, Jim and Heather, both in their thirties, both keen on the business, and asked them what they thought. Like Monopoly board players, they mentally divided up the Maclean Hunter holdings. The Shaws wanted Victoria and south Calgary, which would give them all of Calgary, because they had already acquired the north. "We'd give up Woodstock [Ontario], which is very important to Ted, we'd give up Toronto, we'd take Thunder Bay and the Sault because we wanted to stay in Ontario and we'd give up all the rest. They kind of agreed what we wanted, what Ted might want, what they would like to get."

The following night, JR Shaw made his pact with the devil, in this case Ted Rogers—he would let Ted buy Maclean Hunter, and then do a swap for the assets each of them wanted. The Shaws would pick up 145,000 new subscribers, mainly in the West, and Ted would be able to reinforce his position in Ontario, with more than 600,000 new customers. But the deal, worth about $200 million to JR, was more than that—it was an implicit agreement that these two family companies would be the consolidators in English Canada, that they would have to work together and that they would not rock each other's boat. They were joined at the hip. It would set the Shaws on a growth curve that would enable them, at the beginning of the twenty-first century, to become one of Canada's ruling media families and pioneers in convergence.

With the Shaws out of the picture as a white knight, Ron Osborne and Maclean Hunter's management capitulated, and Ted got the company he wanted, with the cable properties he wanted. To this day, the gentlemanly JR has one regret. Once he had made his decision to throw in his lot with Rogers, he didn't notify Ron Osborne before the announcement of the deal trickled into public knowledge. When he called Osborne, the disappointed MH president said this must mean that JR was in Ted Rogers's camp. "Oh, that did not sit very well because I thought I was in Shaw's camp," says JR, who is fiercely determined not to be Ted's obedient servant. Not that Osborne did badly, as the owner of a whack of MH shares. Osborne, famous in the industry as a class act, stayed on to help the Rogers team work their way through the CRTC hearings and moved on to BCE as president, and then to run Ontario Power Generation, the generating-plant side of what was once the Ontario Hydro utility.

As for JR, he hardly had time to catch his breath after doing his deal with Ted. While he was negotiating the carve-up of MH, he started talking to those minority shareholders of CUC Broadcasting, a big Ontario cable system that had been built by the late businessman Geoffrey Conway. CUC was a private company, but it was clearly in play, as the various ownership interests talked to outside buyers. Some directors were talking to the Audets, the respected family who ran Cogeco, a Montreal-based cable system; others were talking to JR. But the Shaws were finally able to deal with Julia Conway Royer, Geoffrey's widow, and walked away with the prize. The Shaws went straight from the swap with MH to buying CUC, a deal to which Ted was not even invited. It was typical—people just wanted to do business with JR.

Right after the deal for CUC, JR turned around and bought another Toronto-area cable franchise, Classic Communications in Richmond Hill. All in all, JR's little shopping spree in Toronto added up to more than a billion dollars, but it propelled him to a new level, with 20 percent of the Canadian cable market. If there had been any doubt the Shaws were a force, these investments dispelled it. Not only that, the CUC package contained a minority stake in the kids' specialty channel YTV, which in time would become one of the foundations of the Shaws' broadcasting ambitions.

Those were hectic times for the likeable JR, who is the ying to Ted's yang, the anti-Ted. JR is casual and charming—Ted is intense and overpowering. Crackling with homespun humour, and intensely Christian, JR has a chatty manner that belies a razor-sharp mind. He lulls you with those corny phrases "doggone it" or "sheesh" or "Holy geez." He's the innocent-looking rural rube who, while apparently being fleeced by the travelling salesman, is actually quietly picking the guy's back pocket.

JR never saw himself as the visionary, the man who would bring sweeping technological change. The Shaws are great managers, great builders, but not people who are creating the new, new thing in technology. By the time he met Ted at the Toronto Club that night, JR was thinking about good businesses on which to build a strong ownership succession. His two older children, the boisterous Jim Jr. and the more cerebral Heather, were both highly ambitious, and two more, Julie and Brad, were waiting in the wings.

JR knew the importance of giving children a legacy—he got a Ph.D. in business from his own father, growing up in the farming community of Brigden, Ontario., south of Sarnia. JR was the youngest of four kids and used to fight over the radio with his older sister: "I wanted to listen to the hockey game and she wanted to listen to something else." When television came, JR would sneak down to a neighbour's house to watch his first television show—a small-screen version of the Lone Ranger. "So I went from radio to television and I wondered, 'My God, how is this happening?' And it was all out of Detroit, because we were very close to Detroit."

JR eventually moved on to Michigan State University, where he studied business economics. After he got his degree, he went to work for his father, Francis Shaw, who was quite an entrepreneur himself. The elder Shaw, who started out as a farmer, had moved beyond his roots to succeed in a number of businesses, eventually becoming a millionaire. He hauled pigs and gravel, invested in drive-in theatres, and during the boom years of the 1950s got into construction, particularly pipeline construction. JR, then known as Jim, moved around a lot in the early days, helping out in his father's operations in Ontario. With the construction of the Trans-Canada Pipeline in the 1950s, the Shaws had a nice business adding the epoxy protective coating to the pipes used in the web of oil and gas distribution networks. The Shaws began to look westward with the idea of setting up pipe coating operations in the energy industry's backyard.

JR, living in the shadow of his dad and older brother Les, yearned for his own space. He could see there wasn't a lot of room at the top. So he agreed to move west to Edmonton, over the protestations of his young wife, Carol. "My wife just about had a bird when I suggested that—because she was moving away from her family, she was from Sarnia and we were riding Viscounts and Vanguards in those days. It wasn't exactly a Spitfire trip and it wasn't nonstop either. I said I'd do this one thing: 'You can come home whenever you want.' That's the key thing—you say they can go home anytime but after a few trips, they stop and say, 'That's not our home anymore. Edmonton is our home.'"

It was a successful move, and JR established Shaw Industries' coating yards in Edmonton and later Regina. But he still yearned for a business of his own, separate from the energy and pipeline services operation that his brother and father were building. He was also concerned that coating pipes was a "sunset business" that would lose its allure as technology changed and plastic piping became more widely used.

JR's dad, Francis, had been an early investor in cable television in Southwestern Ontario, teaming up with other entrepreneurs, such as Harry Anderson, an enterprising TV repairman, and London's affluent Jeffrey family, who had made their fortune from the insurance industry. As for JR, he could see an urgent need for cable in the West, particularly in his adopted home of Edmonton, where the television viewing was dismal beyond the CBC and CTV outlets. One problem was that Edmonton was too far from the U.S. border to pick up American signals, even with the big antennas used by cable companies. JR kept thinking, "Well, geez, how come I'm so deprived of choice and what difference should it make that I live so far from the border? Estevan had it, Lethbridge had it, you get close to the border and you had it, but you come to Calgary or Edmonton or Saskatoon or Regina, you couldn't get it. It was just really bugging me all the time."

Convinced he could make cable work, he founded a company called Capital Cable Television in December, 1966. Thus began a long fight for the first cable licence in Edmonton, up against the local TV broadcasters, who wanted to keep the market to themselves. But the Shaws were building up cable systems in Southwestern Ontario, as well. In a deal with the Jeffrey family, JR managed to get hold of the Woodstock franchise with its 2,500 to 3,500 subscribers. He and Les paid about $100 a subscriber; thirty years later, his son Jim would pay $3,500 a subscriber for the Moffat cable company in Winnipeg.

JR now regrets that he didn't buy even more cable licences during this period. In fact, it may be the biggest regret of his life that he didn't expand quickly enough. The industry was gradually consolidating as the more ambitious families were buying out the others who couldn't keep up with the intense capital spending demands. Cable systems were going for a lot less money than they would be twenty years later. But in those days, JR was fixed on breaking through in Edmonton. "I just had to persist; it wasn't just going out and putting up an antenna—you had to have some distance mechanism." It would have to be a microwave system, not an antenna, he figured, and the federal government was reluctant to issue a licence for microwave to bring in U.S. signals to compete against Canadian broadcasters.

After four years of lobbying, JR was finally able to apply for a cable licence in Edmonton. He keenly remembers Klondike Days in Edmonton in 1970, and the big parade passing his office at 104th and Jasper, with Premier Harry Strom in the lead car. Right in the middle of the noisy parade, the phone in his office rang. The Shaws had won the licence for half the city, the east side, while another local entrepreneur got the west side. That was the start of cable TV in Edmonton, but it was also the start of what became Shaw Communications.

It also took JR right out of the management of the family pipeline company. He had his own little empire, even though he still owned big shareholdings in Shaw Industries and his brother Les owned a chunk of what became Shaw Communications. "Aggressive brothers work a hell of a lot better 2,500 miles apart," Les says today. "We're a little aggressive. You know, the Shaws are red-headed. JR was red-headed when he had hair. He's the guy who took the company west, he did a hell of a fine job, and we were in this, that and the other thing and one of them was cable. And he took cable and you know what it is today." Les did pretty well with the family company, which became known as Shaw Industries, and then Shawcor, and is now an energy services company with revenues of more than half a billion dollars a year. Les lives in Barbados, and he, like his brother JR, is very wealthy. In 2001, JR finally retired from the Shaw Industries board, and Les planned to leave the cable company board. The two brothers remain close—when I interviewed him at the Shawcor annual meeting, Les was almost in tears over the prospect of not having his little brother on the board anymore.

JR's secret weapon as a businessman was his conviviality, which he quickly put to work in the cable business. Sometimes he was just lucky, too. In 1970, after winning the Edmonton licence, JR and Carol decided to take the kids, Jim, Heather, Julie and Brad, on a celebratory trip by recreational vehicle around northern Alberta and down through British Columbia to Seattle. The trip was an odyssey right out of hell, JR recalls, because the rented RV kept breaking down, starting in the Peace River district. Every time it broke down, the Shaws would get it repaired, and every time it would find a new way of breaking down again. When the Shaw family limped into Penticton in British Columbia's Okanagan Valley, the RV was having problems with its lights. "This was a fiasco trip," JR recalls, except for one little detail: during his Penticton stopover, he walked over to see a friend of his, the cable TV operator in the Okanagan Valley, owner of a small system with 7,500 subscribers.

As the two men chatted, the Penticton operator let it slip that he had just conditionally sold his cable system. JR was thinking that the Okanagan Valley was a fine place to own a cable system—a veritable Garden of Eden. "Sheesh, there was no better place than the Okanagan Valley with the water and fruit and the vegetables and so on. So finally I said, 'If you don't sell that [system], give me a call.' I'll be danged if he doesn't call later. The sale had been turned down, so we started negotiating. So in 1971, that's the first system we buy outside Edmonton—Kelowna, Penticton and Revelstoke."

It would not be the last. JR Shaw, the aw-shucks farm boy, would become the dominant cable operator in the Canadian West and, thanks to some wrangling with Ted Rogers, would split up the country. JR could charm the pants off other cable operators so they would want to sell to him, not to Ted Rogers, who was from Toronto and despite his brilliance was considered pushy and obsessive. Les Shaw, JR's brother, who is the spitting image of Jim Shaw Jr., but thirty years older, says his brother's strength is his negotiating skills and his honesty. He was adept at putting people at ease. But above all, his secret, Les says, is ABR: "Anybody but Rogers." People would want to do business with anybody but Ted.

Randy Elliott, who has worked with JR for more than thirty years, says his boss's strength is his ability to simply talk to people. If JR was going to buy a cable company, he could just walk into the prospective seller's office and sit down and start talking. "He's a guy that you immediately like; it's his nature. Some people have that gift and other people don't."

From the Okanagan Valley and Edmonton, the Shaws began a slow march across the country. They bought Saskatoon for $60 million, and they kept adding new services, new channels to their cable packages. "How many wires are there to the house? There are three and we've got one of them," JR figured. "We're the one that's got that added capacity. You know one thing I've always liked and hated about the cable industry? It's always expansionary, always expanding its services." In the eighties and early nineties, the popular specialty channels TSN and MuchMusic were added to the cable packages. But when CHUM CITY's impresario Moses Znaimer did a deal with JR to add MuchMusic to the Shaw lineup, "he told me that there are only three cable companies to deal with in Canada, and we weren't one of them, I can tell you that. It was Rogers, Maclean Hunter and someone else. We weren't at any table. We weren't big enough." That really bugged JR.

That feeling of insignificance began to fade in 1993, when they picked up the cable properties of Cablecasting, owned by David Graham, whose other claim to fame was having once been married to Barbara Amiel, the journalist, now the wife of Conrad Black. The Graham properties brought into the Shaw empire north Calgary, part of Winnipeg, areas of Toronto along the Humber River, St. Thomas and Strathroy, as well as up along Lake Superior. It was a big breakthrough into the rich Ontario market. It put them on the radar of people like Ted Rogers and Ron Osborne, before the Maclean Hunter deal came up.

JR said his style was a lot different from Rogers's. "I always thought that Ted was the kind of the guy who wanted to be the first doing everything, and I was happy to see that happen, so we'd learn then from either his strengths or weaknesses, his mistakes or his successes." JR acknowledges that Ted has had good managers, people like Phil Lind and Colin Watson, and he has made some daring moves, taking over Canadian Cablesystems, for example. "Ted's an expansionist. I admire him. I respect him. He's a different operator than we are because we want to have a team. He's Ted, and he wants to make all the major decisions. That's the difference in philosophy."

JR likes to leave the impression that he just got carried along with the tide, with every new deal leaving him shaking his head at the price he'd just paid. To finance the David Graham purchases, he went to see his lender at the Toronto-Dominion Bank. "We asked him for $320 million and he gave it to us that day and I remember going out and sitting on the steps of the TD Centre in Toronto and thinking, 'Holy, what have I done—$320 million? I can't believe this.' It was 1993 and that took us from a few hundred thousand subscribers, doubled our size, you know." Before the Graham deal, the Shaws were mainly in Western Canada, but now they were in Ontario in a big way.

JR was a gambler, tenacious like Ted, even though he had no game plan for how the technology would work out. Still, he was an early convert to the fibre networks that could bundle huge amounts of data in minuscule glass wires. He had a keen eye for technical talent. The Shaws have consistently posted better profit margins and exhibited a better grasp of customer service than their Toronto peers. They are not hated nearly as much by their customers. It may be that they are cut a little more slack because they are the West's home-grown operator. They also got caught up in the negative option billing quagmire, but were able to escape with little damage. The Shaws, unlike Ted, don't feel they have to be out in front all the time; they could move with the consumer.

JR says he never really was sure about how the technology would turn out until one day he went to meet Harry Boyle, the vice-chairman of the Canadian Radio-television and Telecommunications Commission in the 1970s and a sage observer of the passing scene. "I'd go down to CRTC, me the guy from the West, sorta hat in hand, and ask, 'How does this work?' You'd want them on your side to kind of help. I said, 'Where is cable TV going?' Harry said, 'Lookit, there will be more and more signals all the time, and you got the wire to the house and the TV set. And whatever comes, comes through you.' That gave me a lot of comfort, all those years."

John Cassaday, the executive JR recruited to run his broadcast operations, says the Shaws should not be underestimated in the vision department. "The thing about JR and people like him is they really do have the ability to envisage a future that is not readily predictable today," says the president of Corus Entertainment. Cassaday sees JR and Ted as being cut from the same basic cloth, although the tailoring is a bit different. "At the end of the day, no one can really appreciate how many times they've been within an eyelash of losing it all. These guys, these entrepreneurial visionaries, unlike most normal human beings, believe they're right all the time. And it's only that absolute belief in themselves that keeps them going."

In Cassaday's view, "Everybody said to Ted, you know you've gone too far, invested too heavily, and you're too much in debt. And JR believed there was some benefit in a cluster of cable systems, and he bet the ranch. He came to Toronto and got a bunch of stuff. He decided he would have to be a consolidator or get out. He couldn't continue to have a nice little comfortable family business in Edmonton. That just wasn't going to happen. He wanted to secure a legacy for his family and he did. You and I will probably never know how close he actually was to succeeding or failing."

JR was heavily influenced by John Malone, the iconoclastic cable visionary in the United States, a former McKinsey & Company management consultant whose Denver-based cable giant, Tele-Communications and its offshoots, have been among the dominant forces in the U.S. media. It was Malone who conjured up the concept of the five-hundred-channel universe. He took a big stake in television programming and spun off a programming investment company called Liberty Media. But he also has detractors who believe he has accumulated far too much power in the U.S. communications world.

JR Shaw agrees that if Shaw Communications is based on any U.S. model, it would probably be John Malone and Tele-Communications. He has three words to describe Malone: "bright, bright, bright." In the early nineties, everyone was talking about telephone companies emerging as the big challengers to cable TV. But inspired by Malone's example, JR decided that satellite would be the biggest competitor to cable. Like Malone, the Shaws decided to have a foot in both camps, so they applied for and, after a long struggle, received a licence in 1997 for a satellite service called HomeStar, which would eventually be merged into StarChoice Communications. The charming JR convinced the federal regulator that, amazing though it seemed, the Shaws would be able to compete with themselves—with cable on one side and satellite on the other.

JR was also listening to a bright young analyst recruited from the cable television association named Michael D'Avella, who was also convinced of the importance of satellite in complementing cable. At the time D'Avella came aboard as a planning executive, Shaw was the owner of a bunch of smaller systems, not yet a major cable player. Still, D'Avella was able to sell JR on the satellite idea. Satellite did not have the interactive facility, and lacked the broadband capabilities, but it was a system that could reach people who couldn't be reached by cable. "We felt we had to own both, and it took us years to persuade the CRTC to let us," D'Avella recalls. When D'Avella had solved the satellite entry issue, he turned his mind to high-speed Internet, and Shaw has been a North American leader in signing up new customers.

The cocky D'Avella has been a key recruit, one of the least known important executives in Canada's communications industry. "People tend to underestimate us and that will be their demise," D'Avella says. "We're extremely tough and disciplined. We've got guys who have been in the business a long time, who have a historical perspective. We don't have committees—decisions are made very quickly and they are usually the right ones. I am forty-two, joined at thirty-two, and I'll retire here. I'm not going anywhere."

JR Shaw is no mechanical genius—in fact, he often exudes the air of the technological *naïf*—but D'Avella says Shaw is smart in being able to buy into an idea, and let his people take it to the market. The brilliant Ted Rogers didn't share the satellite vision with the Shaws, "and now they probably feel they should have been there. Now the horse has left the barn and we're one of two now." (Ted's rejoinder is that the Shaw's Star Choice system was losing buckets of money, was not economical long-term and, as many in the industry believe, will eventually be sold to rival Bell ExpressVu.)

JR, in his folksy way, says he learned an important lesson early in his career: Although cable was a monopoly, it was not a licence to print money—it is, in fact, a licence to spend money. While the industry spits out impressive cash flow, it demands constant capital expenditure—CapEx, in the language of the industry—for upgrading and improving the network. That meant that after-tax profits never look terrific, especially for bankers casting a cool eye over the income statements. People who knew the business realized it was an "ebitda business," which is the financial lingo for earnings before interest payments, taxes, depreciation and amortization.

During the nineties, ebitda became a fashionable and somewhat controversial profit measure, one that is not recognized by generally accepted accounting principles. While all kinds of companies now like to quote their earnings in ebitda, the cable industry was a pioneer, because ebitda measured the company's ability to generate cash, independent of its constant capital spending. For accounting purists, particularly those dismayed by the rash of high-profile corporate scandals, ebitda smacks of snake oil, but JR claims it's a measure that makes sense for certain sectors. "We don't make a profit, it's ebitda, because we are investing so heavily and then you're always upgrading, taking that old stuff out, getting a few cents for it and putting in new stuff. It's just awful," says JR, although it's hard to shed many tears for a man who has seen the value of his shareholdings skyrocket. "We've always spent more money than we made and that's a juggling act."

Even in the early years, JR found one bank willing to lend money on an ebitda basis, and that was Toronto-Dominion. Ted Rogers also borrowed from the TD—in fact, the TD Bank made the cable industry in Canada. The banker who best understood the cash nature of cable was Robin Korthals, a TD senior manager who in time became the president of the bank. This willingness to lend to the cable industry—to both Ted and JR—was shared by Dick Thomson, the bank's long-time CEO. The TD also became a big supporter of cable business in the United States, as well as telecommunications—although this industry became a rough ride for the bank amid the tumult of the dot-com collapse.

But cable can be a tedious business and most cable guys have a hankering to dabble in the stuff they distribute through their pipes. JR liked broadcasting—indeed, his cable system in Edmonton always had a public access channel operated by the Shaws. Television and radio broadcasting were just good businesses, he figured, and they didn't require a lot of CapEx, unlike cable. The Shaws began to build media assets—they bought radio stations and invested in the new wave of specialty TV—but felt they were limited in their financing and scope because they were tied to the capital expenditure-eating cable operations. The ideal situation would be to run them off separate balance sheets, with their own financing, their own focused management. That idea germinated early, and was fed by the Malone experience in the United States. The Shaws always believed more in de-convergence: the media would be run better if they were kept separate from the cable—they were two separate industries with radically different cultures.

JR is a charming man, but his charm has some hard edges. He can be hard as nails when it counts. One example was Shaw Communications' fractious negotiations with the city of Edmonton over fibre lines it planned to bring into its downtown technology centre. The city argued that the agreement it had negotiated with JR in 1970 should be renegotiated and the new lines should now belong to the public, not to the company. That set off four years of negotiations, standoffs and heated exchanges, until JR said enough was enough. The Shaws started to look around for other head office cities, the top candidates being Toronto, Calgary or Victoria. In Victoria, the problem was travel connections. If he moved back to Toronto, JR figured he'd be in Ted Rogers's backyard and "we're not there to compete with Ted or anyone else." So it boiled down to staying in Edmonton or moving to Calgary, and JR made his choice: he told the board the company was relocating to Calgary. None of the directors, including three from Edmonton, protested.

The day Shaw Communications announced it was moving to Calgary was, in JR's view, the toughest day of his life. "You're leaving friends, you built the business there, you'd become successful in this industry because you're in that city. The city also has a feeling that they made you successful too." But JR concluded, "We had to do to our cable plant what was needed to survive and they wouldn't let us do it. They just jerked us around for four to five years and we said, 'Sorry folks, we're moving.'" The day JR made the announcement, he paid a visit to Jan Reimer, the city's mayor, and "I took a daughter along rather than a son 'cause I thought that was the better way of doing it." Mayor Reimer seemed shocked by the decision to leave Edmonton. "I don't think she really understood all the implications to it, but we'd spent enough time talking," JR says.

A lot of Edmontonians were bitter because the new Shaw home was in the rival city of Calgary. JR believes people should get over that feud; he says the two cities are just different—"they've got their own strengths, they just should move on in their own way. I hate [the rivalry], I just hate it. I have been gunned over the past five or six years whenever I go back to Edmonton. People say, 'Calgary doesn't have this or that.' I just hate it, but anyway, you take it, you smile, you keep on going."

He suggests that the company move had a lot to do with succession. "If we had stayed in Edmonton, the company would have always been my company, it wouldn't have been my kids' company. I need to move the identity too." JR had decided early that Jim was going to run the cable empire, and that he would step aside. After all, Jim had showed a fierce interest in the company, had worked in the cable trenches, managed a small cable system in his twenties and helped his dad through the consolidations of the nineties.

But what could JR do for Heather, who was also keenly interested in the business? (Sister Julie studied architecture and now oversees the Shaws' facilities management, and younger brother Brad took up a senior role in the Shaws' StarChoice satellite service.). JR had that figured out, too. Heather was given two startups to run: a cable advertising business, and a digital music service that provided soothing background sounds for restaurants and office buildings. She did well, but she acknowledges that her father was always several steps ahead of her. He was already talking about splitting off the TV, radio, cable advertising and specialty channels, such as YTV, in a separate unit under Heather's supervision.

But Heather had a young family and wanted to spend some time with them, and with her husband, who owns a farm equipment dealership. At the same time, she believed in the Shaws being active owners, not just passive coupon clippers. It was important to have the owners working in the business. Heather explained to JR that she didn't think she was right for the CEO's job, but she would like to be the chairperson. It would mean both his older children would have something to run, just as JR and Les did thirty years before. And that was the beginning of Corus.

So the Shaws moved to Calgary and found a big downtown office building vacated by an oil company, an impressive structure of concrete and rose-coloured glass. JR commissioned a sculpture of a buffalo by Regina artist Joe Fafard to stand guard over the entrance, with the Shaw name prominently displayed. The building's interior opens up into a vast atrium that runs the full height of the twelve-storey structure. Then JR filled up the building with a rich and varied collection of Canadian art—Alex Colville, Mary Pratt, Ken Danby, Fafard and a host of others.

The building is a monument to what JR has built since he left Ontario and made his own way in the West. He has set up a Shaw Communications museum, with old photos, samples of cable gear and "tombstone" announcements of important investment offerings. Visitors can watch a short film about the history of the company, including testimonials from prominent Albertans. "JR Shaw is the Medici of Alberta," says one local worthy. It may be hard to equate homespun JR Shaw with the bankers and benefactors of the Italian Renaissance, but in this place at least, no one is going to argue.

3 ALL ABOUT IZZY

I HAVE CAUGHT UP TO IZZY ASPER ON A JULY AFTERNOON in his sprawling house on Wellington Crescent in Winnipeg, in the black-and-white music room he fills with his George Gershwin music artifacts, his books and his baby grand. It has been a long quest over the past six months: I approached him at first at CanWest's annual meeting in February; I listened to him give testimony in a court case in Toronto; I saw him honoured at a Toronto fund-raising dinner. But on this day in early July, Izzy doesn't remember exactly who I am, only that I am some reporter who wants to talk about convergence, the media and his company, CanWest Global. Izzy, I have been told, has a terrible memory for names and faces.

If there is one place that should spark his memories, it is this house. And the house helps me to understand Israel Harold Asper, his passions and his demons. It starts with the two heavy iron gates that grace the entrance to the Asper estate. The gates are decorated with various metal icons—books for learning, a keyboard for music, a menorah, two men shaking hands. The central icons are a mother, father and children. The message of the gates is clear: the owner of this house loves learning, he loves his faith, he loves his family and in business he is constantly searching for partnership and trust. Anyone who has followed Izzy's life knows that, in business at least, he has not always found what he has been seeking.

Sitting in his beloved Gershwin room, Izzy exudes an unkempt, careless, don't-give-a-shit attitude. He is red-faced, pot-bellied, dressed in a blue-and-white striped shirt, white deck pants and sockless loafers. He has scratches on his ankles, perhaps from tramping through the bush, for he has just driven back to Winnipeg from his cottage on Falcon Lake, on the Manitoba-Ontario border. He sips Diet Pepsi and chain-smokes Craven A's. As he talks, ashes occasionally drop on the leather couch, and he tidily sweeps them into an ashtray.

And what a couch it is, with big bulging cushions in Holstein-like black and white, and a black seat. The room, indeed the house, seems to be all in black and white—black piano, white walls, striped zebra skin on the floor. A bookshelf is built into one wall, high up, at the tall end of the sloping ceiling. There is a ladder that can slide the length of the room to retrieve Izzy's books, which are dominated by historical and political themes. One corner of the room is a shrine to Gershwin— photos, sheet music, even contracts signed by the great George. The sweet sounds of the husband-and-wife duo, Jackie Cain and Roy Kral, two of Izzy's favourite jazz musicians and friends, echo from the stereo system.

This room captures in one place the contradictions of Izzy Asper— a sophisticated man of the world who is fiercely chauvinistic about his hometown. He is very smart but defensive, carrying a two-by-four on his shoulder about being a Westerner and, some say, a Jewish outsider. He is probably the deepest and broadest of the media moguls in terms of intellectual reach—a former tax lawyer, author of a bestselling book on tax policy, a voracious collector of information, a religious man. He is at the same time a shameless vendor of television schlock, whose pro- gramming plunged to such lows that his Global TV was for many years branded "the *Love Boat* network" for its mediocre U.S. fare. Izzy is charming, affable, but quick to sue, to use litigation as a weapon against his partners-turned-betrayers. Yet he is also a family man who enjoys a relaxed and warm relationship with his wife and three children. He is comfortable at his cottage on Falcon Lake or in some smoky Greenwich Village jazz bar. He is Canada's most formidable media tycoon but he still sees himself as a kid from Minnedosa, Manitoba, with his nose always pressed against the window of the Canadian establishment.

Here in his Gershwin room, it is hard to reconcile this charming, likeable raconteur with the dark presence portrayed by his business foes—and by many of his friends. Izzy confesses to me that he loves the media business because the scope for expansion is so infinite that he would never know boredom, "which is my great nemesis." It is this abhorrence of boredom, more than anything else, that may explain the need to conquer new worlds, build new companies, add newspapers to the television empire he already owns. The CanWest story is driven not by some half-baked theory of convergence but one man's restless needs, the drive to expand, to control and, conversely, to never feel at the mercy of anyone else. The fear of boredom explains the non-stop work and the quest for learning, but also the late-night eating, drinking and brooding, which at times have evoked a black and despairing view of the world. He has had health problems, including bypass surgery in his early fifties, which forced him to cut back on his excesses. His daughter Gail says she has watched his physical condition with concern. Izzy Asper gave up a lot for his family, she says.

Now almost seventy years old, Izzy is in his legacy years, when the goal is to leave an indelible stamp on the world. In Winnipeg, the memorials are everywhere: the Asper School of Business and its Asper Centre of Entrepreneurship at the University of Manitoba, the Asper Jewish Community Campus and the Asper Foundation. The house itself is a kind of living museum, of his love of jazz, of his life. Is this room okay for the interview? Izzy asks me, as he gestures around the Gershwin room. There is a boardroom in the basement, he explains, but it's stacked high with books and files. I am told that Izzy is an inveterate collector of the scraps and fragments of his business life. When he dies, his biographer will have a field day.

The street outside, Wellington Crescent, is Winnipeg's most elegant address, a wide boulevard shaded by large elms. Izzy's is one of the newer houses on a street dominated by lofty old mansions, reminders of the years when this was the richest city in the West, the gateway to the prairies, the bustling Chicago of Canada. Izzy's older son, David, lives a few doors down, in a mansion once owned by the Eatons, the faded Toronto retail family that used to send a son or a cousin to Winnipeg to keep an eye on its Western Canadian trade. Next door to David resides Izzy's younger son, Leonard, now the president of CanWest Global Communications, who lives in the former home of the wealthy Riley family. Among the Rileys who grew up in that house was the mother of Izzy's erstwhile business partner Conrad Black.

Izzy moved to Winnipeg from rural Manitoba during high school, then studied at the University of Manitoba. The family lived close to Izzy's current home at the corner of Cambridge and Academy Road in Winnipeg's well-off River Heights. One of his occasional jobs as a university student was to deliver mail. The more experienced mailmen got to deliver to apartment buildings—easy work because you just push the mail into the boxes. Young Izzy got Wellington Crescent with its spacious yards, which meant long walks between houses. But he gets intense satisfaction from knowing that his sons and their families now live in the gracious homes whose mailboxes he once stuffed with letters.

The way the Aspers tell it, Izzy's Ukrainian-born father, Leon Asper, a classical music conductor, immigrated to Canada in 1924, having made his way across Europe in the aftermath of the Russian Revolution. In Canada, he was reunited with his childhood sweetheart, Cecilia Zevert, a pianist, who had earlier left Ukraine with her family. The couple married in 1924 and performed across Canada, first with the Winnipeg Symphony Orchestra and then as players in pit orchestras to accompany silent movies in cinemas across Western Canada.

In the late 1920s, Al Jolson's *The Jazz Singer* hit the screen, talkies were born and the silents went into eclipse. So Leon Asper bought the Lyric Theatre in Minnedosa, Manitoba, where he and Cecilia raised three children, Aubrey, Hettie and Israel. They formed the Minnedosa Little Symphony Orchestra and would perform free public concerts at the Lyric. When the Second World War broke out, Leon Asper was rejected for military duty because he had a wife and children. So he joined up as conductor of the Canadian Legion Symphony Orchestra, which toured the military camps to entertain troops. Cecilia served as the orchestra pianist. After the war, the Aspers built a small chain of theatres in rural Manitoba and Winnipeg. The original Lyric Theatre burned down in 1941, so Leon had it rebuilt in fashionable art deco style, with a modern sound and projection system. The Asper family moved in 1941 from Minnedosa to Neepawa, where Leon operated the Roxy Theatre, and to Winnipeg in 1945. Leon continued to manage his chain of theatres until he sold them in 1954. The second Lyric Theatre was finally torn down on July 6, 1992, although the Aspers have recently revived the name in the form of a bandshell in Winnipeg's Assiniboine Park.

As a young high schooler, Izzy had a crush on a girl named Lorraine, also from Minnedosa, while older brother Aubrey dated Lorraine's sister Marsha. The parents were good friends and it's a wonder Izzy and Lorraine didn't get hitched eventually. But they both moved to Winnipeg, went to university, and as with many high school romances, they drifted apart. Lorraine later moved to the United States, married and became Lorraine Abdul, and had two daughters, one of whom, Paula Abdul, became a Los Angeles Lakers basketball cheerleader, a dancer and singer and a pop phenomenon of the late 1980s and early 1990s. Izzy, the jazz lover, admits he doesn't know much about Paula Abdul. "They told me who she was but, I mean, if she didn't play with Dave Brubeck or she's not Sarah Vaughan, I wouldn't know her." The breakup of Izzy and Lorraine meant that he was available when, in a Winnipeg high school, he met the love of his life, Ruth "Babs" Bernstein. Like the Aspers, the Bernsteins were immigrants from Eastern Europe—Babs's father, Maurice, came to Winnipeg from Poland in 1903, and her mother, Sara, made the journey from Russia in 1913.

There is lots of evidence in Izzy Asper's childhood to suggest that he would become a media mogul. Even as a kid he was a newspaper junkie. As a Grade 10 teenager in Neepawa, he started a newspaper of his own. But Izzy has said that his own father never expected him to amount to much in life. "He kept shaking his head and saying to my mother, 'The kid will never make a living,'" Izzy once said. His father was also disappointed when Izzy went into law. Leon was always remembering the

Dirty Thirties, Izzy told the *Winnipeg Free Press*, when lawyers were paid in chickens or whatever goods their clients could find. Instead, Leon wanted Izzy to take over the movie theatres, but the younger man resisted. Izzy says his father, who died in 1961, forty-one years before Cecilia's death in 2002, was much affected by the Depression; it left him very conservative in his business orientation. Izzy sees his father's reluctance to expand as a symptom of a wider malaise. During the Depression, he says, Winnipeg and Manitoba lost their vigour and their confidence, which Izzy Asper would try to restore through his own business life.

Izzy took his undergraduate and law degrees at the University of Manitoba, where he is remembered as a big man on campus, a ubiquitous presence in debating societies, campus newspapers and variety shows. At one point, his law school attendance was so abysmal that the dean threatened not to let him write examinations. He had to go in and plead his case with the dean, who was known to be a "softie" and ultimately caved in to Izzy's entreaties for a second chance. After graduation, Izzy started practicing law in Winnipeg, where he established a tax and estate practice. In the 1960s he was writing a column on tax for the *Winnipeg Free Press*, *The Globe and Mail* and other newspapers in the national FP Publications chain. He later wrote a best-selling book, *The Benson Iceberg*, a critique of Finance Minister Edgar Benson's tax reform of the early 1970s. Izzy also developed a young protégé named Gerald Schwartz, a very bright University of Manitoba law graduate who articled under Izzy in Winnipeg before going into practice with him.

An active Liberal Party member, Izzy had a compelling interest in public affairs, debating the issues of the day, sometimes passionately. There was a near-legendary dinner party in the early seventies at the home of a local lawyer. The several couples assembled included another close pal of Izzy's, an accountant, who that night engaged him in an intense argument over the minimum wage—Izzy wanted to raise it; his accountant friend was opposed. The debate grew heated, with the two shouting at each other over the dinner table, before the embarrassed host and hostess finally calmed them down. At the end of dinner, dessert arrived in the form of a peach pie. One guest asked for another helping, and the hostess brought a second peach pie and began cutting it. But the pie flipped off the table and onto the floor, and the dish broke into two pieces. Izzy stood up quickly, walked around the table, picked up the bigger piece of pie and shoved it into his antagonist's face. The accountant, pie dripping from his face, picked up the other piece of the broken plate, walked around the table and mashed the pie into Izzy's face. The jagged edge of the plate fragment caught Izzy's nose and he started to bleed profusely. The guests sat, open-mouthed, as his face turned into a unappetizing mess of spurting blood and peach pie fragments. The host whisked Izzy off to a nearby hospital, and the dinner party ended.

Izzy was also fascinated with business, and with Manitoba's place in the broader Canadian economy. He wanted to make things happen for his home province. "So in a series of events which are in retrospect outrageously hilarious I decided to build a distillery in that most natural of locations, Minnedosa, Manitoba," he recalled to a York University audience in 1996. And not just any distillery, he said, but a world-class operation that, according to Izzy's projections, would in time dwarf the industry leader, Seagram. The distillery was immediately profitable for Izzy and his other shareholders, and he was well on his way to his thirty-year plan to exceed Seagram in size. But then the unforeseen happened—a takeover offer came through the transom. Izzy wasn't prepared to sell and he didn't bother telling his other investors. But the other shareholders caught wind of the offer and pressured Izzy to sell, to recoup on their investment after only eight months in business. Eventually, he agreed. "But I learned a terrible lesson—namely, that no matter what your partners agree to going in, ultimately they forget what they had for breakfast when it comes time for lunch. Amnesia, I learned the hard way, is the curse of the business world." The line was delivered good-naturedly, but this early friction with his distillery partners was the harbinger of a business career filled with strife.

Izzy also cherished the dream of becoming premier of Manitoba and delivering the province from the high-taxing, over-regulating NDP, then led by a new premier, Ed Schreyer. Asper managed to win the Liberal leadership in 1970, took a by-election so he could enter the legislature and prepared, he thought, to become provincial premier in the next election. Establishing his credentials as a right-wing Liberal, he laid out a platform that would look good in today's Canadian Alliance party: work for welfare; a triple-e Senate (elected, equal and effective); abolition of capital gains tax; a flat-rate tax system; and constitutional limits on debt, deficits and tax rates.

His battle plan was to become so popular in Manitoba that Conservatives would flock to him, create a united right-wing alternative to the tax-and-spend NDP and hoist Izzy into the premier's job. But that didn't happen—the Conservatives stayed glued to their own party. In the general election that followed, Izzy managed to raise the Liberals' seat count to five from three, but the NDP coasted to province-wide victory again. Izzy likes to joke that he is still known in Manitoba as Landslide Asper for the four-vote victory in his own riding.

It was now clear to Izzy that he would never become premier of Manitoba, and his interest in electoral politics began to wane. His own explanation of why he left politics is that he had to keep repeating his message to the voters, which he found boring—and boredom is the worst thing that could happen to Izzy Asper. He didn't have patience with the short attention span of the voting public. Bud Sherman, an old university friend but also a Conservative political adversary in provincial politics, says Izzy was a great presence in the house, but the Liberals in Manitoba suffered from lack of organization and the cultural strength of the left. There was an idea that to beat the NDP, the right had to be united, and the Conservatives, not the Liberals, traditionally presented themselves as the alternative. In time, Sherman says, Izzy found politics confining, especially for someone with a lot of other interests.

Leaving politics in 1975, Izzy was disillusioned and practically broke at forty, having used up his law practice savings in pursuit of political power. He could have gone back to tax law, but that would have meant a return to narrow precise technical issues, instead of dealing with the big picture, which he had enjoyed in politics. Tax law would also probably force him to leave Winnipeg, which he didn't want to do. Starting a business career from Winnipeg was another option. He already had some irons in the fire, including an involvement in a new television station in Winnipeg. But it was not a clear-cut decision. He remembers that he agreed to a ten-year contract with Babs, which stipulated that after a decade of business, having made his fortune, he would move on to other pursuits, perhaps in public service or academe. That contact was never honoured, Izzy says, because the recession of the early 1980s intervened and other people kept obstructing his game plan.

In his past life, Izzy had always been the trusted adviser to business people. Now he had something to prove, that the adviser could become a doer, that he could be a successful businessman and do it all from Winnipeg. So he poured his energy into CanWest Capital, a holding company he formed with Schwartz to invest in varied businesses, including financial services and Izzy's great love, communications. Asper attracted other investors, including the Toronto-Dominion Bank and the Canada Development Corporation, a federal Crown corporation. In his heart, Izzy dreamed about being a communications magnate, a kind of Citizen Asper. He preferred newspapers, but the fast-growing television industry was attractive, too. Asper came to believe there should be a third force in Canadian television besides the established CBC and the new private network, CTV.

Even before Izzy left politics, he was drawn to the federal government's call for applications to establish independent television stations across Canada, including one in Winnipeg. Stuart Craig, a station owner from Brandon, Manitoba, yearned to tap the much bigger Winnipeg market. The Craig family had broadcasting in their blood: Stuart's father, Johnny, a minor-league hockey goalie and car dealer, had passed up a chance to pick up the lucrative General Motors dealership in Brandon because he wanted to buy part of the local radio station. The Craigs had done well, but they needed other investors and the support of prominent Winnipeggers to win a licence in the province's capital city. So Craig called Paul Morton, a gregarious and well-connected Winnipeg movie theatre entrepreneur. Could Morton come in as a financial partner? But Morton was skeptical that it would ever get off the ground.

The evening after he was contacted by Stuart Craig, Paul Morton went to a Winnipeg garden party and ran into a guy he knew, a local lawyer and politician named Izzy Asper. The Morton and Asper families had done business in the past, for both Izzy's and Paul's fathers had been movie theatre owners. Asper, too, had been approached by Craig, and the two men concluded that they could probably do better than the Craig proposal. The next day, Asper called Morton and asked him if he still felt the same way. The rest is history. Paul Morton and Izzy Asper found themselves in business together, preparing an application for a new TV station in Winnipeg.

In time, the Morton-Asper tandem won the new licence for Winnipeg, and Stuart Craig was demoralized, convinced to his dying day that he had been snookered by the politically connected Asper, who was still leader of the Liberal Party in Manitoba—even while he was seeking a broadcast licence. But Izzy Asper quickly discovered that owning a TV licence in Winnipeg was no slam-dunk to big profits. For one thing, there was this little problem with KCND, a TV station in Pembina, North Dakota, that was making money hand over fist through its unlimited access to the Winnipeg market. It even had a sales office in the Manitoba city to pick up local advertising sales. But the Asper team found a way to effectively block KCND's signals, which led to one of the most storied coups in Canadian broadcasting history.

A central figure in Izzy's early television ventures was Seymour Epstein, a Toronto broadcast engineer whose company, Imagineering, was helping set up the Global television station in Toronto in the early 1970s. Global founder and president Al Bruner introduced Epstein to this unknown guy from Winnipeg who wanted to develop a TV station in his hometown. At that time, Izzy was frustrated because, as the Liberal leader in Manitoba, he felt there was no TV outlet for his views: the

CBC was the NDP's mouthpiece and the CTV station, owned by Winnipeg's Moffat family, was a pawn of the Tories. Bruner, meanwhile, was sympathetic to the idea of getting TV stations going in other cities because Global, an Ontario station, was buying rights to U.S. programs but had no place else to play them.

Epstein, who had once worked at the CRTC, knew the communications legislation backward and forward, and according to his version of the story, he helped Izzy come up with a solution to the KCND problem. (The exact contribution made by Epstein is still disputed by Izzy.) Whoever came up the idea, the upshot was that any new Winnipeg station could erect a transmitter south of Winnipeg that would effectively block KCND's signals. The owners of the North Dakota station realized their Winnipeg gravy train had been derailed, and contemplated selling out. So the Asper group bought the North Dakota station and hatched plans to move it to Winnipeg. Over Labour Day weekend in 1975, they dismantled the entire station, equipment and everything, and moved it north in trucks. The station never skipped a beat, resuming broadcasting immediately as CKND in Winnipeg.

Meanwhile, in Toronto, the fledgling Global TV superstation was on the rocks. Epstein, who had been given a small ownership stake in CKND in return for his assistance, came to Izzy with a sad story— Global, his only customer, was about to go out of business, owing him hundreds of thousands of dollars. Al Bruner, a brilliant marketer but an abysmal businessman, was about to lose his creation. At the same time, Epstein was also talking to a company called IWC, whose investment partners included the wealthy Ivey family of London, Ontario, and a broadcaster named Allan Slaight.

Slaight was a radio pioneer, considered by many the father of rock 'n' roll radio in the country. The son of a newspaperman, he had pioneered the rock music concept in Edmonton and then moved east to become manager of CHUM, a popular radio station owned by former ad salesman Allan Waters. CHUM took off in the late 1950s with the rock 'n' roll revolution, becoming even bigger with the advent of the Beatles, the

Rolling Stones and the Beach Boys. A bit of a rolling stone himself, Slaight left CHUM on a bit of a lark, went to work for a pirate radio station off the British coast and then came back to Canada to run a company that represented CBS in Canada. He joined forces with IWC, which invested in Global, becoming a fifty-fifty partner with CanWest and its bumptious CEO Izzy Asper.

Slaight was Global's on-site manager, but nothing had quite prepared him for having to work with Izzy Asper. Slaight grimaces about how difficult Izzy was. It was always about control, he says. "Did I have conflicts with Izzy? Who doesn't? Izzy is just an impossible guy, as far as I was concerned," Slaight says today, in his office at Standard Broadcasting, his radio company, which has become one of the biggest in Canada, building from its base of the Rogers family's CFRB, the long-time ratings leader in Toronto. "Probably his objective from day one was to squeeze us out, to make life miserable, and it wasn't worth that kind of frustration. . . . He's a brilliant guy but he's just impossible to get along with. You can quote me on that."

According to Seymour Epstein, Izzy either intentionally or accidentally embarked on a campaign to drive Slaight crazy. Asper was a tireless generator of memos and queries, asking for more and more reports on the financial state of Global. Slaight, on the other hand, was a very good hands-on operator, who saved Global by getting its profligate spending under control. Epstein is still puzzled about the whole affair. "What was it between Izzy and Slaight? I wish I knew. You can't say what Izzy did was contrary to his fiduciary role. He was carrying it out in a manner that was difficult to Allan, because Allan wasn't a guy who wanted to write paper reports all the time—he wanted to be out selling. It was fire and water."

The shareholders agreement governing Global TV contained a shotgun clause, which provided a way to resolve the ownership of the company in case of irreconcilable differences. One partner could pull the trigger by making a bid for the other's assets. The other partner then had thirty days to respond with a matching bid. Slaight pulled the trigger in December, 1976, offering $6.8 million for the 50 percent of Global that IWC didn't own. But the Asper group was ready and responded with a matching bid, which allowed Izzy and his partners to take over the network. Slaight and the Iveys were out. Asper, Morton and Epstein were now in control.

Izzy Asper's third career—after law and politics—was now really in motion. He had teamed up with his old friend Morton and his new friend Epstein in running Global. He and his protégé Gerry Schwartz were assembling a nice little group of holdings at CanWest Capital in Winnipeg. Epstein was enthralled with the idea of working with Izzy Asper for a long, long time. "Izzy is the kind of guy who is so likeable that people were wanting to do bad deals with him so they can be working with him. He's bright, he's caring, so it was easy to find a relationship."

If only it were that easy. The Asper-Slaight feud was just the beginning of a pattern that would dominate Izzy's business life. He simply scrapped with a lot of people. It stems from his view of the world: Izzy is an idealist who believes in true love and true friendship, and he is bitterly disappointed with anything that falls short of his ideals. His view of partnership is "my word is my bond." Why has he battled almost anyone he has partnered with? They have all disappointed him. Instead of being partners for life, they have conspired to blunt his ambitions, to muzzle his plans—and that, in turn, has bred an ingrained expectation that in every deal he will be wronged. If necessary, he will sue, and if sued himself, he will not surrender.

CanWest is a powerful business empire built on the simple concept that "they" have let Izzy down. In some cases, "they" are former business partners, or the forces from Eastern Canada, mostly from Toronto, but also from Ottawa or Montreal. "They" include the CRTC, which keeps changing its policies, alternatively giving and taking away what Izzy has rightfully earned. "They" are the cultural nationalists who want everything that runs on Canadian television to be stamped with beavers and maple leaves. Most often, "they" is CTV, whose sole purpose of existence, Izzy believes, is to undermine his dreams—certainly not to make profits.

Underlying all this is the sense of Winnipeg versus the East. This enmity towards Eastern Canada probably arises from Izzy's youth and his career as a young lawyer. Winnipeggers have always moved east to win fame and fortune—in fact, Jewish ex-Winnipeggers have had a powerful impact on Canada's artistic, media and business life—but they have made their careers elsewhere than in their native city. Izzy stayed in Winnipeg and swam against the tide. It rankled him that people believed if you weren't in Toronto or Ottawa, you were a nobody. Izzy Asper was never going to be a nobody.

Asked if he feels like the outsider, Izzy laughs it off. "That's just a media joke—I mean from my perspective. But it gets to be kind of a legend, the myths that grow up." Yet he admits there is something to it, even though "it's not willed, or it's not planned." Many years ago, he says, he committed himself to break the old pattern of someone who would become successful by moving to Toronto. Izzy argues such centralization of power and opportunity is simply bad for nation building. He believes that in his own modest little way he can contribute to the concept that Canada consists of much more than that little triangle of Toronto, Ottawa and Montreal. But that kind of attitude, he says, gets him branded as the chauvinistic Westerner, the guy who automatically frowns on anything from Ontario or Quebec. He insists, "I have contempt for arrogance wherever I find it, and there is, there certainly is." He is scornful of the view that "if it wasn't invented here—in Toronto, New York or whatever—it can't be any good. It impedes what I'm trying to do. I don't resent it philosophically—I smile and laugh at it. But to the extent it gets in the way of where I'm trying to go, yeah, then I battle it and I battle it openly."

This country has, indeed, experienced a shocking centralization of power and elites, which has spawned deep resentments, reflected in the Western support for the Canadian Alliance Party and the rest of Canada's visceral dislike of Toronto and Ottawa. It is a fact of Canadian history. Izzy has spent much of his life trying to level the field. But has it been worth the trouble, the stress, the litigation, the flailing away at shadows? Meanwhile, his critics charge that he has exploited this self-characterization as the downtrodden Western Canadian broadcaster, as a way to have the freedom to thumb his nose at obligations to produce more Canadian programming.

Global TV proved to be very smart about using its money to buy hit programming from the United States. It exploited the peculiar Canadian practice whereby Canadian stations could effectively duplicate U.S. transmissions of hit shows, simultaneously broadcasting the shows themselves and loading them up with their own advertising. Global was able to acquire winners—not only the execrable *Love Boat* and *Dynasty*, but the more acclaimed *Hill Street Blues, St. Elsewhere* and, moving into the nineties, *Friends* and *Frasier*. In time, Global became the largest buyer of U.S. television programming outside the United States. The cultural nationalists might hate it, but Izzy's programmers knew how to stretch their bucks, how to anticipate the hot new show, how to attract advertisers, even if the programs offer appealed to the lowest common denominator.

Izzy's view is that Canada made a huge mistake in tying itself to the U.S. television system by allowing American television stations untrammelled access to Canada on cable systems. "We have wrongly linked our television system to the American system. It's really one of the saddest things that ever happened, but we're back to 1958 there. I spoke against this compatible TV system that allowed over-the-border leakage of signals and then must-carry [U.S. networks] on Canadian cable." He explains that a cable consumer cannot buy the Global television network without also getting ABC, NBC, CBS, PBS and Fox, which are in effect legally Canadian signals. That meant that Canada could not emulate the distinct television system that operates in Australia, for example, where CanWest also has TV stations. "There are really grown-up television operators in that country—and in England. They're not competing against Coca-Cola advertising in Buffalo, because there is no Buffalo in London or in Sydney. We should have developed a purely Canadian television system." The implication is that when Canada made the decision to admit U.S. cable signals, Canadian television operators like Global had no alternative but to compete in the U.S. programming game. Why should Global be pilloried because it played this game so well?

But the other story at Global was the deep divisions within the ownership group, which were perhaps inevitable after Izzy's old Winnipeg partner Paul Morton went east in 1977 so that he could watch over Global Television from its Toronto base. The move distanced him, both physically and emotionally, from Izzy, and brought him closer to Epstein, who became his ally. Friction quickly developed between the Toronto team and the Asper group in Winnipeg about who was really running the company. In time, each wanted the other out, but because each group had a 50 percent voting interest, the company ended up in deadlock.

Cracks also formed in the relationship between Izzy and his partners in CanWest Capital. According to Izzy, in 1979 he saw his chance to fulfill his dream, to realize his great dream of becoming a newspaper publisher. He insists he was never as passionate about television as about newspapers, but he would be continually blocked in his plans—at least until 2000 when he was able to nab the Hollinger papers. In the late 1970s, the FP chain of papers became available, including the *Winnipeg Free Press* and *The Globe and Mail,* and Izzy could have bought the whole chain for less than $160 million. But the board at CanWest turned him down and the papers went to Thomson. Later Izzy would try to buy the *Sun* chain of papers, but again the board turned him down. He would also be squelched in efforts to buy other Thomson papers, but he couldn't be stopped forever.

For Izzy and CanWest, 1983 was a watershed year. Certain CanWest directors, including Gerry Schwartz, wanted to sell some of the holding company's financial services investments. The debate centred on Monarch Life Assurance, based in Winnipeg. Izzy wanted to keep the company, but in the end, Monarch Life was sold. The CanWest assets were split up, and Schwartz moved to Toronto to form Onex, his buyout company. It was a case of the protégé moving out of the mentor's shadow and was probably inevitable, given the magnitude of the two men's egos. Twenty years later, when Schwartz was giving a tribute speech at to Izzy, his tone was teasing but the undertone hinted at the bitter battle: "We started CanWest together and we wound it up in 1983, and there was a moment in time when we were really mad at each other."

With the breakup looming at CanWest, Izzy decided to bid personally for its communications assets—including the holding company's stake in Global TV—but his old partner Epstein submitted a competing offer. For Izzy, this was the ultimate betrayal, and it set the stage for the war to come. Izzy won the bidding for the communications assets, but the stress of the battles with Schwartz, Epstein and Morton exacted a heavy price—as did the Asper diet of fast food, Pepsi and Craven A's. He had a heart attack and underwent bypass surgery in November 1983 at the age of fifty.

The cold war between the two camps continued through the late 1980s, five years of lawsuits, allegations and depositions. The actual legal dispute was about voting control—Izzy held 62 percent of the shares of Global television, but the two sides had equal voting power. And there were other issues, mainly about power and recognition. Izzy felt he wasn't being recognized in Global's Toronto offices for his contribution to the now successful station. The trio's inability to reach agreement ultimately threatened Global's development as the third national TV network. Justice Peter Morse of the Manitoba Supreme Court described the battle between CanWest Ventures, represented by Izzy Asper, and Global TV, which Morton and Epstein ran: "There is a complete lack of trust and confidence between Mr. Asper and CanWest on one hand and Messrs. Morton and Epstein on the other." The atmosphere at board meetings, the judge said, "is very unpleasant and unproductive. Meetings are taped because neither side trusts the other to prepare accurate minutes and lawyers are in attendance. Both Mr. Morton and Mr. Epstein have indicated they do not trust Mr. Asper. Mr. Epstein has stated that Mr. Asper has lied and Mr. Morton has gone so far as to make disparaging remarks in the business community and to friends with respect to Mr. Asper's sobriety, veracity and reliability as a businessman. For a number of years, the CanWest and Morton/Epstein groups have been unable to agree upon the election of independent directors for Global, a requirement of the CRTC, and the so-called independent directors continue in office even though CanWest has lost confidence in them. Nor have the two groups been able to agree on the appointment of auditors and the approval of financial statements or on the holding of annual meetings." Judge Morse observed that Global had prospered as a business despite the almost complete breakdown of communication. But if the parties had been able to agree, the results would have been even better.

Izzy had the dream of building a national network of stations in which he would team up a group of Western stations he already owned with Global in Eastern Canada to take on the established CTV network. Meanwhile, Morton and Epstein wanted to continue to expand Global as a kind of superstation, whose Toronto-originated signal would be transmitted by satellite or broadcast over the air to areas that did not have third English-language service. As long as the impasse remained, Global could not go forward. Judge Morse, reaching judgment on the legal battle, ordered an auction in late 1989 between the two parties. It was the outcome Izzy had been hoping for but, surprisingly, it was not an easy decision for the Asper family, says his daughter Gail. Izzy was in his late fifties, which was late in life to take on the responsibility for managing an entire network. Whoever bought Global would take on a tremendous burden in the programming war with CTV and CBC. "Dad was older than Paul and Seymour. Should he make the decision that they should win the auction, or should he just get his financing in order to win the auction? We had friends calling and saying, 'What are you going to do? Are you crazy, you should be selling out, you can just relax.' And my mom was definitely leaning on the sell side, but obviously that didn't happen."

Outside forces kept changing Izzy's timetable, and he had some unfinished business. "Every time I tried to do something, everybody rose up to stop me. I'm not paranoid but I'm just saying in order to move our Canadian thing along, I wound up having to get into a horrific lawsuit with my Toronto partners. It took five years, so everything went off kilter in terms of my timetable. And as the warfare ended, in 1990 finally, a peculiar thing happened: Gail came into the company."

Indeed, Gail Asper had come back to Winnipeg after five years of practicing law in Halifax, and Izzy had found a place for her in CanWest. Then David, who was in private law practice, and Leonard, who was still at law school, were expressing interest. Suddenly, it was not just about Izzy—it was about providing a place for his family to work, and a business to build for the future. So Izzy bid aggressively for the rest of Global, and won it with an offer of $130 million for Morton and Epstein's stake, which included 40 percent of the equity and half of the voting ownership. Izzy finally had his network.

The timing of Gail's return was also fortuitous because Izzy's lifestyle was taking a toll. Concern about her father is always near the top of Gail's priorities. It was not unusual for him to work away until two or three A.M. Sometimes there are a few drinks and a midnight snack of salami or corned beef or perhaps a takeout from Winnipeg's hamburger chain, Salisbury House. As Izzy worked and ate, he would churn out a deluge of faxes, voice-mail messages or, in recent years, e-mail for senior managers, often painting a dark view of the world, his enemies and the alleged spendthrifts who held the management positions at Global TV in Toronto. Executives would come in the next morning to be greeted by a voice-mail or faxed harangue. It would often blow over later, but it would be disconcerting. For a man who had such gifts, he was driven by considerable insecurity. Izzy's ballast is his wife and the kids, who keep a tight and loving rein on their undisciplined husband and father. At a recent family meeting, the kids cracked the whip, telling Izzy that his unhealthy habits were resurfacing, that he was going longer periods without proper exercise, that his midnight snacks were getting excessive. So they cajoled him into doing something that seems at odds with the Izzy lifestyle—he hired a personal trainer and was to meet him every morning at ten. And Izzy was keeping the appointments rigorously.

Once he took control of Global, Izzy proceeded on his course to becoming the third network in Canada, moving beyond the patchwork of Global, which was essentially an Ontario superstation, and a few stations in Western Canada that had been part of the CanWest assets. But it was tougher than it looked. His relationship with the CRTC was up and down, as Global continued to come up with ratings winners with U.S. programs but was perceived to lag in offering Canadian drama and other hallowed icons.

Izzy describes himself as an economic nationalist, but he is no cultural nationalist. He argues that the cultural mavens would require that domestic television produce fare that is unwatchable as long as it is true to its Canadian roots. Izzy argues that news and sports can be Canadian in content because that is what the Canadian audience wants. But when it comes to drama and music, it is very hard to develop an indigenous product unless you can sell it into world markets, which, Izzy argues, is what Global is trying to do, thus creating jobs and wealth in the country. But the cultural nationalists are contemptuous of popular programs such as the *X-Files* sci-fi series because, even though it was once produced in Canada, it reflected nothing that was Canadian. The reason the show was so successful, he says, is that it attracted a substantial production budget, and that's because it had a U.S. audience. For Izzy, there is a place for pure Canadian drama, but that's the role of public broadcasting. Unfortunately, he says, the CBC does not play the role of public broadcaster—it has become an unfairly subsidized commercial television operation in competition with Global and CTV.

Izzy's views put him into conflict with the nationalist cultural lobby, personified by gadfly Ian Morrison and the Friends of Canadian Broadcasting, a non-profit group. Morrison is a constant burr under Izzy's saddle through his clever sound bites and CRTC testimony. In CanWest's view, the group is an extension of arch-rival CTV, and the

Aspers make much of the fact that Morrison's consultant wife has worked for the rival network.

But Izzy's most bitter foe is perhaps Robert Lantos, a flamboyant film producer who is Izzy's equal in ego and drive. This is a rare Canadian public feud, between two sons of Jewish immigrants, who have both benefitted from government policies or funding, and who have both succeeded remarkably in the Canadian cultural arena. Lantos is a Hungarian-born filmmaker, who began his career in skin flicks, and then moved into legitimate production and distribution. He sold his company Alliance to Michael MacMillan's Atlantis, pocketing $60 million and leaving him free to produce his personal projects. He is a strong Canadian nationalist who makes no secret of his disdain for private broadcasters who, in his view, want the best of all worlds—government-regulated protection, unbridled access to U.S. programming and minimal obligations to support Canadian production. Often, it's Izzy Asper he has in mind.

On November 12, 1998, Lantos let loose at Izzy with both barrels, in a speech at Toronto's Ryerson University which has been reprinted in court documents. Lantos decried the fact that 60 percent of television programming in English Canada was foreign-originated, including more than 90 percent of fiction offerings. But the real miracle, he said, was that Canadian programs managed to attract more than 30 percent of television viewing, even in the face of massively promoted U.S. fare. It was no thanks to most Canadian broadcasters, who serve to undermine Canadian talent through the practice of simulcasting U.S. television shows. "Broadcasters who are nothing but toll collectors between Canadians and their access to popular American shows are just hitching a free ride on the back of the regulator who protects them from true market competition," Lantos thundered.

The speech referred to broadcasters who "walk around, Order of Canada in their lapels, while they call their countrymen losers and urge us to adopt the values of a foreign culture. They talk of free market economies for others, but when it comes to their own business, they are the first to seek the shelter of government policies and programs." He

accused Global Television of stacking the deck against Canadian programming, and particularly the much admired *Traders* series, which
Lantos said was set up to fail in the ratings by being scheduled against
the big U.S. blockbuster *ER*, which was broadcast by CTV.

In late January, 1999, Izzy sued Lantos for libel, alleging that the
speech was defamatory. But more than three years later, the much anticipated libel case still had not proceeded to the courts. Lantos, meanwhile, refused to comment: "I will do this in a courtroom. I have a lot
to say. I'm not going to say it over and over. Asper chose the battle-
ground, not me. I prefer open debate and he chose not to." When and
if it goes to trial, it will be tremendous fun for spectators of the
Canadian culture wars.

Yet the suit itself may have cost Izzy an opportunity to buy a coveted
TV specialty channel. In the mid-to-late nineties, the television market
was being fragmented by the rise of specialty channels that catered to
narrower tastes, to rock music fans, history lovers and sports nuts. The
big networks were seeing their dominance shredded—and in many
cases, the networks themselves were backing the new channels. Global,
distracted by international expansion, had done very little in this area,
until the top specialty station, TSN, became available. TSN had been the
first station in Canada targeting the sports fan, just as ESPN had done
so successfully in the United States. It was controlled by a company
called Netstar, which was owned by Bronfman family interests, other
Canadian investors and ESPN. In 1998, the majority share of Netstar
held by the Canadian investors came on the market and the Aspers made
a bid. It seemed like a sure thing, an offer that would likely meet the
approval of ESPN, which held a veto over the new Canadian partner.
On January 20, 1999, Izzy announced that CanWest had reached agreement with the Canadian investors to buy their shares. But in early
February, Izzy's takeover of Netstar was called off and arch-rival CTV
swept in and snagged Netstar's control position in a $400 million deal.

The yanking of CanWest's offer and CTV's winning bid came only
about a week after Izzy had sued Lantos for libel. It roused speculation that

New York–based ESPN had become nervous about a partnership with the litigious Izzy, and that the nervousness had only been heightened when the Lantos libel action hit the headlines. According to industry speculation, that caused ESPN to drag its heels on the Asper bid and make a call to CTV to gauge its interest in TSN. It wouldn't be the first time Izzy's reputation had come back to haunt him. For years, Asper was unable to forge a merger with WIC, the Vancouver broadcasting company, because WIC's late owner, Frank Griffiths, was wary of the Manitoba entrepreneur's track record in partnerships.

Leonard Asper says the CanWest–Netstar deal exploded because ESPN was asking for a lot of things that the Aspers could not accept. CanWest became concerned that it was paying a hefty control premium for the NetStar stake, but was not getting effective control. ESPN, the 32 percent shareholder, wanted an equal partnership. "Which is fine," Leonard says, "if you've got half the money in the place. They wanted to veto everything so we wouldn't get any of the benefits of controlling it, integrating it. And they weren't wrong—they just wanted an asset that they could sell later."

Leonard also acknowledges that CanWest's reputation, and particularly the lawsuit with Lantos, might have turned off ESPN and led it to approach CTV. The libel suit against Lantos was a principled act, he says, against someone who was attacking the family. He also alleges that there was some history at work: Lantos had offered his company to CanWest at one point, but his selling price had been rejected. "So there are people who don't like us and find ways to attack us and we fight back, and if we lose a deal over that, I'm not worried. I'd rather go to sleep each night knowing who I am, who we are and what we stand for—to know we stood up and didn't back down and didn't compromise our principles for some short-term opportunity." Leonard acknowledges that a lot of CanWest managers say, "'Aw, why do you fight? I know they crapped all over you, but don't fight. It's just messy. People will think you're litigious.' So what? I feel more pure and in the end we are good people and we will win."

CTV president Ivan Fecan says he knows of no whisper campaign against CanWest or any pressure brought by his network on ESPN. "ESPN called us—we didn't call them," he says, adding that the call came to him with about ten days left before the deadline for new suitors. "I think CanWest had been dealing with ESPN and Netstar for nine months and as I understood it, made a deal and then ESPN decided it wanted a different partner. And I was sitting behind this desk in this chair and the guy from ESPN called and said, 'You want to talk?' Why the hell wouldn't I want to talk?"

The youthful Leonard, even more than his father, gets agitated by the alleged treachery of CanWest's rivals. "People have tried to screw us, or sued us. We stand up for our rights, we don't settle, we fight because we stand up for our principles, for what our rights are. We don't say, 'Oh, let's just sweep it under the carpet—it will be messy.' So yeah, you end up in a few lawsuits like that, and people looking it at it from ten thousand miles away will just see a bunch of lawsuits. And there are a group of people in Toronto, our competitors, perpetuating those myths, particularly CTV."

Izzy also found himself blocked in his dream of a national conventional TV network. Most important, he was being shut out of prosperous Alberta. He owned the Ontario-based Global station and outlets in Regina, Vancouver and Winnipeg. Then came a call for applications for a new Alberta licence in 1993–94, which CanWest applied for, along with its old rival, the Craig family of Manitoba. But the CRTC decided not to award any new licence at that time. Frustrated in Canada, Izzy moved offshore more aggressively, buying television and radio properties in Australia and New Zealand. The CanWest formula is the same abroad as in Canada—to buy up ailing broadcast properties and nurse them back to health through aggressive sales and close attention to costs. The first target was New Zealand, where in 1991 CanWest bought an interest in T3, one of the national television broadcasters. In 1997, it increased its stake to 100 percent and in 1997 launched a complementary service called T4. In 1997, it also purchased a private radio group, now called CanWest Radio NZ, and currently operates nine stations reaching about 65 percent of the population.

In 1992, CanWest was part of a consortium that bought Network TEN, the major Australian private TV network, for $208 million. Because of Australian laws, the Aspers have had to retain only a minority voting interest in the network—but they have a majority economic interest. In 1998, CanWest moved into the Irish market with the launch of TV3 Ireland, a television network that has contended against the established three stations as the first privately owned independent commercial station in the republic. CanWest was a contender for a new Channel Five slot in the British market in 1995, but its bid was rejected in favour of the German broadcaster RTL. Prevented by foreign ownership constraints from entering the United States in a big way, Izzy had still become the only Canadian broadcaster with a strong array of international assets.

The Aspers' next big chance for an Alberta channel came in 1996, when the CRTC once again opened the door for applications. This time, Izzy was determined not to be denied. Arrayed against him, as before, were his old sparring partners, the Craig family from Brandon. It was a tough hearing, and one that the Aspers badly misjudged. The Craigs trumpeted their willingness to pump money into local programming, which impressed the CRTC. Bud Sherman, Izzy's old friend, was enlisted to help CanWest try to win the battle of Alberta, but he says that the Craigs basically came in and undressed Global. "With all due deference, Izzy's got to be twice as good as anyone else to win something from CRTC," admits Sherman, a former CRTC commissioner. "He doesn't suffer CRTC too comfortably, and the CRTC is too aware of that." But this time, CanWest was too complacent. Having felt it had been denied unfairly before, it believed it had almost had a divine right to be in the rich Alberta market.

"A lot of the industry felt it was the last piece of the puzzle to fill in Izzy's system," agrees Drew Craig, the son of Stuart Craig and the quarterback of the family's television strategy. The Craigs themselves had ambitions to be a serious national player. This was a big test for them, to determine whether they would be in the game. "They were two very different approaches," Drew Craig says. "Izzy's was that Canada needs another national network: 'Alberta needs Global and we need Alberta.' Our approach was, 'Look, what Alberta needs is its own local stations.'" On November 1, 1996, the Craigs won the licence for new stations in Calgary and Edmonton. Izzy was again shut out of Alberta, but he made one last bid, appealing the CRTC decision to the federal cabinet. In late January, 1997, the CRTC decision was upheld by cabinet. Twenty-five years after losing the Winnipeg television licence to Izzy, Stuart Craig had exacted a measure of revenge. In late 1999, the Craig patriarch died of pancreatic cancer.

Izzy was deeply frustrated about losing twice in Alberta—until WIC suddenly appeared on his radar. WIC Western International Communications was a broadcasting empire built from Vancouver by the enterprising Frank Griffiths, with television and radio stations across Canada, and the dominant TV news player in Vancouver with its ownership of BCTV. When Griffiths became ill and died on April 7, 1994, the divisions in his family burst wide open. The children tried to move into leadership roles, but the widow, Emily Griffiths, was not convinced they were up to scratch. In time, she decided to get out of the broadcasting business, and she put her control position into play. It was a classic crisis for a publicly traded family company—the death of the patriarch, infighting among the survivors and hovering vultures eager to pick at the spoils.

Izzy, rebuffed twice by the CRTC from owning stations in Alberta, saw the opportunity to complete his dream, a network from coast to coast. He felt he had the upper hand because he and Frank Griffiths had had a long and friendly relationship. Indeed, they had talked as early as the 1970s about joining forces in a strong Western broadcast company. After Frank's death, Izzy wooed Mrs. Griffith and felt she would support his bid for the company. But this time he ran into the Shaws, a determined family of Albertans who were not about to roll over and let

Izzy take WIC without a challenge. The Shaws had their own agenda: they were building a substantial media presence, in addition to their cable television empire, mostly in western Canada. It should have been a saw-off—the Shaws coveted WIC's dozen radio stations, its raft of specialty channels and a majority interest in Cancom, the satellite company; Izzy mostly wanted the conventional TV stations. But even for Izzy, a veteran of the wars, the WIC battle was a nightmare: "The WIC stuff was a shoot-out at the OK corral," Izzy says now. He jokes that CanWest was culturally unprepared for battling the Shaws: "We're prairie people, not Albertans—it was one of the toughest that we had to get through."

Izzy says he arranged a summit meeting in a Toronto hotel, where he tried to stike a deal before the war started. He figured he had been through this kind of corporate warfare before as a lawyer and as a student of business. The two sides sat down—Izzy and his younger son and heir apparent, Leonard, with patriarch JR Shaw and his heir apparent son, Jim. Izzy suggested that they cut a deal on the assets right then and there, and it would prevent a lot of time, grief and money later on. But the Shaws said they had never gone through a contested takeover battle like this, and were prepared to take their chances. JR's view was that the Shaws would like to go a few rounds, and just see whether Izzy's prediction of dire consequences would pan out.

The Shaws and Aspers proceeded to do battle and the WIC showdown took on a life of its own. Izzy argues that it was particularly tense because of CanWest's ultimate strategy. To get what he wanted, he had to force an impasse—to reach a situation where both Shaw and CanWest held large stakes in WIC but neither could move without the other. It meant tying up millions of dollars for many months without any return, waiting for a breakthrough. Izzy also admits he made tactical errors. At one point, CanWest seemed to have locked up the purchase of the controlling interest in the voting shares from Emily Griffiths. But CanWest sought to gain seats on the board as a precondition for the deal, which angered Mrs. Griffiths and allowed the Shaws to move back in and make their own deal with the widow. In March 1998, Mrs. Griffiths sold her controlling interest in WIC to the Shaws, which momentarily put them in the driver's seat. Then the Aspers countered with their own takeover bid for all the WIC shares, and the Shaws responded with their own all-share bid.

The saw-off of bids, counter-bids and court challenges added up to a nearly two-year delay in getting a hold of WIC's TV assets, in what Izzy calls "a stomach-crunching fight." Even after the Aspers and Shaws finally made peace and divvied up the assets, the deal was delayed when the tax department shot down the arrangement. It was only in October 1999, more than two years after Izzy and JR met in that hotel room, that the deal was finally done. And it took another eight months before it passed CRTC muster.

The battle also marked the emergence of a new generation in both Shaw and CanWest. Leonard Asper's presence in that room signalled he was taking over from his father—in fact, he was named CEO in the fall of 1999. The feisty Jim Shaw was assuming control from his own father, but Jim's style was different from that of his charming folksy father—he liked to rock and roll. At the most bitter moment in the battle, when the Shaws had seemingly taken control of WIC, Jim Shaw taunted Izzy in a comment to *Globe and Mail* reporter Robert Brehl: "We really shook his peaches," a phrase of indeterminate origin but perhaps adapted from the old Steve Miller Band hit song, "The Joker." The highly competitive Izzy admits that when the deal was finally done, he had to bite his tongue. He was tempted to say, "You're having peaches with sour cream, baby!" Instead, Izzy's line was, "Now it's peaches and cream."

At a cost of $800 million, Izzy finally had his national television system, which was confirmed in CRTC approval in July, 2000. But there wasn't the customary celebratory dinner that usually marks a successful takeover. "It was such a difficult and painful thing, the warfare, that nobody wanted to have a celebration. " It wasn't until a year later that the takeover team would get together for a victory dinner. And by that time the family was knee-deep in integrating its $3 billion-plus buyout of the Southam papers.

4 THE SON ALSO RISES

THE FOCUS OF ATTENTION IN THE VAST MEETING HALL IN Montreal's downtown Place Bonaventure is a handsome dark-haired man moving around on crutches. The occasion is the CRTC hearings to rule on Quebecor's takeover of the cable and broadcasting giant Groupe Vidéotron, and the magnetic Pierre Karl Péladeau is, as usual, the centre of attention. The hearings are an important test of Pierre Karl's drive to dominate the Quebec media scene, and his injury doesn't slow him down as he moves among his managers and advisers, laughing and nodding. During his pitch to the CRTC, commissioner Andrée Wylie slyly quips that even though this is Pierre Karl's first performance before the commission, she will refrain from asking him to "break a leg."

A little thing like a fractured limb doesn't slow down Pierre Karl, a six-foot-tall athletic thirty-nine-year-old, who is Quebec's young man in a hurry. "Even on crutches I was not moving too bad," he boasts later. The crutches, he explains, are the result of a spectacular snowboarding accident on a mountain near Val d'Isère in France. Pierre Karl is an experienced boarder, but "I had a bad fall, carving very fast—I was finishing a curve at high speed," he explains, giving the incident a taste of the proper body language. But the pain of the fracture, he says, was nothing like the discomfort during the ride down the side of the mountain, strapped to a toboggan by the ski patrol. He proceeds to slouch down deeply in his chair, thrusting his body up and down in pelvic bumps and grinds to imitate the ride. But within a month and a half of the accident, he asserts, he was back up water skiing in Quebec. "No, Pierre Karl," protests his media adviser Luc Lavoie. "Yes, I was," the younger man insists. "The first time that I did it, I had a bit of a pain, but two weeks later it was fine." The water in early May is pretty cold in Quebec's Eastern Townships, he admits, but Pierre Karl dove right in.

It is an image of Pierre Karl Péladeau that resonates among those who know him: daring, a bit out of control, risking injury in business and in life. He is emotionally turbulent, moving from calm analysis to childish delight to torrential profanity in the span of a minute. It would be too facile to dismiss this as simply Gallic emotion. No one does Gallic quite like Pierre Karl. And yet despite this erratic personality, he manages to come out of it appearing charming and roguishly likeable—and ultimately very smart. The brightest of all the media moguls is reputedly Ted Rogers, says one executive who has worked with many of Canada's communications titans. Yet this executive also says, "Pierre Karl is just as smart as Ted, but his youth and inexperience work against him."

These two men, Péladeau and Rogers, found themselves in the middle of a no-holds-barred six-month battle for Vidéotron, Quebec's largest cable company, with its 1.5 million subscribers and controlling share of TVA, the province's biggest private TV network. It began in early February, 2000, with Rogers making a $5.6 billion stock bid for Vidéotron. After lawsuits, injunctions and some of the most heated rhetoric in Canadian takeover annals, Pierre Karl won the battle with a $5.4 billion all-cash offer, in a controversial partnership with the massive pension fund, the Caisse de dépôt et placement du Québec, which already owned 17 percent of Vidéotron.

That is why Pierre Karl is here today in Montreal, putting his case before the CRTC panel. Of course, he must also show the obligatory corporate video proclaiming the abundant public benefits of Quebecor's takeover of Vidéotron. The video consists of a stirring rhapsody of classical music and eloquent testimony by Quebec artists and musicians about how Quebecor's ownership of the cable and broadcast company would give them a stronger voice in the province's media life. But the film also shows a black-and-white film clip of a scruffy, long-haired man conducting a symphony orchestra. It is, of course, Quebecor's eccentric founder, Pierre Karl's music-loving father, Pierre Péladeau, who has been dead for more than three years. The clip is an appropriate touch, for even in death, Pierre Péladeau is still a force in the company he founded fifty years earlier.

Pierre Karl has played a lot of roles in his young, turbulent life, but one of his most frequent portrayals is that of the sullen, rebellious son, trying to escape his father's image and expectations. In an interview, Pierre Karl's one moment of shy hesitation comes when he is asked, "Do you manage like your father?" The answer is halting and skittish: "I don't know, it's tough for me to comment. . . . Ask others who are in a better position to answer." But at other times, he readily invokes the memory of his father, who died in 1997 at age seventy-two. Pierre Karl often talks about "what my father did" in certain situations, or what "my father said." There is clearly a complex relationship here. "PK has his demons," says a close friend. "He is still trying to exorcise his father."

His father, of course, was a hard act to follow, a wildly controversial figure who built up a gigantic media, printing and publishing empire. He was just as famous for his personal life, as a shameless womanizer, separatist sympathizer, alleged anti-Semite, reformed alcoholic and manic-depressive engaged in a constant tussle with mood swings. But he was also an intellectual, a student of philosophy and a classical music buff whose hero was Beethoven. For years, he was the biggest benefactor of the Orchestre Métropolitain du Grand Montréal. He was the Québécois version of Ted Turner, the founder of CNN, another media genius and innovator who is buffeted by emotional disorders and a turbulent personal life.

Pierre Péladeau, who was born in 1925, liked to leave the impression that he had to climb up from lowly roots in the tough slums of east-end Montreal. But according to journalist Kevin Dougherty, in a 1992 article in *The Financial Post,* he was in fact born in the upscale neighbourhood of Outremont, where his father made and lost a fortune in the flooring business. Pierre's father, Henri, died when his son was ten, but the family managed to hang on to their Outremont address. Pierre enjoyed the typical education of an affluent Quebecer, going to the elite

Collège Jean-de-Brébeuf, then on to the University of Montreal. At U of M, he obtained an advanced degree in philosophy before moving on to take a law degree at McGill University. Pierre always said that his law and philosophy training were the ideal background for a tabloid newspaper publisher.

Fresh out of graduate school, he bought his first newspaper, a failing weekly called *Le Journal de Rosemont,* in 1950, using $1,500 his mother, Elmire, had borrowed for a down payment. Through the 1950s and 1960s, he kept acquiring and launching weeklies, as well as establishing his own printing operations. He was a millionaire by the time he was thirty-four. In 1964, *La Presse,* then Montreal's leading circulation daily and controlled by the powerful investor Paul Desmarais, was shut down by a strike. Péladeau leaped into the void by starting *Le Journal de Montréal,* a flamboyant tabloid, a paper so lightweight in its aspirations that even today it does not run editorial opinions. It quickly grew to 80,000 in circulation, but when *La Presse* returned to action seven months later, *Le Journal* slipped back to 10,000 readers. However, the tabloid's formula of sensationalist crime, entertainment and sports took off from that point, until it overtook *La Presse* and reached 330,000 circulation in 1981. It is now the largest newspaper in French Canada.

Pierre Péladeau formed Quebecor in 1965, taking it public on the American Stock Exchange in 1972, because, in his view, the shares would then be more highly regarded by U.S. investment analysts. But not everything he touched was golden. He thought his *Le Journal* tabloid formula was exportable, so he launched the *Philadelphia Journal* in 1977. But it never caught on and closed in 1982. Similarly, in the late 1980s, he started a tabloid English paper, the *Daily News,* to take on the *Gazette* in the Montreal market. He had to pull the plug on it, too, after a flood of losses.

His personal life was a paradox: Péladeau gave the impression of being the cultured intellectual, but he drank heavily and caroused late into the evening. According to Dougherty, he once owned a Montreal cabaret where he used to bend his elbow with *les vedettes,* the stars of the

Quebec pop scene. Then in 1974 he suddenly quit drinking and joined Alcoholics Anonymous, becoming what his biographer Colette Chabot calls "the least anonymous" alcoholic in Quebec, as he shared his drunken experiences in a kind of public catharsis. But Pierre's personal demons seemed to stalk the rest of the family. His first wife and the mother of his four oldest children— Erik, Pierre Karl, Isabelle and Anne Marie— died in 1976, herself the victim of addiction to alcohol and prescription drugs. Over his lifetime, he fathered seven children with three women, and carried on a host of affairs. His last child was born in 1991 to a companion in Paris. "We have interesting family reunions," Erik, his oldest son, once noted dryly.

Until 1974, Péladeau was an atheist, captivated by Nietzsche's ideas of the death of God and the notion of a Superman. But while boarding an Air Canada flight in Val-d'Or, Quebec, to return to Montreal, he suddenly had a mystical experience. He thought about the plane's pilot, who was holding Péladeau's life in his hands. "All of a sudden, it became clear to me that if the guy was controlling my life, someone else was controlling his life. I said to myself that God was controlling his life and I experienced a profound feeling of security."

Conversion or not, his political incorrectness—some would say his bigotry—knew no bounds. Péladeau faced accusations that he was an anti-Semite after a 1990 interview in *L'actualité*, in which he said that Jews "took up too much space" in Montreal's fashion industry. He later explained that he was trying to advance the cause of Francophone designers in a world dominated by Anglophones, and not just Jews. He also expressed sympathy for Quebec separatism, although he explained that he simply shared the ambiguous feelings that a lot of Quebecers hold towards Canada. And his views about women were that they were essentially playthings. In 1989, he attracted harsh criticism outside Quebec when he said, "The big problem with women in business is this: They try to seduce too much." But the more he angered non-Quebecers, the more he seemed to be loved in Quebec, where he was embraced as the little guy standing up to the establishment, and overcoming his battles with alcoholism and mental illness.

As he developed the company, Péladeau began to expand its operations in the printing sector. He hired good people, including Rémi Marcoux, a smart young manager from the entrepreneurial Beauce region in eastern Quebec. Marcoux rose high in the organization, but eventually left to form his own company, to the incredulity of his boss, who kept trying to lure him back. Marcoux's company, GTC Transcontinental, became a competitor to Quebecor, a smaller version of the company Péladeau had formed, the second largest magazine publisher in Canada, and itself a participant in the convergence trends of the late 1990s and early twenty-first century.

In the 1980s, Péladeau became a partner of the Czech-born British publishing magnate Robert Maxwell, also a man of large appetites and controversial style. In 1987, they collaborated to buy control of Donahue, a large Quebec forest products firm; this gave the Quebec entrepreneur a measure of integration with his printing and publishing business. In late 1988, Péladeau bought the printing subsidiary of BCE, which brought him the choice contract to print many of the telephone directories in Canada. The head of that operation was Charles Cavell, an in-your-face Anglophone manager who Péladeau clearly took a shine to. The bumptious Cavell agreed to stay on for six months to run the company in transition, but he wasn't interested in sticking around in a Canadian printing industry that looked doomed under the new Canada–U.S. Free Trade Agreement.

"When Mr. Péladeau challenged me, I said I didn't want to stay," Cavell says. "I said the only thing that would get me to stay is if we were as large in the U.S. as in Canada before the full implementation of free trade. He looked me in the eye and said, 'Okay, you do that.'" Péladeau told Cavell to work out his contract terms with another top Quebecor executive, but Cavell still wasn't convinced he should take the job. He went home that night and told his wife about his dilemma—leave the printing industry or stick with Péladeau and try to create a world-class printing operation. "My wife said I'd kick myself if I didn't take it," he recalls.

Cavell stayed with Péladeau, and two years later they did a deal that was very significant in terms of what Pierre Karl is trying to achieve with Vidéotron. After the mysterious death of Robert Maxwell in the ocean off his yacht, Quebecor bought Maxwell Graphics in the United States for $500 million, with the Caisse de dépôt coming in as a partner. The Maxwell assets were bundled together in a new printing company, highly leveraged with debt, with plans to take it public within a few years. Péladeau and Cavell went in, cleaned up the printing operations, cut costs and created synergies, and the initial public offering of Quebecor Printing two years later was the biggest in Canadian history until then. In a sense, it was just what Pierre Karl expected to do with Vidéotron, again in partnership with his old ally, the Caisse.

As the two men built Quebecor Printing into what would become the world's largest commercial printer, Cavell says he quickly learned that Pierre Péladeau had a gut feeling for business, a gift for being able to assess strategic opportunity, not only intellectually but instinctively. "He had this sixth sense about when it felt like it made sense and when it didn't." Now a key lieutenant of Péladeau's son, Cavell says the younger man has a bit of that sixth sense as well. Perhaps that's what Pierre Péladeau saw in the younger of his two older sons. Erik and Pierre Karl eventually joined the company, but it was not easy working in the shadow of a strong-willed father. Erik, tall, dough-faced and amiable, drifted in and out of the company, liked technology, but perhaps lacked the killer instinct and the obsessiveness of his brother and father. Although Pierre Péladeau took his time about designating Pierre Karl as his successor, he clearly saw the younger son as the one most like him, an instigator, a doer. But they had a stormy relationship for many years, fuelled by a flammable mix of love and jealousy.

Pierre Karl was fifteen when his mother died, an event that turned him into a moody, inwardly focused kid. He was sent away to live with another family, the Laframboises, in Cartierville, a well-off area of Montreal. According to journalist Luc Chartrand, writing in L'actualité, his siblings felt that was Pierre Karl's salvation—he was removed from the turbulence of Péladeau family life. And yet in personality he was much more like his father than the rest of his siblings.

Pierre Karl's early manhood was spent in open rebellion against his father, as he zealously espoused left-wing causes. He took up the spelling of his second name—it was originally Pierre Carl—because of his admiration for Karl Marx. He studied philosophy at the Université du Québec à Montréal, where he developed a taste for communism, even distributing leaflets for the party. But four years later, when he was twenty-two and working on a master's degree in philosophy in Paris, he suddenly experienced a *volte face* and entered the study of law. Pierre Péladeau used to say that a long birthday lunch with his son in Paris led to this conversion to capitalism. Pierre Karl says it was just a natural youthful evolution. In any case, he returned to Canada in the mid-1980s and threw himself into the family business, now a committed convert to capitalism.

The company Pierre Karl entered had risen to the top ranks of Quebec's business elite. The Péladeaus were among the entrepreneurs who formed the core of Quebec Inc., the term popularly used to describe the chosen instruments of Quebec government contracts and assistance, along with financial backing from the Caisse, the large provincial pension plan. To its critics, the Quebec Inc. network represented a cozy club of sweetheart deals and uncompetitive relationships that defied the discipline of the market. But for many Quebecers, Quebec Inc. was a natural response to living on a French-language island in the middle of English-speaking North America. Many of the Quebec Inc. elite prospered, including Quebecor, transportation giant Bombardier and Vidéotron, the province's dominant cable company, controlled by the tall, slim patrician-looking André Chagnon and his family. In this club, it was inevitable that Chagnon and Pierre Péladeau would get to know each other—in fact, they were quite good friends, although Péladeau's son would not find the relationship so agreeable.

In fact, Péladeau and Chagnon had occasionally talked about doing business together, but nothing ever came of it. Pierre Péladeau had always said how much he liked cable TV, not because he saw any potential synergies with his newspaper chain, but because cable seemed to be a solid cash-generating business. When Pierre Karl Péladeau came home from his Paris university education in the mid-1980s, he found files on his desk, left by his father, analyzing the business prospects for cable companies. Pierre Karl jokes that his dad would say they should be in "le cable," but he points out that "le cable" also means the ropes around a boxing ring. The boxing analogy works nicely, because the son eventually had to engage in a knock-out battle with Ted Rogers—as well as André Chagnon—for control of Vidéotron.

But a boxing match could also describe the tumultuous relationship between Pierre Karl and his father. As Pierre Karl laboured on in Quebecor, working his way through various jobs, his father played with his emotions, behaving like the typically complex father-entrepreneur, viewing his son as a potential successor but also as a threat. Isabelle, Pierre Karl's sister, who also worked for a while in Quebecor, was quoted as saying, "My father would often say, 'that little whippersnapper, he's not going to show me.'" According to the article in *L'actualité* by Luc Chartrand, Pierre told a family business conference in 1993 that he was in no hurry to hand over the reins, that he might wait until he was ninety before passing down the business. The cruellest part of the speech was the judgment Pierre pronounced on his two sons: he praised Erik to the hilt, while dismissing Pierre Karl with the remark "He's harder to figure out." Chartrand wrote that after the conference, Pierre Karl's close associates noticed him sitting in his office, obviously in turmoil. He later admitted that his father's comment was a slap in the face.

Still, Pierre threw him into some tough situations. In 1993, the thirty-two-year-old Pierre Karl was given the job of negotiating the layoff of press operators at *Le Journal de Montréal,* after technological changes had rendered them redundant. Rather than agree to a union deal, as his father would have likely done, Pierre Karl set up a battle plan with a lockout clearly on his mind. He secretly sent Quebecor managers to learn the basics of press operation and found an abandoned factory in nearby Cornwall, Ontario, where they could print the paper. Pierre Karl was ready when the lockout came, hunkering down with the managers at the Cornwall plant and helping put out the paper. But after the stalemate had dragged on for five months, Pierre Péladeau stepped in and negotiated a settlement that put the workers back on the job within forty-eight hours.

One common view is that after the failed lockout, Pierre Karl was banished to Europe. But Pierre Karl says he was simply tired to hearing the whispers that he was a beneficiary of blatant nepotism. He wanted to run his own show. He was appointed president of the company's European printing operations, which were almost non-existent at that point. Pierre Karl made Quebecor a force in Europe, and Europe, in turn, made his career. In four years, he turned the company into Europe's largest printer, with $800 million in annual sales. He also made a reputation as a savage cost-cutter, one who could take over a bankrupt business and make it hum again with profits.

His big coup was taking over Jean Didier, the largest printing operator in France. It was a fat company with huge debt and a bloated, elegant head office, where Pierre Karl mercilessly trimmed the fat. He says today that he finds it ironic that the press makes so much of his layoffs and terminations of managers at the former Vidéotron. It's nothing compared with the cutting at Didier, but no one in the Canadian media paid much attention to him in those days. He also closed the opulent managerial dining room at Didier, which was a hallowed perk in this very French company. "You can't go from drinking vintages to drinking maple syrup," one former manager complained to Chartrand. "This guy is not very subtle." The pattern was repeated in acquisitions of troubled companies across Europe. Pierre Karl had a reputation as an indefatigable, merciless turnaround artist.

As a manager, he is very much a product of those days. Despite a flamboyant lifestyle, he sees himself as essentially a nuts-and-bolts printing guy, comfortable with the industry's pattern of heavy capital expenditures and obsessive attention to costs. "The printing world is big pieces of iron and lots of unionized workforce who come and go, just numbers on the page," says a manager who once worked in Quebecor. People are fodder in this industrial model—there is not the sense of massaging egos that you get in knowledge industries, such as television. the Internet, or even newspapers. High management turnover is a fact of life. "The whole printing operation went through management like shit through a goose," the executive says. "There was a big search in Europe and in the United States; they went through a lot of management." Pierre Karl is, of course, highly skilled at the cost management part, but it invites suspicion that he is no visionary—essentially, he is an old-economy, bottom-line manager, and a very good one. It's ironic when you consider the economic straits he has found himself in as a result of venturing into something as futuristic as media convergence.

Pierre Karl's successful European interlude ended dramatically in December, 1997, when Pierre Péladeau suffered a massive heart attack and slipped into a coma. Pierre Karl flew back to Montreal and sat for weeks beside his father's hospital bed. On Christmas Eve, Pierre Péladeau died. An interim management team of Péladeau loyalists, including Charles Cavell, took over the company, but Pierre Karl was already making his mark in other places. Even before taking over as president, the younger man, who was chief operating officer at Quebecor Printing and vice-chairman of parent Quebecor, took his scalpel to the U.S. operations, closing plants and the U.S. head office in Boston. He also slashed though budgets at *Le Journal de Montréal,* eliminating jobs in the process.

If there was any question about who was in charge at Quebecor, it was quickly dispelled in late 1998, when Pierre Karl was at the centre of a takeover battle for the Sun Media newspaper chain, including its flagship, *The Toronto Sun.* There had been a lot of history in the relationship between the feisty tabloid Sun newspapers and the feisty, tabloid Quebecor group. In 1996, Pierre Péladeau *père* had launched a takeover offer for the Sun chain, which debt-strapped Ted Rogers was trying to unload. Péladeau was immediately confronted with an angry reaction from the newspapers' outspoken columnists, who recoiled at the idea of having an avowed separatist as a boss. A typical response came from Allan Fotheringham, a columnist for the Sun-controlled *Financial Post*, who wrote that the "idea of Péladeau for a boss would be too much to stomach."

According to Fotheringham, "he is, for starters, an ex-alcoholic, a closet separatist, and has slurred Jews. He has credentials for all those categories. The thought that a chap whose separatist views are no secret in Quebec could own and run thriving and lively newspapers in Alberta and Ontario is too much to bear."

Quebecor lost the battle for Sun Media, prompting Péladeau to charge that he had been the victim of a smear campaign by the Sun papers. The winners were a management team led by Sun president Paul Godfrey, which acquired control of the chain. But Sun Media was now widely held, and nakedly exposed to another takeover in the consolidating media industry. Two years later the *Sun*'s bitter rival, Torstar, owner of the left-leaning *Toronto Star*, made a bid for the chain. It was repugnant to the *Sun* loyalists, who knew the *Star* bid was not only ideologically distasteful but held the possibility of heavy layoffs due to duplication. The irony was huge, as the once despised Quebecor actually came in as the white knight, spiriting Sun Media away in a $1 billion takeover.

Leading the negotiations for Quebecor were Pierre Karl and Charles Cavell. They paid three times what Pierre *père* had offered in 1996, but Cavell and Péladeau both insist now that it was a great deal. It gave Quebecor an asset with a strong cash flow and a publishing presence across Canada. But for the Sun management, who became very rich in the takeover, the deal left a bit of a sour taste. Before the Quebecor takeover, the Sun management had essentially traded *The Financial Post* business daily to Conrad Black—and it became the linchpin of his new *National Post* daily. In return, they got a group of newspapers in Western Ontario, including *The Hamilton Spectator, Kitchener-Waterloo Record, Guelph Mercury* and *Cambridge Reporter*. "We now had *The Toronto Star* surrounded in the richest market in Canada," one Sun manager recalls. But Quebecor seemed oblivious to the possibilities. In an effort to reduce its takeover costs, it offloaded these four papers, led by the *Spectator*, to arch-rival Torstar—which incidentally contracted Quebecor's printing presses to print many of its Harlequin romance novels. This undercutting of the Ontario strategy was a slap in the face to the Sun Media crowd, and accelerated the departure of the now well-heeled top managers from Sun.

The purchase of Sun Media also delivered a 60 percent interest in Canoe, a Web portal developed under *Sun* guidance that was a front-runner in the emerging Internet economy. Canoe, which had dreams of being the dominant Canadian Net portal, had attracted a band of smart, committed managers and employees, many from the Sun chain. For Pierre Karl, the printing plant cost-cutter, this slice of the New Economy would be both intriguing and dangerous. He would never really master the promise of Canoe.

Pierre Karl became president and CEO of Quebecor in February, 1999, rising to the position that his father once said he could not possibly attain. He came in full of piss and vinegar. Hard on the heels of the Sun Media takeover, he bought the U.S. printing giant World Color Press for US$2.7 billion, and combined it with his other printing assets to form Quebecor World, now finally the largest commercial printing company in the world.

Cavell observes that Pierre Karl manages in the manner of a younger man, which is quite different from the style of an older person like himself. "You have an interest in moving quickly and sustaining pressure," he says. But don't you need that measured approach? "Yes and no," he says. You need the energy of young impatient men like Pierre Karl, leavened with the wisdom of the older types, Cavell avers.

But Pierre Karl was gaining a reputation as a volatile mix of talents. He was known for his rages and for screaming at subordinates, in some cases even throwing things. He would carry his cellphone to meetings and allow himself to be interrupted by calls, and would indulge in side conversations, often yelling at the person on the phone, while the other meeting-goers quietly stewed in silence. But above all, he was wildly mercurial in his actions, which some found charming and others simply unnerving. Once, Pierre Karl ordered a meeting with executives of another company, but there was no way the other company's managers could meet him at the specified time. When this was pointed out, Pierre Karl suddenly dropped to the ground and kissed one of his employee's shoes. "Do you expect me to kiss their feet?" the president and CEO of Quebecor looked up and asked. The group of employees laughed nervously.

"He's a yeller, he's a macho guy," says one former Quebecor manager. "He's out to prove he's twice the man his father was—you get that real sense with the big cigars and macho stance." At the same time, Pierre Karl, trained as a lawyer, often relied on the threat of suing people or using the narrowest possible interpretation of business contracts to gain his ends. "His idea was to push it right to the edge, use every measure, the letter of every word in the every contract. He was very aggressive, in a literal legalistic way."

What was clear was that the Marxist rebel had now become, at thirty-eight, the corporate chief. His personal life was also changing. The hard-charging chain-smoking Pierre Karl had led the life of the playboy until the late nineties. Then he married Isabelle Hervet, the daughter of a French banker, and the two had their first child: a daughter, Marie. By all accounts Péladeau had become an indulgent dad.

But his father had left a difficult personal legacy. In mid-1999, the two brothers Pierre Karl and Erik were in the headlines, as they sought to have their sister Anne-Marie cut off her from her allowance as a means to pressure her into a drug rehabilitation program. Anne-Marie, who admitted to a cocaine addiction, was seeking an injunction to restore a $10,800 monthly payment from the family trust, which had been cancelled. She also charged that $21 million worth of shares that she owned had been sold by her brother without her permission. "What they are doing is not being done out of love," Anne-Marie told *La Presse*. "They are doing it for control and power. It's cruel and unjust."

Anne-Marie's case, hotly seized upon by the non-Péladeau press, uncorked a flood of unpleasant publicity, as the brothers faced a raft of lawsuits from half siblings and their father's second wife. They also had to contend with a public quarrel with a retired judge to whom their father had given the power to vote the brothers' shares if they ever came to an impasse. The brothers sought to remove the judge from his position, but he fought back. The various disputes eventually faded away from the public arena, and most of them seem to have been quietly resolved.

But then came the year 2000, the year of media convergence, and Pierre Karl was back into the public spotlight. This time, he was looking ahead to see what his role would be in the dramatically changing landscape. He took his run at Vidéotron, which pitted him against Ted Rogers. These were two antagonists who actually had a lot in common. Both men are haunted by the memories of their brilliant, idiosyncratic fathers. Both are used to living on the edge, certainly in terms of debt. But while Ted is a battle-scarred veteran, Vidéotron would be a test of Pierre Karl's young leadership. Winning the prize was only a small part of the challenge. He would also have to prove he could manage it, and overcome the whispers about his allegedly tempestuous management style—and perhaps finally lay to rest the ghost of a father who never quite gave him the credit he deserved.

5 THE FULL MONTY

JEAN MONTY IS PEEVED AT THE WAY THE WORLD SEES THE managers of the holding company for Canada's largest telephone company. Ted Rogers and JR Shaw, the cable barons, get lots of credit for being daring and entrepreneurial. But his company just gets grief for being a ham-handed conglomerate, with telecom managers who can handle switches and networks but are prone to disastrous diversification moves. Okay, he admits, the old BCE did make some questionable forays into property, trust companies and pipelines in the eighties. "We all got involved in real estate, which was a mistake. We got involved in a lot of things that didn't work out very well. And people just assumed from there that we were a bunch of shitty managers, to use the expression," Monty says, then catches himself. "Don't use that word, please. Use 'poor managers.'"

The legacy of Bell Canada hangs heavily over Jean Monty, who is not a shitty manager, who is in fact one of the country's best professional managers, but who must now contend with all kinds of questions about the wisdom of his dramatic diversification moves. Monty, his bald dome framed by grey-flecked reddish hair, is sitting on the tenth floor of Bell Canada's Toronto headquarters, an anonymous office building that corners one of Toronto's splendid little sanctuaries, Trinity Square, behind the sprawling Eaton Centre. As he does once or twice a week, he has flown into Toronto for a day of meetings, and has found time for a journalist. Two hours with Jean Monty is an experience that mixes Jesuit logic, evangelical enthusiasm and flashes of hot anger. He is alternately bullying and wisecracking, charming and defiant, often peering out at his inquisitor over his tortoiseshell glasses.

The topic is the purchase of CTV and *The Globe and Mail*—the bundling of these two decidedly non-telephone properties with his Internet portal, Sympatico, to create a company called Bell Globemedia. Is this just BCE being stupid BCE, flush with a steady income from its core telephone business and overpaying for assets, then badly mismanaging them and being forced to exit in dispiriting shame? Or is it the beginning of a new era, as BCE thrusts out in front of the convergence game, a model for the telecommunications world?

Monty launches into a defence of BCE as a technology leader and innovator. It has given Canada so much: its first commercial satellite system, digital technology, and no matter what we think of Ma Bell, commendable customer satisfaction—much better, he insists, than his cable rivals. "In our business model, customer satisfaction is part of my bonus, as CEO of BCE. We can't get our sight off the basics of the business and that's where our strength is—we can deliver." Monty argues that the telecommunications culture is superior because it delivers in execution—his favourite word—and that in the long term is what allows you to succeed. "The cable guys are more flamboyant. Rogers goes out there and makes a big thing about small things. We don't talk about small things—we get it done." He concedes that "what we have to add to this now is a bit of flamboyancy," then he quickly adds, "but not too much." One example of his "bit of flamboyancy" is something called a ComboBox, which he says will delivers the Internet, satellite television and the personal video recorder to a single TV screen. He was targeting the product for a launch sometime in 2002, as a weapon against the cable companies "who claim they are the only ones who can carry various forms of content, voice, data or video, and make it simple for consumers. We'll be able to say, 'They're not the ones. We're the ones.'" In the past, he says, BCE would have hemmed and hawed over introducing the ComboBox, but Monty ordered the box's U.S. manufacturer to forge ahead, even if he didn't exactly know how it would all work. "How do you do this stuff and get a reputation for being innovative?" he wonders aloud. "They don't think we're as leading edge as we should be, they don't think we're as innovative as should be. We think we are, but in the end perception is reality. We have to be more aggressive." That aggressiveness, he says, is reflected in BCE's daring convergence initiative, which, he promises, will change the world's perception of BCE, even though it will take years to work out.

The intensity of this soliloquy shows just how much is riding on the strategies Monty is putting into place—and it goes beyond just salvaging the reputation of telephone company managers. It will determine BCE's future and Monty's own place in history. Will he be another Jean de Grandpré, BCE's smart but flawed conglomerate builder of the 1970s and 1980s who failed to build great value in the disparate assets he accumulated? Or will he be the man who propelled BCE into a growth phase as a new-age supplier of content, connections and electronic commerce capability?

He insists that past attempts by BCE to create conglomerates consisted of trying to put together unrelated businesses. This time, he is assembling a number of related businesses. He quotes an analyst who argues that if BCE succeeds in this endeavour, it won't really be a conglomerate anymore, since the whole will be greater than the sum of the parts. Monty clearly likes that. "What I see is that because these pieces fit together, they will fit so well that they produce better results together than if they were four to five pieces apart." He adds, "I believe that's true, but I have to deliver it."

The weight of BCE's history, its past triumphs and failures, presses hard on Jean Claude Monty, a son of a Montreal stockbroker, who has worked his way up the ranks, over twenty-five years, to head one of Canada's biggest industrial companies. In a sense, Monty can trace his managerial lineage all the way back to the inventor of the telephone, Alexander Graham Bell, who was also the progenitor of Bell Canada, and now BCE. On June 2, 1875, at his Boston laboratory, Bell and his assistant Thomas Watson were in separate rooms undertaking experiments with an advanced form of telegraph, when Watson accidentally transmitted a sound to the other room. It wasn't perfect replication, but the telephone was born.

It is an intriguing footnote that the merger of Bell Canada and *The Globe and Mail* might have happened more than 125 years earlier, if not for the short-sightedness of the *Globe's* legendary founder, George Brown. Author Lawrence Surtees tells the story in his book *Pa Bell: A. Jean de Grandpré and the Meteoric Rise of Bell Canada Enterprises.* Alexander Graham Bell had sold the U.S. rights to his invention to his future father-in-law, a Boston lawyer named Gardiner Green Hubbard, but the rights to the telephone outside the United States were still up for grabs. In 1875, Bell paid a visit to his father's homestead outside Brantford, Ontario, in search of a buyer and happened to have a conversation with his father's neighbour—Brown, the publisher of the *Globe.* Bell inquired about possible buyers of the rights to his new "telephone," and Brown indicated his interest. But Brown procrastinated about making a final decision. He was excited about Bell's prototype for a new form of telegraph but wasn't that interested in this new gadget, the "telephone." In a letter to his wife, quoted in *Pa Bell,* Brown said, "my present inclination is to go no further in the business." An opportunity was lost, and it took another 125 years for the *Globe* and Bell Canada to get back together. One can only speculate whether the timetable of convergence might have speeded up if George Brown had been more imaginative.

In the end, the Bell Telephone Company of Canada was created in 1880 as an offshoot of the U.S. Bell system, and in time became a regulated monopoly in Central Canada. A sister company, Northern Electric and Manufacturing Company, later called Northern Telecom and now simply Nortel, was formed in 1914 as a telephone manufacturer, to make the equipment that Bell Telephone used on its network. The Bell-Northern partnership was a textbook case of vertical integration. For years both were controlled by American Telephone & Telegraph, or AT&T, the owner of the U.S. Bell system.

But that changed after 1956, when an anti-trust consent decree between AT&T and the U.S. Justice Department led to the severing of the Canadian Bell system and Northern Electric from its longtime U.S.

owners. Set free from Bell Laboratories and its telephone technology, the company that eventually became Northern Telecom was forced to undertake its own research and development. It also realized that it could not survive and grow as just a supplier to its sister phone company. It had to go out into the world and beat the bushes for customers.

In the 1970s, a tough Bell Canada president named Jean de Grandpré became frustrated with how the CRTC was blending the government-regulated Bell Canada with its unregulated enterprises, thus impeding the company's ability to expand its revenues and profits. He created a new corporate structure, which would separate the core telephone utility from its sister companies, placing them all under the umbrella of a holding company Bell Canada Enterprises, which was born in 1984, and later became known as just BCE.

The BCE model had its ups and downs. In the eighties, de Grandpré, and later his successor, Ray Cyr, took the company on a bizarre diversification drive into other businesses, including a trust company, a property company and a major chunk of a pipeline utility. These companies, as Jean Monty remembers so painfully, were ultimately divested, leaving a cloud over BCE diversification to come. But while BCE was diversifying and de-diversifying, its telephone technology subsidiary Northern Telecom was becoming a significant global player on the strength of its formidable research organization.

Thus there developed a creative tension between staid Ma Bell with its stay-at-home regulated telephone business, and the kid sister Northern Telecom, which stayed out all night and came home with boyfriends and baubles. Bell Canada provided the social and cultural role, supplying Canadians with relatively inexpensive phone service. Northern dabbled in the black arts of wireless, data transmission and ultimately the Internet.

For Jean Monty, there was an implicit balancing act in the Bell Canada–Nortel relationship: "For decades our story was simple: dividend with Bell, grow with Nortel, great R&D support for Canada with Nortel, great social policy support with low prices and high penetration of telecoms through Bell." Bell at home was able to provide the low-cost, high-penetration telecom services that are needed by society. Nortel's growth abroad allowed the export of Canadian technology and the employment of engineering talent at home. This golden era for BCE extended from the early 1970s to the end of the century.

But that tradeoff contained an inner contradiction: conglomerates like BCE are by nature underestimated by the stock market. Investors today like clarity, and simple stories. Thus, assets locked in a holding company usually trade at a discount to the the total book value of their component assets—and BCE was no exception. The growth of Northern was not fully recognized in BCE's stock price—or, alternatively, Bell's other assets were overlooked by the market. Also, the link between Bell Canada and Nortel became problematic as business became more global. Nortel began to supply companies that were, in some markets, rivals of Bell Canada. The executive who would finally confront this paradox was Jean Monty, who had come to work for the company in the mid-1970s. You can draw a straight line from Nortel's development as a twentieth-century technology powerhouse to Jean Monty's decision in 2000 to make his startling bid for the CTV television network.

When he joined Bell Canada, Jean Monty was the classic son of middle-class Quebec: he had gone to school at Montreal's Collège Sainte-Marie, a Jesuit institution, where in typical fashion he spent eight years—from age eleven to age nineteen—and ended up with a BA. The strength of the Jesuit education is that it gives students a certain rigour and discipline in their thinking, and there is no doubt that has influenced Jean Monty. But he is mostly remembered as a quarterback on the football team, a star hockey player and an enthusiastic participant in the organized mayhem known as lacrosse. "He was certainly a leader on the football field and on the ice," recalls Michel Racicot, a Montreal communications lawyer who was a fellow student at the college. "He was the guy calling the shots." Monty was extremely fit and energetic, and only began to distinguish himself as a student in his last few years as he approached his degree. When he discovered economics, he threw himself into academic life with the same fierce competitiveness he showed on the football field.

The athleticism stayed with him, even into the hectic life of a CEO at BCE, when golf was his major form of release from the pressure of business. While the sport has become the favourite networking pastime of the managerial class, it is more than that for Monty. He has about a ten handicap these days—very decent—although it has been lower in the past. "He has a extraordinarily long ball," says a friend, describing Monty's mighty drives. He is probably one of the few Canadian CEOs who wouldn't feel entirely out of place on the same course as superstar golfer Tiger Woods. In fact, in 2001, Monty issued a controversial invitation to Prime Minister Jean Chrétien to join him in a privileged foursome with Woods and a Montreal stockbroker at the Bell Canadian Open in Montreal. The invitation sparked allegations of conflict of interest, but the match went ahead. The spectators at the Royal Montreal Golf Club certainly recognized Tiger Woods and they knew Chrétien, but who were these two other guys? Then Monty impressed the crowd with a stunning first drive, and a tidy putting game.

As a student in college, Monty developed a reputation as a fun guy to be around, not the life of the party, perhaps, but full of jokes. His old friends seem puzzled in recent years to see the sober visage of Monty, the corporate leader, grimly delivering another technical speech on telephone rate caps or addressing a news conference. After his degree at Collège Sainte-Marie, he went on to the University of Western Ontario in London, where he obtained a master's degree in economics in 1969. He then entered the University of Chicago's business school, ostensibly to pursue a Ph.D. in finance. According to a 1997 profile of Monty in *The Financial Post Magazine*, he switched gears three months into the program when he contemplated that it might take him five years to complete his doctorate. He wanted to start a career in corporate finance right away, so he transferred to an M.B.A. program and graduated from Chicago in 1970. In between the Western degree and Chicago, he took three weeks off to marry his long-time girlfriend, Jocelyne. "She is the girl of his life," says a friend, describing Monty's thirty-year marriage, which has produced two sons, now grown.

Fresh from school, Monty took a job in New York as a corporate underwriter with Merrill Lynch. He came back to Canada in 1972 as a vice-president of Merrill Lynch Royal Securities in Montreal. He was a promising executive, but he also felt, as he confided in a 1989 interview with *The Globe and Mail,* that essentially "I was a well-paid salesman." Still, investment banking seemed like a natural career for a man whose father came from the investment business and whose brother Rodolphe had also become a stockbroker.

Then, Jean Monty jumped to Bell Canada in 1974, to become a lowly staff supervisor in the company's financial analysis section. To some it seemed an odd move, getting off the fast track at a major North American investment dealer to join the creaky bureaucracy of Bell. But friends say an uncle in senior management at Bell convinced the younger man that he would have an opportunity at the giant phone company. And he did advance quickly to become assistant vice-president of finance, and in 1976 became president of Telebec, a troubled Bell subsidiary that owned two small struggling rural telephone services in northern Quebec. He had never been a telephone company manager, but he turned the small business around in three years—valuable training for later running the mother ship. During regulatory hearings, he was a frequent witness before former classmate Michel Racicot, who had become a Bell lawyer. "Within a few years it became quite obvious that he had a good shot at the president's job," recalls Racicot, now a lawyer with McCarthy Tétrault in Montreal. Most important, he had caught the eye of Jean de Grandpré and his lieutenant, Ray Cyr. As a reward for his Telebec turnaround, in 1979, Monty was sent to attend the one-year leadership program at the National Defence College in Kingston, which was at that time a common training ground for senior Bell executives. He would later say that the program gave him more of a world vision than he had ever had.

Monty returned to Bell as deputy controller of operations, with responsibility for customer billing, financial accounting and auditing systems. This was the beginning of a progressive series of promotions as he moved closer to the top echelon of the company. As a protégé of Ray Cyr, in 1987 he took the job as executive vice-president of BCE, becoming one of six executives who ran the powerful holding company.

One of Monty's roles was the creation of new businesses, including the emerging cellphone unit known as Bell Mobile. BCE was one of two pioneering cellphone operators licensed in the mid-eighties by the federal government. The other was headed by, perhaps inevitably, BCE's *bête noire*, Ted Rogers, who teamed up with Montreal media entrepreneur Philippe de Gaspé Beaubien and Vancouver's Belzberg family to form Cantel, now Rogers AT&T Wireless. During this period, Monty was instrumental in merging Bell's fledgling cellular business with National Telesystem, a paging company controlled by the young Quebec entrepreneur Charles Sirois, who became president and CEO of the newly merged Bell subsidiary at just thirty years old.

From that time on, Monty and Sirois became one of the intriguing teams in Canadian business, with Sirois providing the entrepreneurial flair to Monty's managerial depth. According to insiders, Sirois has exerted a strong personal influence on Monty, and BCE has in turn invested in Sirois's businesses, often to BCE's profit, but not always. Sirois became a kind of proxy entrepreneur for Monty and BCE. The two friends had neighbouring summer homes on Lake Memphremagog in Quebec's picturesque Eastern Townships, a playground of the Montreal business elite.

Sirois, a native of Chicoutimi, is a charming curly-haired dynamo who speaks in staccato bursts and is often seen as the most visionary of the entrepreneurs who came out of the Quebec Inc. factory of the 1980s and 1990s. An M.B.A. graduate from Laval University, he bought his father's Quebec City paging company for $150,000 and went into business for himself very successfully, before teaming up with Monty and BCE. He was the golden boy—for a while whatever he and his holding company Telesystem touched seemed to make a lot of money for himself and his investors. For some observers, he was considered the most likely candidate to be one of the moguls dominating the communications landscape. Like Ted Rogers, he was always a step or two ahead of the market, but sometimes it was dangerous being out ahead. He tripped badly on the dot-com and telecommunications blowout of 2000–2001, when his collection of wireless businesses in Europe and North America—which included a stake in Microcell, the operator of Canada's Fido cellphone product—came under heavy financial pressure.

As the century ended, his influence on Jean Monty was thought to be waning, largely because of the experience of Teleglobe, which has been both Sirois's greatest triumph and his Achilles heel. Teleglobe, the company that once held a monopoly on Canada's overseas telephone calls, was privatized by the federal government, and in 1987 ended up in the hands of a Montreal company, Memotec, with Bell holding a minority interest. In 1992, with BCE's support, Sirois was able to take over the company, install himself as CEO, and guide it through the deregulation that ultimately eliminated its monopoly over international calls. He was converting Teleglobe into a worldwide marketer of telecom services and its share price rose spectacularly. But in 1999, Sirois over-reached by buying a Texas-based telephone services marketer called Excel Communications for $4 billion. Excel was a direct marketing company, an Avon of telephone services, run by a flamboyant Texan named Kenny Trout. But the acquisition, which was intended to take Teleglobe into the consumer market, was difficult to digest, and Sirois's star began to fade. Even so, in early 2000, along came BCE, which paid close to $7.4 billion for the 77 percent of Teleglobe that it didn't already own. It was a big payday for Sirois, who walked away with hundreds of millions of dollars in BCE stock, but it would create nothing but headaches for Monty.

Sirois, to his credit, has a strong grasp of his limitations and his strengths. "I am not a manager," he says. "Sometimes I don't do enough in detail. I don't like details. Sometimes I hit myself because maybe I should have looked at details and the devil is in the details." What he brings to the table is a powerful intellectual curiosity. "I am always interested in a new thing. I cannot stay quiet with something." But his greatest asset, he maintains, is his ability to stay calm through stress, the kind of stress he faced as his wireless properties were under siege at the beginning of the twenty-first century.

"People around me will fall on the floor, but I will go and have a nice supper, go to bed and sleep after three minutes." He explains that this basic serenity was learned from his mother, who was a yoga teacher for twenty years. "It doesn't mean I don't have stress, that I am not conscious about it. Some people don't have stress because they don't have a concern about what's going on. I'm in full knowledge of what's going on, but in the end I believe you need to always look at the facts." He argued that while the telecommunications market was collapsing, and his wireless investments were tanking, he was confident that his shares of BCE would hold up rather well, and that Microcell would ultimately prosper.

But BCE continued to experience severe problems with Teleglobe, raising doubts about its investment, about Teleglobe's purchase of Excel, and whether the two old allies, Monty and Sirois, were still as close as they had once been. When I talked to Sirois, he was still convinced that buying Excel had been the right move. "The strategy was very simple and I still believe that it works," he told me. "It's a complex machine to make work, and it needs a lot of time." He felt that when he bought the Dallas company, it was the best way for Teleglobe to diversify its revenue sources to expand into worldwide retail markets. He says in retrospect he still would have bought it but wished he had waited for a while. Nonetheless, BCE was forced to write off $2.2 billion of the Excel purchase price and then unloaded the Excel unit for only US$227.5 million in early 2002. Charles Sirois may still become Canada's convergence king, but the golden boy had taken on some tarnish and it had rubbed off on his friend Jean Monty.

But back in 1989, with the help of an odd cast of people, including Sirois, de Grandpré and Ray Cyr, Jean Monty had risen to the post of president of Bell Canada, the top job in BCE's flagship operating company. He had shown that he was a bright and versatile manager who could operate in any of BCE's many war zones. He was ready to move again when BCE needed him to shift into Nortel for a rescue mission. The telecommunications equipment company was going through a rough patch under its chief executive officer Paul Stern, a Czech-born, U.S. trained engineer who had impeccable U.S. contacts—he was a friend of U.S. president George H. Bush. But Stern presided over a disaster at Nortel, bringing in an imperial style that alienated and demoralized the troops. The company tumbled into decline because of strategic decisions that eroded its hard-won status as a global leader. Research and development spending had been cut back, as Nortel pursued short-term profits ahead of long-term viability. Monty was airlifted into the head office in Brampton, Ontario, to become Nortel president in mid-1993, pushing Stern into the chairman's role—and eventually out the door.

His turnaround of Nortel was the making of Jean Monty's reputation. He restored R&D spending and, supported by a bright engineer named John Roth, drove Nortel harder into new technologies such as wireless telephony and broadband networks in these early days of the Internet. He knew that traditional telecom switching, Nortel's core business, was a low-growth kind of operation. He helped guide the fixing of a nagging software problem that was harming Nortel's digital multiplexer switches. He aggressively expanded international business, particularly outside the North American market. He sold off unproductive assets and laid off workers, all of which bolstered the bottom line. He put the company on a growth trail again.

Gedas Sakus, a Nortel executive at the time, says that Monty valued customer loyalty and wanted Nortel to find ways to regain that eroded loyalty. "It had been defocused before," he says, and there had been huge morale issues during the Stern era. Monty also showed his characteristic style: "He's extremely decisive; he doesn't waffle. He picks a direction and he goes for it," says Sakus, now retired, living in Toronto, and sitting on the board of BCE's electronic commerce subsidiary. With Roth as chief operating officer, the two men formed a strong team: Roth knew

Nortel and its engineering culture, while Monty, coming from the telephone company side, understood the customer perspective.

Then in 1998, it was suddenly announced that Monty was leaving Nortel for an unspecified job in the BCE constellation, and that he would be replaced as president by Roth, an engineer with a taste for fast cars who had spent almost his entire career at Nortel. By the fall, it was official: Jean Monty was the new president of BCE. He had won the hearts of the board and above all, of Lynton (Red) Wilson, the powerful former banker and public servant who was chairman of BCE. Monty joined a crowded executive suite, with John McLennan, the outspoken president of Bell Canada, Ron Osborne, the former boss of media giant Maclean Hunter, and John Macdonald, a smart young engineer who had positioned the company technologically. Monty's arrival was a signal that the BCE succession was set in place, and gradually the others moved on.

Among Monty's prime challenges at BCE was to decide what to do with Nortel, the company he had just left. The holding company had been talking informally for more than a decade about spinning off its 39 percent interest in its technology arm. But as Nortel's share value soared in the hot tech market of the late 1990s, the choice became clearer. Monty says he came to a decision about Nortel, "not because it was a failure but because it worked too well, because of its unbelievable success. Nortel's worth hundreds of billions of dollars. Our shareholders are saying, 'Give us the value—you're locking up the value,' and we're saying, 'Geez, if we're unlocking the value, what about the rest of BCE, which we've never pushed before?" In the past, he said, BCE had actually held back on its expansion in services because of concerns that it would be competing too aggressively with companies to which Nortel was supplying telephone gear.

In the early nineties, BCE had considered taking a run at MCI, the giant U.S. long-distance phone company. "We never did anything about it, but just in reflection, one of key arguments was, If we did a deal for MCI, what does that do to Nortel?" The Bell people could anticipate

Sprint and other major Nortel customers protesting that their supplier was part of a corporate family that included their most bitter rival, MCI. "Even in Canada it was difficult to manage because Rogers was building networks and others were building networks, so why should they build networks with Nortel's technology?"

Monty insists this discussion about spinning off Nortel didn't start with him but had been going on for a decade under Red Wilson and Ray Cyr. "It never got to the point of saying we're doing something. It was more like 'We know we will have to do something about it.' They knew it, we just didn't know when." The "when" arrived with Nortel's phenomenal stock market success in the late nineties, as the company moved into the hot technologies of broadband and wireless technology. As its stock soared, it used the shares as currency to buy into new technologies, often at maniacal paper prices. As Nortel skyrocketed ever higher in market value, "that forced our hand, and in May of 2000, we spun it off," Monty says.

In the perfect vision of hindsight, that was the most brilliant investment decision made by any Canadian CEO in recent years. Monty managed to issue BCE's Nortel shares out to shareholders as dividends at a price of $78 a share. He held back about 2 percent of the shares for Nortel's own treasury, which ultimately realized $4 billion. Added to the proceeds from selling 20 percent of Bell Canada to Chicago's Ameritech—which itself was taken over by SBC Communications—it gave Monty a tidy war chest of $7 billion.

The timing was brilliant, if entirely accidental. Within months, Nortel was in freefall, a victim of the great high-tech bust and its own excesses. It was laying off half its workforce and writing off the acquisitions it had acquired for billions of dollars in now-discredited shares. As Nortel stock dropped far below $10, from its peak of more than $120, the once heroic John Roth retired in a blaze of ignominy. But Jean Monty, this time very lucky, was free and clear of the carnage.

This, of course, is all hindsight. At the beginning of 2000, Jean Monty didn't know this would happen, he just knew that he was determined to spin off Nortel—he could not see how the rest of the story would unfold, that this great tech bubble would burst and his own company would come under pressure in a collapsing, overextended telecommunications market. He was concentrating on the strategic challenge that faced him: "So what do we do to make BCE a growth engine?" he was asking himself, now that Nortel was gone. That was what brought him to buy CTV and *The Globe and Mail,* and to become what BCE had never been in all its incarnations—a major investor in media content.

PART 2 **THE DEALS**

6 BELLS AND WHISTLES

FOR A JOCK LIKE JEAN MONTY, IT WAS THE KNOCKOUT punch, the long bomb, the hole in one, a bid so huge and so stunning that it blasted any lurking competitors right out of the water. It was the kind of move Jean Monty loved to make, the kind that won admiration from his supporters and derision from his critics, whose visceral hatred for his huge company, BCE, knew no bounds.

Monty was sitting on the stage of the John Bassett Theatre in downtown Toronto's Metro Convention Centre, announcing his $2.3 billion takeover bid for CTV, Canada's largest private television network. It was an uncontested $38 a share in cash for a company that had been languishing in the low twenties not long ago but had been trading higher recently in anticipation of a rumoured takeover offer. It was the first time in history, anywhere in the world, that a major telephone company would be buying a significant entertainment broadcaster. The Bassett Theatre was an appropriate venue for the announcement, for the late John Bassett was one of the founders of CTV, a television network that had persistently failed to deliver on its promise under a co-operative of deeply divided owners. CTV's divisions were so pronounced that the network's former president, John Bassett's son, Doug Bassett, used to say that his definition of a network was "a bunch of people quarrelling." Recently, however, the network's feuding satraps had been consolidated under a former CBC programming whiz named Ivan Fecan (pronounced Ee-VAHN Fetz-AN), who had brought coherence to the network and its collection of TV stations and specialty channels.

CTV had become a hot item in the early days of 2000, when content was king and the stock markets were still booming. In the small

Canadian television industry, CTV seemed like a rich mine of content—or at least an aggregator of other people's content. As well as the network, it owned and operated twenty-five television stations, the Atlantic satellite service ASN and the specialty TV channels CTV Newsnet and Talk TV. It also had major stakes in the specialty channels the Comedy Network, CTV Pay Per View Sports, CTV Sportsnet and Outdoor Life Network. It was awaiting CRTC permission to buy the majority stake in Netstar, a company that controlled the Sports Network (TSN) and the Discovery Channel.

On this February morning in 2000, Monty, the chairman and chief executive officer of BCE, was convinced he had no choice but to pack a powerful punch of an offer. BCE, whose cash cow was Bell Canada, the country's largest telephone company, had to buy CTV to deliver on his newly developed convergence strategy—to distribute new media products based on brand-name Canadian content through BCE's communications networks. "We couldn't deliver on our strategy of being in content without having bought CTV," he would say. He felt he had to come in with a bid so fat that it would knock potential rivals out of the race.

Monty, fifty-two, the intense and impatient former college football quarterback, wasn't the only one in this game. All the Canadian media barons had watched the blockbuster AOL Time Warner deal in early January with interest, and all roads suddenly seemed to be leading toward CTV, a company with no controlling shareholder. "The AOL Time Warner deal forced us to react faster," Monty recalls. "It didn't tell us what the strategy should be—it pushed us to move faster. If we hadn't done the CTV deal I'm sure someone else would have."

The most likely candidates to challenge BCE were a gang of entrepreneurs and family businesses that Monty knew only too well. The list started with the tough and tenacious Winnipegger Izzy Asper and his CanWest Global Communications, which owned CTV's arch rival, the Global television network, and had just purchased about 10 percent of CTV. Another 10 percent of CTV had been picked up by the Shaw family in Calgary, which ran the largest cable TV system in Western

Canada. The ambitious Shaws were also building a media powerhouse in a new company, called Corus Entertainment, run by the savvy John Cassaday, who happened to be CTV's former president and a one-time managerial rival of the wily Fecan.

The Asper and Shaw families had, after two years of gruelling warfare and wrangles with tax authorities, finally cut a deal to carve up WIC, Western International Communications, a big Vancouver-based media company. As part of the deal, Izzy had acquired the conventional TV stations for $800 million, which allowed him to realize his thirty-year dream of owning a national TV network able to truly take on CTV. The fast-rising Shaws ended up with WIC's radio stations and specialty TV channels, and control of the Cancom satellite company. Monty was thinking about the WIC carve-up as he contemplated buying CTV: "So we have to go after CTV, but it's expensive and not only that, Izzy Asper's got 10 percent and the Shaws have 10 percent. And they're waiting to do another WIC on CTV, which is basically to buy this together cheap and split the assets and really make a lot of money."

In the months leading up to the CTV offer, Monty also knew that other possible suitors had been sniffing around. Pierre Karl Péladeau, the mercurial Quebec media heir, had visited Ivan Fecan in the fall, and nothing had come of it—but the unpredictable Péladeau and his company, Quebecor, could not be counted out of any bidding war. He already owned a television network in Quebec, a bunch of tabloid newspapers and a world-scale printing operation.

And all the time, Monty was thinking about another giant who could join the party if sufficiently prodded: "I'm convinced that in time Rogers would have been interested in CTV—his issue was how to finance it." By Rogers, he means, of course, Ted Rogers, the over-the-top visionary who runs Canada's biggest cable company, a major wireless company and some of its most prized media properties. Indeed, financing was always an issue for Ted Rogers, who had more irons in the fire than the busiest village blacksmith. At that moment, he was distracted by his takeover bid for Vidéotron, a Quebec cable company.

The relationship between Ted Rogers and BCE is one of the most volatile and fascinating in Canadian business—a case of the individual entrepreneur raging against the corporate machine. The history is long and bitter, going back to disputes over running Rogers cable lines on Bell Canada poles in the 1960s, continuing through rivalries in the wireless market and culminating in the costly, futile attempt by Rogers and his partners to loosen the telephone companies' iron grip on long-distance telephone service in the nineties. If anyone would want to scuttle BCE's plans it would be Ted Rogers, although he and Monty admire each other personally. Jean Monty sums up the relationship this way: "Ted has been up, he's been down, but he's always there. He's our nemesis and we are his nemesis. He would prefer that we wouldn't exist."

But BCE does exist; in fact, they all do—these five moguls of Canadian media—and they all took at least a glance at CTV in the fall and winter of 1999–2000. All the threads of this story weave their way through CTV. BCE's takeover of the network was the first big deal that ignited the Canadian media deal explosion of 2000. It opened a floodgate of takeover activity and cross-media consolidation that changed the landscape of communications in the country forever.

It is appropriate, perhaps, that Monty moved first, for he is the odd man out in this unruly Wild Bunch. As the CEO of a widely held public company, he is the hired gun—it is not his personal money on the line, but it is his considerable pride. He is the only one who is not part of a family business. He is the president of the industry's three-hundred-pound gorilla, a colossus by Canadian standards, which in revenue and range of operations dwarfs the other contenders. In the year 2000, Montreal-based BCE was the largest Canadian public company in terms of profits, earning $4.8 billion on revenues of $18.2 billion. It employed seventy-five thousand people and ran the country's largest phone system, a strong wireless franchise, a major Internet portal, a satellite television service, a fast-growing e-commerce business—plus having a 39 percent ownership interest in telecommunications giant Nortel Networks.

But it was a strangely unbalanced giant: Much of its cash flow came from huge Bell Canada, whose core business was the basic voice telephone service in Ontario and Quebec—a reliable cash machine but a low-growth enterprise, built on a traditional monopoly that was being challenged but was still overwhelmingly dominant. In fact, BCE's growth in recent decades had been powered by its minority interest in Nortel. Believe it or not, Monty was determined to get rid of that interest. It seemed counter-intuitive—Monty, the former chief executive officer of Nortel, was plotting to divest a stock market darling, a technological phenomenon and Canada's chosen instrument in the red-hot telecom gear market. But Nortel's massive success in the overheated dotcom markets had created an equally massive anomaly. The Nortel holding accounted for almost the entire value of the BCE stock: its dominant phone franchise wasn't even given a value by the market. Under pressure from investors, Monty had announced in January that he would be liberating his Nortel holding, issuing it to shareholders as a dividend. Monty knew it was the right thing to do, but it left a void in his strategy. How would BCE grow now?

In Monty's vision, BCE's future growth would not come from plain old telephone service but from high-margin, must-have services for businesses and consumers that could be moved along phone lines or over satellite and wireless systems and the Internet. For businesses, that would mean data and video, electronic commerce or wireless communications. For consumers, it could mean sports, news and entertainment delivered on-line, perhaps to a wireless device, to a computer, a TV set or to a new kind of device that would combine high-speed Internet, satellite TV and sophisticated video recording. The content would come from all kinds of places—from CTV, TSN or, perhaps, from *The Globe and Mail* newspaper, which was owned by Thomson Corporation, but had been the subject of ongoing talks between the two organizations.

As the curator of a Canadian artifact, Monty might be expected to be a cautious steward, but at heart he is a gunslinger. Monty is fanatical about execution. The right strategy is important, he concedes, but the real test is in just doing it. He once told students at University of Chicago

Business School that his favourite leadership attribute is action. "Strategy gets most of the lip service these days but my view is that it accounts for about 10 percent of results. The other 90 percent is execution. The only thing navel gazing will do is give your competitors time to pull ahead and thumb their noses as they go past." He quoted Arnold Schwarzenegger, of all people: "Nobody got muscles by watching me lift weights."

Few people know Monty better than Charles Sirois, the Montreal entrepreneur who has done a number of deals with the BCE boss over the course of a close twenty-year relationship. "I think Jean Monty's best quality is he is action-driven. He will not sit," Sirois says. "He prefers to make a wrong action than no action at all." Sirois is always impressed by Monty's ability to take a very complex set of facts and move quickly on a decision with far-ranging impact. "It will just be boom, boom, boom!" Sirois exclaims, with a characteristc burst of enthusiasm. "And if this is wrong, he will just change it. Sometimes this can be confusing for a large company like BCE."

Another executive who knows Monty says this action orientation, and speed of decision making, is accompanied by a short attention span, a mind that is easily distracted from the task at hand. But, he adds, "what I like about Jean is his ability to do huge things with no fuss. Whether they're right or wrong, the proof of the pudding is in the eating. But his ability to do the big things and just get on with it with no muss or fuss is really quite startling. He's just a ballsy guy." The famously action-oriented Izzy Asper, no fan of BCE, admires what Monty has done. Normally, when a company is the size of BCE and no longer has a controlling shareholder, management will never take the necessary risks to move it along— it just stays still. But Izzy agrees that "Jean Monty acts like an owner. You need someone who thinks like an owner."

But as boss of rich BCE, Monty has had trouble winning respect, and the CTV takeover is a case in point. It was another example, critics say, of BCE vastly overpaying for an asset. As the country's richest company, they say, there is no discipline on its willingness to spend, and spend mightily. As a regulated utility for many years, it had a corporate culture that had always assumed it could simply factor the costs of its profligacy into its cost base for the next rate change, these critics say. The result had been some famously wrong-headed investments, particularly in the 1980s when BCE lavished billions on plays in real estate and financial services—which it had to divest after indifferent returns or even huge losses. To further demonstrate BCE's seemingly bottomless pockets, the same month Monty made his bid for CTV, he moved to take over Teleglobe, the international carrier of telephone calls, in what would turn out to be a $7.4 billion stock deal for the 77 percent of Teleglobe that BCE did not already own.

Whatever his critics' complaints, Monty's preemptive strike on CTV was successful—no other bidder emerged, and on March 13, 2000, the CTV board voted to accept the offer. BCE announced that it would retain the network's senior management, including Ivan Fecan. The deal was cleared by the broadcasting regulator, the Canadian Radio-television and Telecommunications Commission (CRTC), on December 7, 2000. This was an important decision because it allowed a major distributor of content—in the form of BCE, which owns the Bell ExpressVu satellite service—to buy a significant repository of broadcast content. And by that time, the fast-moving Monty had already added other pieces to his mosaic.

In September, he struck a deal with Toronto's Thomson family to create a multi-media powerhouse that would comprise CTV, Bell's Internet portal Sympatico-Lycos, and *The Globe and Mail,* Canada's major national daily newspaper. The thrust of the new company, eventually called Bell Globemedia, was to capitalize on established brand names to create content that could be carried on BCE's distribution systems. Again, there were few neutral views—BCE was either the great lumbering incompetent of Canadian industry, or a shrewd visionary for the twenty-first century.

Despite Jean Monty's celebrated decisiveness, Bell Globemedia was not made in a day. All through 1999, he had been thinking about the future, with or without Nortel. He would assemble his top team of managers to plot growth strategy in BCE's offices on rue de la Gauchetière in Montreal. The group often included John Sheridan, the head of Bell Canada; Michael Sabia, the up-and-comer who was running Bell Canada International but who would eventually become BCE president and Monty's successor; and Ida Teoli, the communications vice-president. Prominent in this group was Peter Nicholson, the in-house savant at BCE who carried the title chief of strategy officer. The holder of a doctorate in applied mathematics from Stanford University in California, Nicholson says his title represented a grab bag of jobs, including surveying the horizon for new ideas. He was an early champion of BCE's convergence game plan, but he also admits his title was a misnomer. The real chief strategy officer at BCE was Jean Monty.

Nicholson says those strategic planning sessions started with the assumption that BCE needed growth engines for its underdeveloped services business, and that the Internet would develop into the ultimate platform for all communications. In Nicholson's view, the Internet would subsume everything, including the voice telephone system, and what is now television. "It's not that print will disappear, or there won't be broadcast television, but the Internet as a medium of communication will just become more and more ubiquitous and universal as the underlying technological capability improves. We wanted to be part of that transformation."

As the team focused on the Internet, it was aware of BCE's basic strength—it had the ability to connect customers through its telecommunications and satellite links. This "connectivity" was a business BCE was already in. But to deliver something of significant value, BCE had to move up the supply chain—and that meant owning distinctive content, plus a facility to offer electronic commerce over the Net. So connectivity, content and commerce became the underpinnings of a new growth strategy. "While we may not have articulated it right away, we had a view there would be these three C's in our future," Nicholson says.

BCE already had a fast-growing e-commerce business, called BCE

Emergis, which catered to business customers and in those heady days of 1999 looked like it would be a winner. It also had a company called Nexxia that provided Internet network capability. The next step would be to own content to feed through its connective capability. BCE was also aware that the big U.S. Internet portal companies, such as Yahoo! and AOL, were attracting huge stock market valuations. "I wouldn't say we were exactly caught up in the euphoria but we knew in the longer run this was the way in which our industry would evolve," Nicholson says.

BCE's strategy in capturing business customers would be to target an international market—for example, BCE Emergis was moving into the United States, selling companies network access to electronic invoicing, billing and training. But the consumer-based strategy had to be Canadian. BCE would pursue a "national champion" approach built around established brands. Monty figured BCE didn't have the firepower to become a big global entertainment provider. It couldn't take on Bertelsmann, News Corporation, AOL, or Vivendi Universal in that game, but it could wrap up the Canadian market if it moved quickly.

"We felt we had to be on that learning curve, we felt we had to be in that laboratory, because we knew that something new would have to be created and it would evolve," Nicholson says. "We knew that with Sympatico as a portal and with our Internet service provider function, we had a couple of the important elements of the Internet of the future, but we didn't have all of the elements." The key missing parts were the more sophisticated content and information, plus the right kind of branding. "We needed some of those skills to bake this cake. We didn't know what the recipe was but we knew what some of the ingredients were and we didn't have them all."

The crucial question was who would own the content ingredients that would go into this recipe. Would it be BCE owning the pieces or would it have to enlist allies and partners? This almost ideological issue dramatically divides the communications industry. On one side is the view that a carrier like BCE gets no benefit from owning a film producer or a newspaper. Wouldn't BCE want access to all the best content, not just what it might own? And why would a content player want to be tied to one distributor, such as BCE's satellite unit Bell ExpressVu? Not to mention the cultural problems of meshing together the different worlds of content and pipes.

But Monty had another take: BCE would have to be in the business of developing entirely new content products. How could this be done without owning the whole creation process? Alliances are fine, but not when there is so much uncertainty about the process as well as the end result. And BCE's on-line competitors such as AOL and Microsoft weren't farming out much of this important work.

BCE was already moving into the new high-speed access market, based on the telephone industry's ADSL format. But Monty needed another brand-name portal partner, which would lend heft, applications and content to Sympatico. The industry was gravitating towards these broad portals, with home pages that link and organize the immense amounts of Internet data. The portals addressed the consumer's big headache: How can I get someone else to surf the Web efficiently for me?

A proud man, Jean Monty keeps a close eye on what is written about him, and in late 1999 he was getting a whipping from the press for BCE's perceived inertia. "You probably remember the articles, that we had no Internet strategy, that 'you guys are for the birds.'" Monty grimaces as he remembers one article by then-*Globe and Mail* technology writer Mark Evans that said flatly, "The problem is that BCE doesn't have a clue about the Internet."

"It is very difficult when you are developing a strategy to tell the world you have a strategy," Monty would say later. "Basically you are not sure what that strategy is going to be; secondly, you want to put it in place before someone else does it, because if you tell everyone your strategy, they'll know what your targets are. Then the prices go up or someone else will buy them before you. So we had to be quiet. It was a difficult period for us."

Monty and his team were quietly negotiating with well-established U.S. portals to complement BCE's own high-speed connection. BCE had talked with AOL, for example, but the U.S. giant wanted to control the entire relationship with the consumer. Monty was adamant that he would not hand over the Canadian customer on a platter to someone else. "We stepped back and said who would partner with us so we could continue to own the customer relationship?" Among the major U.S. portals, Lycos was the one that met Bell's conditions. BCE made its partnership deal with Lycos on February 2, 2000, three weeks before the CTV bid. Sympatico became Sympatico-Lycos, with Bell holding 70 percent of the partnership.

Once the portal problem was solved, the BCE team focused on how to win eyeballs away from the on-line competition, led by Microsoft and AOL. "We concluded the way we win is by being Canadian, and I'm not being cute," Monty says. He means by providing Canadian content, national and local, along with general applications such as Web hosting and gaming. One of Monty's future partners would describe it this way: "It's a Fortress Canada business. We're going to bring the world to Canada and we're going to bring Canada to the world."

BCE began to search for a content partner. Ted Rogers, of course, had media assets (magazines, radio and some TV) but he was a perennial rival, and he was plotting his own takeover bid for the Quebec cable company Vidéotron. Monty admired the Shaws as managers, but it was more likely that the Shaws and Rogers would emerge as leading figures in an anti-BCE movement, perhaps partnering with Telus, the western telephone company based in suburban Vancouver. Monty looked at media baron Conrad Black's newspapers but couldn't see a nice fit. The Aspers were pursuing their own media growth agenda, which would ultimately lead to their purchase of Black's major daily newspapers.

The search led to Canada's richest family, the Thomsons, and to Geoff Beattie, the boyish tousle-haired custodian of the family's business interests. Beattie is the president of Woodbridge, the key holding company for the personal wealth of Kenneth, Lord Thomson of Fleet. A prime asset in Ken Thomson's $20 billion-plus fortune is a controlling interest in Thomson Corporation, the company founded by his colourful father, Roy. Thomson Corporation was born as a radio and a newspaper company, but over the years had traded in and out of a variety of assets, from travel agencies to North Sea oil to the Hudson's Bay Company, a large department store chain. In recent years, it has been moving aggressively into electronic information, including specialized databases designed for professionals and financial analysts. Its legal home is Toronto but its operational hub is in Stamford, Connecticut.

The Thomsons were also moving towards a dynastic change, as Ken prepared to pass the torch of leadership to his older son David. The elder Thomson is a gentle soul, and a passionate collector of Canadian art, whose shyness often obscures a perceptive mind. Early in his life, he made the decision to be an owner, but not an owner-manager, to stay out of day-to-day operations. It was a decision that has richly rewarded him. Conrad Black says of his friend Ken Thomson that "taking over a very large fortune and making it a great deal larger is an amazing achievement, as amazing in his way as his father's."

The next family leader, David, a slim man in his early forties, was still largely an unknown commodity, an aesthete and collector of fine art like his father, but in public appearances he seemed moody and intensely conflicted by his role. Even so, Ken had announced that David, who has a sister and a brother, was to become the chairman of Thomson Corporation in 2002—and thus, the next generation's leader—just as the family moves into a new media era.

On the surface, there are no organizations more different than Thomson and BCE. The Thomsons are renowned for an obsessive dedication to cost discipline, reflected in their newspapers' legendary expense controls, which extended to the careful monitoring of newsroom pencil usage. With only occasional lapses, they have bought and sold with an eye for value. BCE, on the other hand, has been known to pay heavily for assets and later discard them with mixed financial results. But both companies see themselves as longer-term players that have stood the test of time. While Izzy Asper and Ted Rogers are phenomenal entrepreneurs and traders, there is always the suspicion that their empires might not last long beyond their own lives.

Geoff Beattie's boyhood nickname is Ernie, but he is the antithesis of the small-town operator that name seems to suggest. In his early forties, he is the perfect *consigliere*, smart and loyal with just the right touch of aggression—the kind who would pick up a phone and berate a reporter who might have got some details wrong about the Thomson family interests. It is one of the family's special talents to find astute advisers like Beattie and establishment lawyer John Tory Sr.—who also serves that other media baron Ted Rogers—and tough operating managers like Michael Brown or Richard Harrington, past and current presidents of Thomson Corporation.

In the late nineties, Beattie undertook a mission vital to the future health of the Thomson fortune. He had spent the better part of the year trying to figure out where the family should go in the new media world, in an age when the business of conventional newspapers was not growing and the Internet held such exciting and dangerous promise. Beattie visited a number of media and communications players that were grappling with the same kinds of questions. He developed a picture of a world where the old intermediaries, such as the great newspapers, no longer held such sway over public opinion. In the age of the Internet, information and ideas were easily obtained, from more sources, and this was somehow more democratic. But with all this abundant information, there was an enduring power in trusted brands and knowledgeable sources. At the same time, the most valuable media properties were those that distributed compelling live content, particularly sports and news.

So the Thomson family confronted the challenge of marrying their mature and trusted brands with the new Internet medium. You could call it convergence, but in the Thomsons' view it was old-fashioned strategic thinking, the kind the organization had always practiced, now transferred to the age of broadband. And they found a willing soulmate in the person of Jean Monty.

As Monty and Beattie held early discussions, the Thomson team was also pondering what to do with its remaining North American newspapers. Although the business had reached maturity, their newspapers still carried great symbolic weight for the family—indeed, for the entire newspaper industry. Many North American journalists started their careers on mediocre small-town Thomson papers, and remembered the experience with a blend of horror and fondness. It was like a badge of honour. The Thomsons had been selling papers, but Ken Thomson loved *The Globe and Mail,* a prestige paper that he had bought in 1980 and pledged he would never let go. Meanwhile, the *Globe* itself was making a stronger push into electronic information, on-line news and investment services as well as television, through the new ROB-TV financial channel. It was clear to the Thomson leadership that a newspaper, even one as storied and distinguished as the *Globe,* could never survive as a stand-alone orphan business. "We can't kill it with sentimentality," Ken Thomson would tell the *Globe's* Jacquie McNish. "We have to look after it properly."

The Thomsons and BCE first talked about collaborating to buy CTV, the largest private television network. It was hard to believe that CTV would be an attractive asset, as it was lagging behind the smaller Global system in profitability. But it had picked up a number of the emerging cable specialty channels, including the industry leader TSN. The controlling shareholder, the Eaton family, beset by troubles in its department store empire, had sold its CTV interests, leaving a widely held company. *The Globe and Mail* also became part of the conversation—Monty saw it as a news source and a national brand to add to his Fortress Canada. The Thomsons would deal, as long as they kept a piece of their sacred trust.

But the Thomsons couldn't move nearly as fast as Monty wanted. As 1999 wound down, the family and its managers wanted to delay any action on CTV, mainly because they had a lot on the table. They were preparing to unload their extensive U.S. newspaper holdings, as well as their small remaining band of Canadian papers. It would be confusing if the Thomson organization announced it was lurching into television, in partnership with BCE, even before announcing its intentions for these newspapers. Recalls Monty: "We had talked about going in together in

CTV, they decided they weren't ready to make the move, and I said Geoff, 'We'll make our move and if you want to talk to us later, we're open.'"

Monty just couldn't sit still. Rumours were circulating that CTV was "in play," meaning someone was about to make a bid. Then came the AOL Time Warner deal, which accelerated his plans. "We said, what do we buy?' Monty recalls. "If you're BCE, you want to be the leader—you're not going to buy Global, you're not going to buy CBC or buy a small TV station here and there. So the real call is we have to buy CTV because it's the only one available that's got a national strategy."

Monty was often working on his own, without the full knowledge of his team back in Montreal. Nicholson, the chief strategy officer, says he heard about the CTV deal long before it happened, but "it went away and then it came back, and frankly when it came back, it was late in the game." He explains that isn't as strange as it sounds. A lot of ideas were drifting around the group—"they wax and they wane and they come and they go. We're a small group, we each have our own thing to do and we don't debrief each other every night."

Ivan Fecan also insists he didn't see BCE coming until fairly late, although he knew Monty personally and was undoubtedly relieved when the big holding company alerted him that it was prepared to make a move. "I was sort of in the middle of the storm and would have been the last one to know," says the cool and careful president of CTV. All through the fall and winter, he heard people were building positions in CTV, but the trigger was the announcement by Corus, the Shaws' media outfit, that it owned 9.9 percent of CTV. "It turned out CanWest also had 9.9 percent and all of a sudden, the question was not if we were bought but by whom and when. It was a rumour a day, and BCE was among those rumoured, but frankly I didn't know what was going to happen."

If BCE had not stepped in, he insists the company would have been broken up. The Aspers coveted TSN, for which CTV had recently out-bid them in a bitter battle. Corus was interested in the raft of other specialty channels, and maybe the network—or the network might have gone to other hands. "I believe it in my heart it would have been split up," Fecan says. "Maybe Péladeau would have kept it together, but I'm pretty sure Corus and CanWest would not have. Canwest wanted the suite of specialty channels, we beat them on [TSN] and they were sore about that—understandably, they thought they had it and they didn't."

In the wake of the AOL Time Warner deal, Fecan was holding a series of private talks with communications executives to discuss the impact of the blockbuster merger on the future of the industry. Monty was one of those executives, and the two men knocked around a number of potential alliances. Monty suggested a second meeting. A few days before the bid was announced, the two men met at a Toronto restaurant, where Monty slid the $2.3 billion offer onto the table.

Fecan defends BCE's bid price, which was clearly inspired by the hyped-up atmosphere and the still booming stock market of early 2000. "You can overpay and underpay, and get nothing. I think in the media space they paid the going price at the time, and frankly, as far as the CTV thing, I believe there are others who would have paid a little more if it wasn't BCE bidding. I think with BCE bidding, you have to think long and hard about how far the thing's going to go."

Indeed, the going price for prime broadcast assets would be bid up even higher in subsequent months. Corus would pay $205 million for WTV, the Women's Television Network, which was barely in the top ten among specialty channels. "We overpaid?" Monty snorted a year after the CTV bid. He then parodied his critics' carping criticism: "So Big Bad Bell has so much money—it can pay $38 when a year before CTV was in the low 20s? What is this, these guys are stupid?" Monty pointed out that arch enemy Ted Rogers paid more to buy control of Sportsnet—in terms of a multiple of earnings before interest, taxes, depreciation and amortization.

Another executive close to Monty says the pre-emptive strike says a lot about BCE's leader. He is truly visionary, but he doesn't worry a lot about the financial details—for Monty, it is all about power and owning things. He is a man of action, a master of the *coup de grâce*. "I don't think Jean ever pored over financial statements in this business. It was more about, 'What is it going to take to own this business?'" Some observers see this approach as classically French Canadian, pointing to that other big spender, Pierre Karl Péladeau and his $5.4 billion takeover of Vidéotron. But it also reflects the constricted Canadian scene: there aren't enough brand-name properties to go around, and in early 2000, in Monty's mind, you had to move with speed and authority.

So in February, 2000, BCE had locked up CTV and the Thomsons had put their remaining U.S. and Canadian newspapers on the block. The two parties went back to talk again about *The Globe and Mail.* This time it was harder to keep the talks under wraps, and by early September rumours were rife that a deal was developing. By that time, the media world had shifted in startling ways, with the CanWest purchase of many of the newspapers owned by Conrad Black's Hollinger *Globe and Mail* business columnist Eric Reguly broke the story on the *Globe's* front page on September 9, 2000, telling the world that BCE and the Thomsons were about to join forces to create a monster media company that would vie with AOL Time Warner, CanWest and Rogers.

By the morning of September 15, when the early-arriving staff of the *Globe* were called to a meeting, there were no surprises. The newsroom, circulation and advertising personnel were greeted by a phalanx of heavy hitters, including Ken Thomson and his two sons, David and Peter, along with Richard Harrington and Geoff Beattie. They laid out the details: the *Globe* would be folded into a new $4 billion company with CTV and Sympatico, which would be 70 percent owned by BCE, 20 percent by Thomson Corporation and 10 percent by the Thomson family's Woodbridge. It would be headed by CTV's president, Ivan Fecan.

It was an unusually tense meeting for such a triumphal event. David Thomson appeared distracted, standing slouched against a wall while the rest of the head table was seated. At one point, he responded testily to a reporter's question about the potential for meddling by the *Globe's* new master, Ivan Fecan, in the paper's editorial independence. David snapped that he had recently "broken bread" with Fecan and had found him totally acceptable. "If he meddles, it means he cares," David declared.

Other *Globe* employees seemed puzzled that Ken Thomson, who had expressed great love for the newspaper, would break his vow never to sell it. But the courtly billionaire made it clear that was not his interpretation. "I do not regard this as the sale of *The Globe and Mail*," he said. "We regard this as a superb partnership." But in effect, the control of Canada's major national newspaper had shifted from Canada's richest family to one of its largest industrial corporations.

For Jean Monty, this deal was not about buying a newspaper, or owning a television network. It was about owning big brand names, extracting the content they produced, repackaging it and distributing it over the Internet. In time, as Peter Nicholson predicted, most communications would move to the Internet, and BCE wanted to be in that game. It was certainly not the paper-and-ink *Globe* that quickened Monty's pulse. He was more attracted by GlobeandMail.com and GlobeInvestor.com and a raft of properties being developed by the *Globe* interactive team.

"We bought *The Globe and Mail* because I felt in terms of content, a newspaper is basically a producer of content," Monty would say. "It's news. And when you look at segments you want on the Internet, it's news, it's entertainment and sports, comedy a little bit. The porn you forget—it's going to happen in any case. But in terms of real value, you want news first, finance, sports, travel and comedy. So how do you get all this stuff? Well, in news, *The Globe and Mail* fit perfectly."

In seven months, BCE had leaped from out of nowhere to take what it considered a leadership position in the Canadian convergence landscape. It had already accumulated portals, satellite systems, wireless and land-line telephone connections—and, now, it owned that magical content. There were some gaps—it did not have a strong local news presence—but in the words of Richard Stursberg, a veteran satellite and telecom executive, BCE had "the dream team" in Canadian convergence. Yet there was still a prevailing sense—which Monty himself confirmed—that the company had no clear idea how all this would blend together. This was still one big fat bet on an unknown future.

Peter Nicholson, the strategy guru, knew that BCE was out in front in the convergence sweepstakes, but he also knew that was a scary place to be. "I remember telling the board at one point during the convergence discussion that the good news is that we're not really behind AOL Time Warner. But the bad news is that we're not really behind AOL Time Warner."

7 CITIZEN ASPER

ON APRIL 26, 2000, COPIES OF THE MORNING NEWSPAPER thumped on the doorstep of the Vancouver hotel rooms where Izzy Asper and his sons, Leonard and David, were planning for the most important days of their lives. The CRTC was about to open hearings on their bid to acquire the television stations of WIC Western International Communications, a national media company whose assets included valuable TV outlets in British Columbia and Alberta. It had been a bitter three-year struggle for WIC. The Aspers had battled and eventually bartered with the Shaw family. Izzy Asper, who already owned Global Television and a collection of other TV stations, as well as TV and radio networks in Australia, New Zealand and Ireland, was about to realize his dream of a national network based in Western Canada, a counterweight to the cultural and entertainment establishment in Toronto, Ottawa and Montreal.

But the morning newspaper screamed out headlines that would change the Aspers' lives in more significant ways, that would set them on a path to becoming media pioneers in converging print and television assets, but would also load them up with huge debt, put them under the glaring spotlight of journalistic inquiry and make them household names—not just in Winnipeg, but right across Canada. If you hadn't heard of the Aspers yet, you soon would.

The news was that newspaper baron Conrad Black and his company, Hollinger were preparing to sell their smaller Canadian community papers, a group that included such titles as the Belleville *Intelligencer*, *The Peterborough Examiner*, and the St. Catharines *Standard*. The controversial Black had become one of the world's largest newspaper publishers, with international titles that included London's *Daily Telegraph,* the *Jerusalem Post* and the *Chicago Sun-Times.* In a massive buying spree in the nineties, he had accumulated more than half of Canada's daily newspapers, including the old Southam chain and many of the former Thomson papers. But Black was concerned about the strength of his balance sheet with the economic recovery showing signs of faltering. As he pondered a sale of assets, the politically conservative press baron was also growing more negative about the political and economic scene in his native country. Black felt he was overexposed to newspapers and overexposed to Canada.

But if Black was souring on Canadian papers, Izzy Asper was anything but. Asper had always loved the feel of newsprint. The Aspers had long coveted the *Winnipeg Free Press,* the hometown paper now owned by Thomson Corporation. What's more, the CanWest team had identified newspapers, along with television, radio, Internet and outdoor advertising, as their five targeted areas of expansion in a strategic plan devised in 1998. So far, in Canada, the Aspers were strong only in television. Izzy Asper had been trying for almost three decades to become a newspaper publisher, and suddenly, the chance had materialized to become the largest newspaper owner in the country.

The Aspers were not yet disciples of convergence, the onrushing *zeitgeist* in the media industry. They were not spouting buzzwords about "repurposing" content, or integrating "content" and "carriage." But they knew things were happening fast. Three months earlier, they had watched as AOL announced a massive merger with Time Warner in a formidable combination of print, Internet and cable assets. Earlier in April, the powerful telephone holding company BCE had locked up the Aspers' bitter arch rival CTV in what was touted as a convergence play. Rumours were swirling that other big media deals were coming, and that the most prized assets would soon be snapped up.

Not only that, but the Aspers saw themselves as specialists in advertising-based media, and by broadening the base of this business—to newspapers, for example—it would be harder for any national or local advertiser to ignore them—or, in the lexicon of the ad industry, "to buy around them." The Aspers were concerned about the growing consolidation of the advertising and media buying business, as agencies have been merged and bought up, and more and more of the buying decisions have moved to New York. In the view of boyish-looking thirty-six-year-old Leonard Asper, who had recently become CanWest's president, the number of ad agencies he was dealing with had fallen from twenty-five to about half a dozen in recent years. To get the attention of these fewer ad buyers, and to bargain more effectively, a media company had to come to the table with a wide range of what Leonard would call "platforms," or media.

Another concern was the growing fragmentation of the television market, whereby newer, more narrowly focused channels were chewing away at the audiences of old conventional networks such as Global and CTV. Indeed, since 1991, the percentage of total viewing hours devoted to English-language conventional networks had fallen from 52 percent to 35 percent, while specialty and pay channels had risen from 12.5 percent to 30 percent, according to Nielsen Media Research. After a rocky start, the sixty or so analog specialty channels such as TSN, MuchMusic, Home and Garden, History and CanWest's own Prime, had won over viewers' loyalties, and a deluge of at least forty digital channels was on the way for the fall of 2001. Specialty channels provided an attractive dual stream of revenue—generating both advertising dollars and, more important, steady subscriber fees from cable operators, a source that was less buffeted by economic ups and downs than advertising.

But in the Aspers' eyes, there was still one surviving mass medium, the local newspaper, which in some cities penetrated 40 to 50 percent of households. The Aspers felt that this franchise wasn't always well run by the current breed of local newspaper publishers but they could see the potential of rich synergies combining local TV, local newspapers and ultimately local Web sites, all of them feeding off each other. If they could just add to their specialty TV lineup, and build some radio and billboard holdings, they would be on top of the Canadian media world.

In fact, the Aspers were already looking at the small stable of Canadian newspapers that had been put on the market in mid-February by Thomson Corporation. After more than sixty years in newspapers, the Thomson family saw a better future in electronic databases. David Asper recalls that when Thomson announced that it was going to sell its dwindling supply of Canadian newspapers, one of which was the *Winnipeg Free Press,* he approached his father about buying it himself, or even managing it as a family investment outside CanWest. The decision was made to go after the *Free Press,* and see what else might fall into place.

But the talks with Thomson were not going well, and the two sides, both notoriously hard bargainers, differed about price. Then the Hollinger papers miraculously surfaced. As the WIC hearings were swirling around them that April morning, the Asper family were already talking to Black and his shrewd colleague David Radler about an involvement in Hollinger's Internet properties, which included the Canada.com portal. As the Aspers thought about it, they began to form an idea: Why not go back and pick up the conversation on the larger newspapers as well, prime properties such as *The Ottawa Citizen, Calgary Herald, The Edmonton Journal,* Montreal *Gazette* and Vancouver *Sun?* This time, they would be going after the major newspapers in Canada's largest metropolitan centres—with the possible exception of Toronto, where Hollinger did not seem eager to part with Conrad Black's beloved *National Post.*

Izzy was also drawn by the identity of the seller: Conrad Black, a man as transparently different from him as any businessman could be. Izzy is Jewish; Conrad is WASP Anglican converted to Catholicism. Izzy is Winnipeg, Conrad is Toronto and London, but both men are great lovers of New York, just different aspects of New York. "Conrad likes opera, I like jazz. That's a huge chasm for me—imagine schlepping him around to New York clubs," Izzy says, rolling his eyes, musing about his famous nocturnal jaunts through the Big Apple's smoky jazz hangouts.

Now in his mid-fifties, Black had a storied career, the subject of constant turmoil and media speculation in Canada and abroad. Indifferent about school as a youth, he became a passionate student of history and a well-regarded if ponderously wordy biographer of Maurice Duplessis, the iron-fisted Quebec premier of fifty years ago. He burst into public view at a young age by wringing value out of assets as varied as supermarket chains and mining companies; by the time he was fifty-five, he was the subject of three large books, including his own autobiography. But his great love was newspapers, from the day he bought his first weekly paper. His old friend and partner David Radler—only half joking—claims to have invented the three-person newsroom—in which two of the three were ad salesmen.

As he reached middle age, Black, a rare intellectual among businessmen, became more avid in his enthusiasms, which included uniforms, ceremony, right-wing politics and a highfalutin vocabulary replete with grandiose and obscure words. He was always a favourite sparring partner of Canadian journalists, and he could dish it out with uncommon gusto: "My experience with journalists authorizes me to record that a very large number of them are ignorant, lazy, opinionated, intellectually dishonest and inadequately supervised," he once told a royal commission on the media. His greatest business accomplishment was his stunning turnaround of the *Daily Telegraph*, the fusty old British quality daily that had been in decline until Black rescued it in the 1980s. In recent years, he had dramatically consolidated the Canadian newspaper business, first acquiring of the Southam chain, the largest in the country, and then adding many of the Thomson and Sifton families' newspaper holdings. He founded the conservative daily the *National Post* with the idea of tossing a stink bomb into the complacent liberal political consensus in Canada. But, on this morning in April, 2000, he was suddenly selling newspaper properties, which suggested that the restless Black was growing tired of the game, particularly in Canada.

The wannabe aristocrat Black, who coveted a seat in the British House of Lords, seemed an unlikely partner for the down-to-earth Izzy Asper, owner of the Love Boat TV network. But they both saw themselves as outsiders when it came to the dominant soft-left, soft-nationalist elite. There was another indisputable link. "We both came to recognize that the other person's word was gold—we demonstrated that in the 1970s," Izzy says. Back in those days, Izzy and Gerry Schwartz were on an acquisition binge, with a particular interest in financial services companies. A thirty-three-year-old Conrad Black had managed to wrest control of the industrial conglomerate Argus Corporation away from its founders' families, and decided its 54 percent interest in Crown Trust was expendable. Izzy bought the Crown Trust holding on the strength of a handshake, in a deal that didn't close until a year later. Izzy keeps a small decorative pane of glass with the etching of two hands shaking. Whenever he looks at it, he says, it reminds him: "That is the Crown Trust deal." For the idealistic Asper, always searching for the perfect partner, Conrad represented that rare person who could be trusted. This is the essence of Izzy. It is not ideas or politics that drive him as much as trust. He has spent his entire career being disappointed by partners. He is like Diogenes the Cynic, carrying his lamp, searching for an honest man and continually disappointed with what he finds in the real rough-and-tumble world.

Before venturing into a deal, he likes to know the people, their background and history. He had just been through a bruising battle with the Shaw family of Alberta for control of the WIC assets. Izzy remembers trying to tell the Shaws—patriarch JR and his son Jim— that the split-up of assets could be amiably solved in the early stages, but it dragged on, costing the two families millions of dollars more than they needed to spend. "When the war started, it became clear that if the Shaws knew me, they would know I was willing to fight the battle to the end. But they didn't know me, I didn't know them, and I didn't realize that they were as determined, or gutsy, as they were."

Conrad was different, a known commodity, although there was no question he was also shrewd and determined. In addition, Izzy wasn't so enamoured of Conrad that he wouldn't pull his leg a bit, lampooning his self-parodying pomposity. Izzy recalls giving a speech in Sydney a few years ago to an advertising convention, soon after Black's failed campaign to buy full control of Australia's Fairfax chain of newspapers. Black, frustrated by foreign ownership limits, had left Australia in a cloud of controversy, and Asper, who was acquiring assets in Australia, feared that the local community would direct some residual anger towards another Canadian. They would assume, Izzy figured, that "he was just another Conrad, that he'd pee all over us."

At the convention, Izzy observed that Black would soon be writing his biography, which would be called "the Ten Greatest Media Barons in the World and My Impression of the Other Nine." Izzy recalls that his old ally didn't really enjoy the joke but, Asper says, "if life wasn't funny we'd all kill ourselves." The relationship clearly could survive a little leg-pulling.

As for Black, he, too, felt comfortable doing business with Izzy. "We'd always got on fine, although I know he's got a reputation as a difficult man. The fact is, [the Aspers] are not the easiest people to deal with but they're not the worst," Black says. "They have a considerable talent for making small issues [into] large issues. They have great sensitivities, they get very impatient and have the tendency sometimes to think if they don't get everything they want when they want it, it's for reasons that aren't legitimate. But when all that is said, I've found them on balance to be rather pleasant people and intelligent."

But the biggest differences would seem to be political: Izzy is a Liberal—he was once the Manitoba party leader—while Conrad eyes Liberal Prime Minister Jean Chrétien with the loathing one might normally reserve for the anti-Christ. Black founded the *National Post* largely as a tough-minded, partisan Conservative antidote to the one-sided Liberal consensus that he felt had gripped Canada for most of the twentieth century. Still, while much is made of Izzy Asper's Liberal leanings, his is a very pragmatic Liberalism, and much of his personal credo would find favour with Conrad Black. Izzy's Liberalism is also tinged with the same sense of Western Canadian outrage that drives many members of the Canadian Alliance party, which Black's *National Post* backed so ardently. When he was the Manitoba party leader, Izzy had espoused policies to the right of the Liberal mainstream. He was not hesitant to take the party and the government to task when they strayed from what he saw as the proper free-market course. But Izzy's political career had forged important personal relationships in the Liberal Party, and he has remained essentially loyal to these people. It is a loyalty based as much on friendship as on ideas. It has also been a useful relationship: as the governing party for most of the last half-century, the Liberals have had much to say about the direction of broadcast policy in this country.

Leonard Asper says if his family has a philosophy, it is based on the ideas of John Stuart Mill, the British political and social thinker of the nineteenth century and author of *On Liberty*, one of the most eloquent expressions of intellectual liberalism of his age. Mill set a clear distinction between the realm of society and that of the individual. The individual should have complete and absolute autonomy over his own affairs, Mill wrote, except in those matters that affect others. In those cases, such as defence and policing, government does indeed have a role. In Izzy and his two sons' view, public life was all about maintaining those boundaries, preventing the state from sliding into areas where it was not needed. That is why on almost every economic issue, Izzy finds himself far out on the Liberal right.

As for Black, he insists that in early 2000 his motives for selling his newspapers were mainly financial—an outcome of his heavy debt load and a suddenly negative outlook for the economy and newspaper advertising. He also felt that given Hollinger's lacklustre share price, he could not issue new shares without seriously diluting existing shareholders. "It's like a Venus flytrap—it is closing on me," Black was thinking through the winter of 1999–2000.

For Black, the key moment came in mid-February, when he got a call at his London home from John Tory Sr., the close adviser to Ken Thomson, saying that Thomson Corporation was selling the rest of its newspapers except for *The Globe and Mail.* "He was clearly hoping we were a buyer, but we were a long way towards thinking it was time for us to do some selling," Black recalls. "That was a real catalyst for us. We thought if Thomson is heading completely for the exit, we should try to get there first because there is going to be too much product otherwise floating around."

Although Hollinger was formally offering only its small papers, it was, in fact, open to all offers. "We were up for anything," Black says, but in order to cause as little alarm as possible among employees, it was dressing up the deal as only a sale of the smaller units. "That was just baiting the lure," Black would say later.

The bait attracted one very large fish. After musing about what would happen if the bigger metro papers owned by Hollinger were up for sale, Izzy finally told his sons, "I'll talk to Conrad and see what he thinks." The Aspers' early thought was that they would buy Hollinger's Regina and Saskatoon papers, and combine them with the Thomsons' *Winnipeg Free Press* to create a little prairie collection.

Izzy remembers how the momentum picked up: "All of a sudden, Conrad called me about negotiations on Canada.com. 'You and I have to break this logjam,' he said, and we started talking about it."

"If you are putting up your little papers, what do you need Regina and Saskatoon for?" Izzy asked.

"I'll consider it," was Black's reply, to which Asper suggested, 'Maybe Alberta?'

Black observed that might mean breaking up the Southam/Hollinger chain, although clearly he was not entirely distressed by the idea.

"Then why don't we talk about the whole chain?" Asper added.

On May 12, Leonard and Izzy were on a plane to New York to meet Conrad and Dan Colson, the Hollinger vice-chairman.

The Izzy and Conrad show took over at that point, a marathon of talking, drinking, faxing and e-mailing that took place over two continents, at luxury homes in Canada and Florida, in Europe and in summer cottages over the next five months. The conversation shifted quickly to a discussion of all the major Canadian newspapers, except, at first, for the *National Post*. "We kind of nursed it along," Izzy says. While Black was initially not inclined to sell the bigger papers, he came around to the idea fairly easily. "We tried to catch the last train leaving the station. Izzy Asper was the only buyer of any big size," he says.

Was it a convergence play? For Izzy, it was more of a "shouldn't we be in this business?" play. Despite his ownership of Global, he was never a broadcaster at heart—his great passion was newspapers. He only got into television because he was continually blocked from owning print. "I had tried, all my life, from the time I was a teenager," says Izzy, rhyming off his years running high school and university papers, then writing a tax column for *The Globe and Mail* and other newspapers for the FP Publications chain in the sixties. In the late 1970s, he had tried to buy the FP papers but had been thwarted by his board, and the chain had gone to Thomson Corporation. He was later nixed by the board in an attempt to buy the Sun newspapers, and they eventually ended up with Quebecor. One of the prime attractions for Izzy was the newspaper's ability to offer a forum to communicate his views. "It's the opportunity to make a difference and make sure a perspective that isn't always presented is there," Izzy insists.

So was he motivated more by his pent-up desire to own a newspaper or by this thing called convergence? Both, he says. "A: I wanted a newspaper group. B: It does tie in beautifully on what is euphemistically called convergence." But was owning a newspaper his primary goal? "Fundamentally, yes. If the government had a public hearing and said no more concentration of interests, go spin off the newspapers from the television, I'd be there [personally] buying the newspapers."

Izzy does not use the language of platforms and convergence, but he does talk about continually broadening the stages on which CanWest is an actor. First, there was his Winnipeg television station, CKND. "But I knew I had to be part of a national group, then I had to be international. In 1991, I had to go public, to my regret. Now we're absolutely nowhere in terms of where we want to go. What I love about the business is that it is infinite."

Izzy's view is that if you're going to concentrate on advertising-based media, you have to have a number of properties that overlap and create an increasingly broader base. You could no longer be in just one medium, such as television. You had to be in all of them. Izzy also realized that he had experienced terrible wear and tear to get where he was. Companies always have finite resources, and there were a limited number of prime media properties in Canada. "Yet here was an opportunity in one fell swoop, at one time, to do what took me twenty-five years in broadcasting—it was irresistible."

As the negotiations with Black picked up steam, security was extremely tight. Izzy was fearful that news would trickle out, sparking another bid. Neither Black nor Asper had informed his board that preliminary negotiations were underway, since that would have required public disclosure. Torstar, owner of *The Toronto Star,* and perennial bridesmaid of Canadian media deals, was sniffing around, and the behemoth BCE was always there in the background. Jean Monty had talked to Conrad about many of the same newspapers Izzy was eyeing, but had backed away. "Conrad had approached us to see if we could do a deal with them," Monty says. "We thought it was too much for us to buy the whole of Black's papers. We didn't have the expertise and we thought in terms of concentration and markets. It was too much and I'm not sure it's efficient."

By late May, the security-conscious Izzy was hand-writing a document describing the deal's concept in about fifty pages. Famous for his nocturnal hours of work, Izzy had hidden himself at his cottage on Falcon Lake, scratching away at the document until about four in the morning and getting up as late as eleven. He had it typed outside the office for security reasons, and sent it around to Leonard, Tom Strike, CanWest's chief operating officer, and a few others, who went through it and massaged the text.

There was no business model for a television-newspaper convergence—this had never been done before on such a scale. Still, the Aspers were convinced that even if the big synergies didn't come, newspapers were ultimately good businesses. If there was any model, it was the Tribune Company, of Chicago, with its blend of newspaper, television and content assets, including the Chicago Cubs baseball team. The Aspers saw themselves as the *Tribune* of the North, and CanWest executives spent time with *Tribune* chief executive officer John Madigan studying the Chicago-based company's model—although one CanWest executive said his main discovery in visiting *Tribune* was that it hadn't yet found a way to make media convergence work.

Secret merger negotiations take code names to maintain their confidentiality, and these talks became known as a Canterbury Tale—after Canterbury Lane, the street address of Izzy's Palm Beach, Florida, winter home, which was once owned by Conrad Black. Media observers later made much of the image of Chaucer's collection of ill-assorted pilgrims wandering towards a shrine, in this case, the dubious shrine of media convergence. In that sense, all the Canadian convergence plays should have been called Canterbury Tales, because they all had uncertain outcomes.

After early conversations, Black invited Izzy to join him in Brussels at the elite Bilderberg conference on economics and politics in early June. The Bilderberg meeting, much reviled by anti-globalization activists, was the kind of high-level meeting of powerful minds that Black revels in. The 2000 gathering drew such figures as Black's friend Henry Kissinger, financier George Soros and the Agnellis, who own Italy's Fiat car empire. Izzy was in Israel at the time and, armed with his concept document, hopped a plane to Belgium where he hoped to work with Conrad on the major points of the final agreement. The Brussels talks turned into a comedy of errors as Black and Asper tried to find some quiet moments away from the constant schmoozing at this elite gathering.

The hope was that the two Canadian media tycoons would meet after dinner in the bar of the luxurious Château du Lac Hotel, where the conference-goers were staying. Both Conrad and Izzy are night people, and they figured the other conference-goers would go to sleep, but the meeting was so interesting and the bar was so popular that it was impossible to find a private moment until after 1 A.M. On the day the conference broke up, Izzy was "zonked" and trying to catch some shut-eye, when Black dropped by his room. The two decided it was time to stop talking and nail down the key points. "We went straight from that to eight hundred pages of paper," Izzy marvels. Black was happy with the results: "At the end of that meeting, we knew all the outstanding points." In fact, Black says, "I've never had an un-cordial moment with Izzy. Occasionally, our guys get impatient with their guys, but at that level it was not a problem."

As the conversation evolved, Black talked of taking a big ownership stake in CanWest or possibly merging the two companies. "It went through all kinds of iterations," Izzy says. "And because I didn't want to share control of CanWest, it gravitated towards what we did." The idea was that Conrad would hand over Hollinger's ownership of the Southam papers for a chunk of cash and a significant minority ownership in CanWest, and a management contract would allow Black, Radler and their team to continue their role at the newspaper chain.

One possible sticking point was the fate of the *National Post*, Conrad's great love, perhaps even before his second wife and political soulmate, the conservative journalist Barbara Amiel. Black had been viewed as a brilliant businessman but essentially a collector and trader of assets, not a founder. The *National Post* newspaper was his bright and shining creation. At that point, Conrad Black still felt committed to the *Post*, despite losing more than $100 million in the newspaper war with *The Globe and Mail*. Yet as the Aspers developed their dream of a national newspaper chain to complement their TV assets, they were adamant that they needed an entry into Toronto. The *Post* was a necessary piece of the puzzle. So Black relented, agreeing to part with 50 percent of the newspaper. The significance of this will be debated forever: Was it a way for Black to grease his exit from the *Post*, which showed no signs of becoming financially viable? Was the cohabitation of the conservative Black with the friend-of-Chrétien Asper doomed from the start? Black insists that at this point, he was still fiercely committed to the *Post*, even though he wanted to reduce his exposure to Canadian newspapers.

Through the early summer of 2000, a lot of the work took place at cottages. The Aspers are never far away from each other. Izzy's cottage on Falcon Lake is right next door to David's. Leonard's place is at Lake of the Woods, near Kenora, Ontario, just thirty miles up the road. Izzy loves his cottage—in fact, all his major moves have been orchestrated to some extent at the cottage. He bought it forty years ago for $9,000, and wrote his master's thesis in law there. He used the cottage to write *The Benson Iceberg*, his critique of Liberal government tax reform in the early 1970s—"a book that had to be written," he says.

The stunning thing is that news of the deal never leaked out. It had become public knowledge, David says, that CanWest was doing due diligence at the small Thomson papers, which they eventually passed up buying. But with the Hollinger papers, the CanWest team was very careful about who went where. David was a fairly safe bet, because he was not in the public eye, but Leonard had been getting a lot of ink since becoming president of CanWest in late 1999. There was a dangerous moment when David Asper was challenged by a Montreal *Gazette* security guard, who was supposed to have been informed that important—and anonymous—visitors were coming that day. The Asper team managed to talk their way around that one. Izzy is still amazed that nothing found its way into the press, "Here was the biggest media deal and there was no leak. We were terrified of a bidding war."

As they combed through the Hollinger assets, the Aspers began to realize that television and newspapers were not alike. They had a different economics and, even more important, different cultures. The key Southam papers consisted of fourteen major local businesses plus 50 percent of the *National Post*. "The more we got into it, the more we realized how much more complex than television they were," David said, in a comment that ominously presaged turbulent times ahead.

While much of TV programming is purchased, newspapers create their own content, and that requires many more people than the Aspers were used to having employed. David Asper was amazed: "Then you realize why all the people are there, what this business does every single day. And then you see those rolls of newsprint, and you go to see the presses—this is a manufacturing business. What it takes to get those words and those ads and everything else in the paper, that is just staggering. We went out to watch the press run in Vancouver and it's staggering, it's staggering."

In just three months, CanWest and Hollinger had managed to assemble thousands of pages of documents, enough to occupy three rooms at a Toronto law firm. Leonard couldn't help comparing it with the more than *eighteen months* it had taken to decide on a split of assets with the Shaw family, including a delay over the tax structure of the deal. In the case of Hollinger, the participants knew each other right from the start. "It was the full Marquess of Queensberry Rules," Leonard says. If one party detected something in a document that would benefit it, but harm the other side, it would point it out.

As CanWest's corporate secretary, Gail Asper, Izzy's daughter, was watching all this unfold from Winnipeg, she found it hard to keep her distance. Deal making is the great game of corporate life, the adrenaline-pumping reward for all the hard slogging. "There is that camaraderie of being in the office at midnight, then you go out and you celebrate like everything. I have to say I really do miss that. The experience is like hell, but then you see John Maguire [CanWest's chief financial officer] so happy, coming in with that exhilarated look, that all their hard work was positive, for something good, and they've closed the deal." It's a lot like acting, says Gail, who is a frustrated thespian. "For all the insecurity, there is also the incredibly intense joy of being on stage."

The morning of July 31 was indeed showtime for the Aspers, as they signed the final documents paving the way for the biggest deal in Canadian media history. The final stack of papers was eighteen inches high, Izzy recalls, and "there was still biting and chewing and scratching over these documents right up to the end." Newsrooms are quiet places in summer and this day started out no differently, until the buzz started to rise that a big deal was in the works. Reporters huddled nervously as rumours circulated that the Aspers were about to become big players in their industry. Then came the invitation for journalists to come to the News Theatre, a press-conference venue on the Esplanade in downtown Toronto. There Izzy and Leonard, father and son, greeted the press, posing for pictures as they mock-read the *National Post*, announcing the $3.5 billion deal (later reduced to $3.2 billion) that would make CanWest the first major TV network in the world to buy a large national newspaper chain.

CanWest, in addition to its large television holdings, would now become a huge newspaper corporation—comprising 14 major metro dailies, 126 small newspapers, 85 trade publications and 50 percent of the *Post*, as well as a newspaper ad site and four other Internet properties. Combined with the takeover of the WIC properties, which had been approved the previous month, this deal meant the Aspers now literally owned urban British Columbia, with three daily newspapers in Vancouver and Victoria and two major television outlets, including the news ratings powerhouse BC TV. The initial price included $2.2 billion in cash, $700 million in debt; and about $600 million in stock, making Hollinger a 15 percent minority owner of CanWest.

At the press conference, Leonard, as president of CanWest, took his place in the foreground, while his father, now executive chairman, appeared to play a supporting role. But everyone knew it was Izzy's relationship with Conrad that got the deal done. Black was not available—in the final negotiations over the *National Post*, he had been exchanging memos with head office while attending the annual Wagner opera week in Bayreuth, Germany. Occasionally, the negotiators would get faxes that would begin, "It's intermission at the opera . . ."

For Leonard, it was his first big deal as CEO, and he was almost kiddishly exultant over how things had turned out. He insisted the new CanWest could find $50 million to $150 million in annual savings or revenue increases through synergies among the media properties. Most of the gains, he said, would be on the revenue side—by selling cross-media ad packages—and not by cost-cutting, although the Aspers were drawn to the possibilities of using multi-purpose journalists across a spectrum of media. As Leonard said later, "It just seems like we have so many toys in our sandbox—that's what it feels like, or to use a military analogy, we really feel like we have a navy and airforce and artillery. When you need one you always have it—you can either have a concerted attack, or if necessary, an air attack only."

But there was an unavoidable question hanging over the deal with Hollinger: Why would Conrad Black sell if this was such a great business? Black's argument was that he was over-invested in newspapers and in Canada, and that the Aspers, as television owners, were better positioned to make a breakthrough in the newly converging media world, where the Internet would become the prevalent delivery mechanism. But paying as much as CanWest did as a multiple of earnings, how could it hope to make a significant rate of return on its investment?

That was what David Galloway, the CEO of Torstar, was asking after the deal was announced. Torstar had looked at a Hollinger deal, but "we thought it was pretty expensive. We had enormous respect for Radler and Conrad and how they ran those papers and we didn't think we could do better." With the multiples that Torstar would have to pay, consistent with newspaper prices at the time, "We [would have] loved to own the properties but we didn't think we could get a return."

But Leonard Asper argues that the Southam chain, under Hollinger ownership, was still an unfinished canvas. Southam did not operate as a real company but as an agglomeration of separate entities. The Hollinger people had gone a long way towards changing that, but before they finished the job, they had launched the *National Post*, and its challenges had then preoccupied the top Hollinger managers. Leonard believed the job of integration was not finished. Furthermore, Hollinger had an unwieldy management structure in Canada that, according to Leonard, "was not conducive to maximization of profits as it could be."

The day after the deal was announced, *The Globe and Mail* ran a front-page cartoon showing Izzy Asper with a maple-leaf flag as a bib, dining on Conrad Black, roasted in the manner of a stuffed Thanksgiving turkey.

There was an air of gloating glee that the Aspers had devoured Black, and that he was leaving the scene in humiliation. But as the CanWest debt load mounted, the economy slowed down and share prices tumbled, perceptions shifted to the view that the wily Black had seen the Aspers coming and taken them for a ride. That view was bolstered by the deal's fine print—that CanWest was paying Black and his aides a $6 million annual newspaper management fee—plus an $80 million non-competition fee, for Black's promise he would not compete with Southam until at least 2005.

Conrad Black insists neither representation was accurate, that it was a case of both parties getting the deal they wanted. He got a good price and the Aspers got solid properties—in his view, much better assets than a Canadian television network, such as Global, which was basically a flim-flam game based on a shaky business model. A Canadian TV network's core business depended on simulcasting the same programs that were appearing on the U.S. networks, while inserting its own Canadian commercials. This device, aimed at commercially protecting Canadian television networks, could not last, Black says. "Over time, Izzy bought first-class assets from us, whereas a Canadian television business is essentially a fraud while a Canadian newspaper business is not. The newspapers are easily comparable with those of similar size in the United States, while I don't see how these Canadian television stations won't ultimately become the network affiliates of American ones, apart from the CBC. This was a real quantum leap for Izzy and I think it was a good deal. He paid a fair price and I don't think it was excessive."

The Aspers also knew that the strange economics of Canadian TV broadcasting could not continue forever—at some point, the United States networks would surely make an attempt to do business directly in Canada, instead of using Canadian networks as proxies. The Internet was already threatening to create a global TV marketplace. The fragmentation of the media would continue, and CanWest still had some serious gaps in its five-media strategy, particularly in Canadian specialty

TV and in radio. And they wanted to do something about it quickly.

A couple of days after the Hollinger deal, Allan Slaight, one of Izzy Asper's many estranged business partners and now owner of radio giant Standard Broadcasting, got a phone call from his old nemesis, inviting him to lunch. Slaight, a former Global TV partner who had split with Asper twenty-five years earlier, agreed to the meeting out of curiosity. They got together at the Rosewater Supper Club, an upscale eatery in downtown Toronto, directly across the street from Conrad Black's Hollinger headquarters. Izzy, puffing madly on his cigar, tried to convince his old partner that he should sell him his chain of radio stations. Slaight was amused, but he declined: he had his own plans to become a much bigger radio station owner. Izzy was thwarted this time, but he would probably be back again. Right now, he had an awful lot on his plate.

8 VIDÉOTRON GAMES

THE WAR FOR VIDÉOTRON BEGAN INNOCENTLY ENOUGH, IN informal conversations around the boardroom table of the Toronto-Dominion Bank, the bank that acted as the primary lender to Canada's cable TV industry. Two of the TD Bank's veteran directors, Ted Rogers, the hyperactive Toronto cable baron, and André Chagnon, his dignified Montreal counterpart, started talking to each other about the future of their industry, and one thing just led to another. In the late 1990s, both were aware of the pattern in their industry: The cable business had evolved from a collection of small Mom-and-Pop shops to a clutch of very large operators, all of whom knew each other well and did deals together, trading assets back and forth. In Quebec it was down to two major players, the industry leader Vidéotron—André Chagnon's company—and Cogeco, another large family company, which was 12 percent owned by Ted Rogers, and also had substantial holdings in Southern Ontario.

So when Chagnon, the seventy-two-year-old founder and controlling shareholder of Vidéotron, looked around for a business partner, it was inevitable that he would start talking to his fellow TD director Ted Rogers, who had become the industry consolidator in Eastern Canada. After several decades of building the country's third largest cable system, the always forward-looking Chagnon was finally convinced he would never be big enough to compete with giant rival BCE in breadth of communications services. He still felt that cable provided the most flexible access to the home, because of its potential to transmit vast amounts of data, voice and video, now offered through the digital format. But BCE's near-monopoly dominance in plain old telephone communications gave it a tremendous financial and marketing advantage. It could use its monopoly profits from its phone service to subsidize its money-losing but fast-growing ExpressVu satellite system and high-speed Internet offerings. The only way to knock BCE off its perch was to team up nationally with another big player, and the logical choice was Ted Rogers. "We could grow with Ted," André Chagnon was thinking. "We could compete efficiently across Canada." At first, the two entrepreneurs talked about integrating the two companies to form a combined operation with the scale and scope to fight BCE on every front. When they couldn't make that work, they decided that they should merge the two firms, and it made sense that the bigger Rogers would make a friendly takeover bid for the Chagnon assets. There was no sense that Pierre Karl Péladeau's Quebecor might be ready to jump into the bidding.

The fact that Ted Rogers was actually alive and solvent was something that amazed a lot of people who knew him. In the mid-1990s, he had been perilously close to ruin, the victim of overreaching and crushing debt. But he had divested assets, sold equity and bounced back to such an extent that in late 1999, he could look at a new acquisition, particularly one that would let him cluster his networks and sell bundles of cable, wireless services and media properties into new markets. He would offer an all-share deal that would not load extra debt onto his still highly leveraged balance sheet. At the same time, he was talking about another big cable swap with the Shaw family, which would mean giving up the rich Vancouver market, but adding some key Toronto suburbs, as well as large swaths of the Atlantic provinces. Ted was also thinking about sports, and a run at the Toronto Blue Jays, and a television channel called Sportsnet, in which he owned a minority stake but expected to buy the controlling interest from CTV, as a result of a regulatory ruling.

Ted Rogers and André Chagnon had a lot in common—people often spoke of them in the same breath as the technological pioneers of the cable industry, dreamers and risk-takers who had a bigger vision than the others. Like Rogers, Chagnon had enjoyed a monopoly business for many years, but his company rarely enjoyed the strong margins of other cable providers, mainly because he was always pumping his money in the next big idea. His great dream was to provide basic telephone services over the Internet, taking on BCE in its monopoly phone business. Chagnon was ahead of almost everybody, including Ted Rogers, in this still unproven technology of Internet telephony, which was another reason why buying Vidéotron appealed to Rogers so much. "I was convinced that with the scale and scope of Ted, it was the greatest opportunity we had in Canada to compete with the giant Bell Canada," Chagnon said later. "We could not compete with a company that had a monopoly in telephony if we could not offer those services, too. I am still convinced today it was the best deal for Canada."

To Chagnon, a self-effacing man, all this talk of being a visionary was somewhat amusing. He felt his innovative drive came not so much from big dreams but from sheer business necessity. Although he had run a highly successful business—and his debt was under control—cable television had not penetrated the Quebec market to the same extent as it had conquered the English-language population. Only about 62 percent of Quebecers subscribed to cable television in the late 1990s, compared with 85 percent of other Canadians. Chagnon understood the reason—French-speaking Quebecers were not as tempted by the big packages of English channels and programming that the cable companies typically offered. They were relatively well served by the local French-language stations that could be picked up off the air, without cable. So Chagnon felt he had to add more and more non-TV services to entice buyers and boost Vidéotron's revenues. Internet telephony would, he hoped, be part of that offering someday. "Sometimes you are a visionary because you have to do something," Chagnon says. Meanwhile, the rival satellite TV systems—owned by Shaw and BCE—began to ramp up activity in Quebec, spending huge amounts in a quest to lure away cable subscribers. This new battle intensified the pressure to add services, capital spending requirements were rising and a Rogers-Vidéotron deal seemed to make sense.

By late 1999, it was an open secret in Montreal that Chagnon was thinking about selling the cable network to concentrate on broadcasting, through his ownership of TVA, Quebec's largest private television network. Montreal media sources say there was also some concern in the Chagnon family that André's handsome silver-haired son Claude, now Vidéotron's president, lacked his father's entrepreneurial dynamism. According to this view, Claude did not have the drive to push the cable company to the next stage of growth that would have been needed to survive. André's decision to sell, they said, was motivated by a need to protect his family investment and the huge charitable foundation he hoped to build. But others dispute this—the main reason André Chagnon was looking for a buyer, they say, was because Vidéotron would never have the size to flourish in the new media world, especially against a rival with the abundant resources of BCE.

Daniel Lamarre, a former journalist and a senior public relations executive, had come to work for the André Chagnon in the mid-1990s as the president of TVA. He had barely known his new boss before joining the Chagnon fold, but "I just fell in love with the man when he approached me for the job. He was so smart; he was a visionary." Lamarre believes that if Chagnon had lived in the United States, in Los Angeles or New York, he would have enjoyed a reputation as big as that of Bill Gates for his pioneering work on convergence. "When you look at what's happening now on e-commerce and Internet and all those things, this guy had figured it out ten years ago. He was too avant-garde for this time, and in too small a market."

By doing business with Ted Rogers, Lamarre says, Chagnon saw a way to sell off the cable assets, but by holding shares in Rogers Communications, he would be a minority owner of a much larger entity, which would compete on a national scale. Also, he still wanted to own TVA, which he planned to build into an international broadcasting force. "He kind of fell in love with content and he thought we could become a significant player in the industry and he knew it was impossible to become such a big player in the cable business. So the deal with Rogers was perfect for him and perfect for me," says Lamarre, who under this scenario would have continued on as president of a Chagnon-owned TVA.

Ted Rogers was not the only one talking to Vidéotron. In fact, in the heady days of late 1999 and early 2000, everybody in the media business was talking to everyone else. Pierre Karl Péladeau certainly liked cable television because it threw out lots of cash, and Vidéotron had a good physical network. But he was not looking to buy—yet. However, Pierre Karl was checking out André Chagnon on the possibility of combining Vidéotron's new high-speed Internet access with Quebecor's Web portal, called Canoe, which he had acquired with the Sun newspapers in 1999. Pierre Karl saw the potential to marry Canoe's home page and news content with a cable partner that could provide the high-speed pipes to the home. He was being urged on by Canoe's managers in Toronto, who felt their portal, now five years old, was on the front end of the oncoming Internet bonanza.

Pierre Karl was always open to deals. After all, he had already bought Canoe's former parent, Sun Media, wresting it away from Torstar, and he and Charlie Cavell had taken over a U.S. printer, World Color Press, propelling Quebecor to the top rank among the world's printing companies. At one point, he considered a takeover of CTV, a ripe target because of its lack of a controlling shareholder. Indeed, after buying the Sun newspapers, Pierre Karl could see that CTV might be a nice match in English Canada. He met with Ivan Fecan but never took the plunge. "So someone came in with a bigger cheque, a knockout punch, and it worked," Pierre Karl says. That someone was BCE.

Even so, Péladeau was never impressed with CTV's economics. It was one of several highly competitive players, including Global, in the English-language conventional network game. "These two giants were looking for the same dollars. But when you look in Quebec, you do not have that kind of competition." Beyond Quebecor and Vidéotron, Bell was active on the Internet side, the Desmarais family owned some newspapers and Radio Canada, the French-language arm of CBC, had a strong presence. But Quebec was the kind of place where one player could, with a strategic takeover, become dominant very quickly.

Pierre Karl also approached Ted Rogers about linking up with Canoe, but to no avail. Rogers Cable, he felt, should be interested in Canoe as the home page for its high-speed Internet service—after all, Canoe was first developed at Sun Media in the early nineties when Rogers controlled the newspaper company. There were promising conversations with Rogers cable boss, John Tory Jr., and its media president, Tony Viner, but Ted Rogers was determined to cast his lot with Excite@Home, a California company that had emerged as his high-speed Internet partner—and where Melinda Rogers, his daughter, was actually employed for a couple of years.

All this talk of broadband and portals was exciting for Pierre Karl Péladeau, who had come to the tech game relatively late in his young life. His brother, Erik ,was always the technology wonk, running a group of assets in the 1990s that carried the name Quebecor Multimedia. But in the European printing operations where PKP cut his teeth, the technology was always of the Old Economy type. When he returned to America in the late nineties, Pierre Karl was suddenly exposed to the high-tech world and he was like a kid in a candy shop. In the late nineties Erik introduced Pierre Karl to a twenty-four-year-old technology whiz, Alexandre Taillefer, who had sold his own Web design firm to Quebecor. Pierre Karl, the Luddite, was fascinated by the world that Taillefer unfolded before him. "I think that was the moment Pierre Karl really came to understand the Internet's potential," Taillefer told the *Report on Business Magazine.* Others who have worked for Quebecor say Pierre Karl was in the thrall of the charismatic Taillefer, who had a superb grasp of on-line technology. Pierre Karl was also a willing learner: He began to make investments in technology companies, although he insists he was always cautious in the ones he chose.

"The euphoria was so high, we got caught up a bit. I got caught up in the Internet," he acknowledges. "I thought that was a very interesting and maybe because I was curious myself, I liked to learn and to understand things." In his earlier career, "I didn't have a computer, I was in the printing business, and I never worked with a computer. Then I started working with e-mails and things like that. I got interested in the New Economy."

His other inspiration was Canoe (short for Canadian Online Explorer), which was run by a messianic team of Webmasters and former newspaper types in the *Toronto Sun* building in Toronto. Inside the *Sun* papers, huge excitement was building around Canoe, a pioneering Web portal with Canadian content. There was talk of expanding it rapidly and going public with an initial share offering to capitalize on the dot-com bandwagon of the late nineties. The Sun Media brain trust saw tremendous potential in this and pressed PKP to—in the new jargon—"monetize" the locked-in value.

For a while, PKP seemed to be on the same wavelength, and took an active hands-on interest in Canoe. "At first, Pierre Karl loved Canoe. He's got this multi-billion-dollar corporation and he's running Canoe person-ally—he took an office right in the place," one former Quebecor official recalls. But the public offering never happened, and Pierre Karl's inter-est in Canoe seemed to shift into cutting huge amounts of the Internet unit's costs, rather than building it into a New Economy force. His heavy hand alienated the tight Canoe team, and many of its champions quit, led by the president of Sun's new media unit, Wayne Parrish, a respected former senior journalist with *The Toronto Sun*. Pierre Karl insists he never changed his mind about Canoe, although he says he did come to resist the growing, costly demands of the Canoe team. For many, it was a classic example of Pierre Karl's fickleness, his ability to blow hot and cold on a project. The former Quebecor official recalls the sudden turnaround: "He had [Canoe's executives] running down this road, saying acquire this and acquire that. They had to do deals with this guy and that guy. Then it was a case of 'look at all this stuff you've done.'" It raised concerns about his ability to focus, as well as his understanding of how the New Economy worked.

But Péladeau sees the Canoe controversy as yet another example of what happens when journalists get talking to other journalists. "They go have a beer, and then do some PKP-bashing and the day after, it's in the newspaper. If I were producing sandwiches or shoes, I wouldn't worry that I'm going to be in the middle of discussion. But we're just running a company efficiently."

He says that the Canoe's expenses were in danger of careering out of control—although former Canoe managers insist Pierre Karl himself was the source of a lot of that heavy spending. Péladeau points to one particular example: Canoe managers wanted to move out of the *Toronto Sun* building, and find new quarters downtown. "They are telling me that they needed to move because if they have to be in the *Toronto Sun* building they'll lose their soul," he says mockingly. He shakes his head. "People, you know, they are dreamers." This high-spending mentality prevailed at other dot-coms, he says, and many of those companies don't exist anymore. In his view, Pierre Karl held the line and saved Canoe, which he argues is still a strong product. "We didn't change our mind [about Canoe], we said that this business, the way it was growing, is not sustainable. The revenues are not going to be there but you are spending, spending, spending. At a certain point, no one will buy that. They were looking to grow the company by two hundred people and do things and buy other companies."

In time, he would merge a dramatically slimmed-down Canoe with Netgraphe, a Web company acquired in the Vidéotron deal. For the ex-Canoe staffers, it was a huge lost opportunity to create a dominant Canadian portal. While Canoe the product survived, the dream effectively ended in April, 2002, when Quebecor cut sixty-seven staff, most of them Canoe editorial employees. From that time on, the site would have no original content, but would be used as a "showcase" for Quebecor's newspaper content, including articles from the Sun Media chain and *Le Journal de Montréal* and *Le Journal de Québec*.

In the middle of his Canoe phase, in 1999, Pierre Karl remembered an earlier conversation with André Chagnon, who had once spoken of his great admiration for Pierre Karl's father and had suggested that the two companies should try to do some business together. At the time the comment was made, there was nothing much to discuss, but when Pierre Karl was pondering the future of Canoe, he once again visited André Chagnon.

Péladeau explained that he was now setting up Canoe.qc, a French-language version of Canoe.ca, which could be fed with content from Quebecor's strong stable of newspapers. He pointed out that Vidéotron was weak in content for its own high-speed Internet service still in development. "I said, 'You don't have any content—the only content you have is TVA.'" Pierre Karl was also unimpressed with the "Berlin Wall" that prevented the people in the Vidéotron cable company from talking to the TV broadcaster. "They were not even buying computers with each other. I think that is not the right approach, all the components should work together."

But the talks went nowhere, Péladeau says, because Chagnon demanded control of the content that would be displayed through the Canoe portal. He was appalled by the older man's presumption, and he pointed out to Chagnon that Quebecor's primary expertise was content. "We've been in newspapers and magazines and portals, and things like that, newspapers for twenty-five or thirty years. This is a partnership and you should treat the partners as partners. . . ." He indicated that "we created Canoe.qc, one of most highly visited sights, a carbon copy of canoe.ca. When we go to advertisers, we can sell a national platform." The two men walked away from each other frustrated.

What happened next was an unusual rupture at the highest levels of the Quebec Inc. community. Pierre Karl says he did not talk to André Chagnon again until he learned that Ted Rogers was bidding for Vidéotron and that the Chagnon family had committed their shares to the Rogers bid. But the exact circumstances under which he found out are intriguing, and point to the powerful influence of the Caisse de dépôt in setting the corporate agenda in the province.

Late on Friday afternoon, January 28, 2000, Pierre Karl was in the Quebecor building on rue St-Jacques, when his chief financial officer, François Roy, invited him to come in to his office. There he found Jean-Guy Talbot, a senior Caisse executive, who was delivering an important message. Talbot, who had worked closely with Pierre Karl on an earlier takeover, said that it was possible that the Chagnons might be making a transaction concerning Vidéotron. The Caisse was a minority shareholder of Vidéotron, and had two seats on the board. According to Pierre Karl, Talbot did not mention the identity of the suitor or the price being offered. Pierre Karl disclosed this meeting in discovery proceedings in May, 2001, for a legal dispute in Quebec Superior Court involving Vidéotron, Rogers, Quebecor and the Caisse. What the testimony suggests that the Caisse was prodding Pierre Karl towards action, but that the young Quebecor president was also very willing to be prodded.

Péladeau said he was surprised to hear that the Chagnons were getting out of Vidéotron, and the information piqued his interest in the cable company. The following Friday, on February 4, the stock exchanges slapped a cease-trade order on Vidéotron stock, which had been trading heavily on takeover rumours. That Sunday morning, Péladeau met Claude Chagnon and asked for time to develop Quebecor's own response to what seemed to be a pending sale of the cable company. According to Pierre Karl's testimony, Chagnon said it was too late for that.

On Monday morning, February 7, Rogers Communications announced a $5.6 billion bid for Vidéotron to create a massive cable and broadband communications group. The deal included $4.9 billion in Rogers stock and the rest in cash, plus a $241 million lockup fee—an amount payable to Rogers if someone else were to acquire Vidéotron. It was the ultimate follow-through on Ted Rogers's and André Chagnon's conversations around the TD boardroom table. The Chagnon family recommended that all shareholders accept the bid, which would see TVA spun off to remain in the Chagnons' hands. But storm clouds were already gathering. The Caisse's chairman, Jean-Claude Scraire, mused publicly that "the transaction with Rogers is not complete," spurring rumours that a Caisse-led counterbid was in the works.

When the Rogers deal became known, Péladeau immediately responded. Taking advice from Michel Nadeau, the powerful assistant director-general of the Caisse, he explored the idea of a partnership with another cable company to take over Vidéotron. Pierre Karl insists the initiative was inspired by good financial reasons, not politics: "It was a business takeover, 100 percent." Pierre Karl, an overnight convert to convergence, was eager to do a deal, and the Caisse was keen to keep Vidéotron in Quebec hands.

After the Rogers bid was announced, Péladeau says, "We needed to work. We needed to find out how we can arrange this transaction, how we can arrange a deal. We started flying around the world to find how we can find partners, try to find money and we found partners and money." According to his court testimony, he talked to a number of parties, including Gerald Levin, the CEO of AOL Time Warner, about the possibility of a joint bid. None of these talks bore fruit. In late March, he developed a plan and took it to the Caisse.

And why wouldn't he? Pierre Karl asks. The partners knew each other well, having linked up to acquire printing assets owned by the late British tycoon Robert Maxwell in the early nineties. "We had a very decent, strong and successful experience, so why not? I've been personally negotiating with Caisse de dépôt since 1992." But the Rogers bid was surely a good offer? "It was a good bid for Rogers," Pierre Karl snaps. "I'm not sure it was a good bid for Vidéotron shareholders." Most of the price was to be paid in Rogers shares, which made the value more volatile, more uncertain, than the all-cash bid that Quebecor was contemplating.

Pierre Karl also couldn't see the great synergies in a Rogers and Vidéotron hookup. The language differences meant there were limitations on how much costs could be cut. "I can't see a technician from Scarborough [Ontario] installing cable in Jonquière. That's where Vidéotron's manpower is located, in technicians and call centres. Sorry, but in Toronto, they're not going to be able to answer in French. Yes, there's synergy but not a lot of it. In fact, I think there are more synergies for Vidéotron in a large media conglomerate based geographically in the same area than with a cable company." And that media conglomerate would be Quebecor.

Other industry watchers suggest that the Rogers bid was perhaps not motivated entirely by possible synergies, which were always elusive in the cable business, particularly between French and English companies. Instead, Rogers simply wanted to bulk up its cable assets. Some suggest that when foreign ownership rules are relaxed, it could offer any buyer a huge volume of subscribers in a concentrated area. The possibility of foreign ownership is always a factor in the cable guys' estate planning, and Ted Rogers is not entirely immune to it.

As PKP was developing his plans, the Caisse's campaign against the Rogers bid was firming up. A Vidéotron special shareholders meeting, called to approve the merger, was adjourned when the Caisse, with its 17 percent interest, won a court-ordered delay on the grounds that the deal would violate a longstanding shareholder agreement. Its agreement, the Caisse argued, gave the pension fund an effective veto on any sale of the company.

On March 27, Quebecor tabled an informal $5.9 billion counterbid, and the Chagnons mounted a counter-challenge in the courts. That set off a long, nasty legal and public relations battle as the Caisse, Rogers, Quebecor and the Chagnons engaged in a messy war of words over the future of the company. They held talks to try to negotiate a compromise, but the talks fell apart. The English-Canadian press had a field day with charges that the Caisse was playing politics with the private sector. It didn't help that at one point, Jacques Parizeau, the former Quebec separatist premier, declared that Rogers buying Vidéotron would be the same as "Toronto buys Montreal." It was not a high point in Canadian business.

This was a confrontation that typified a lot about Canada, and about the Canadian media. The debate that raged around it was about regions and ethnicity, even in this supposed modern borderless world of Internet and satellite communications. Ted Rogers is not a cable czar, he is a *Toronto* cable czar, and the Shaws are a *Western* cable family. Izzy Asper cares deeply about being from Winnipeg and about creating a Western voice. In Canada, it matters that Quebecor is from Montreal and Rogers is from Toronto. In fact, that was what the battle of

Vidéotron was all about. No two actors fit the casting call better than Ted Rogers, the sixty-eight-year-old WASP descendent of Quaker loyalists, and Pierre Karl Péladeau, the thirty-nine-year-old son of a separatist sympathizer.

Pierre Karl defends the Caisse's role in the affair, arguing that its longstanding shareholder agreement with the Chagnons had been ignored in the Vidéotron-Rogers arrangement. "When you have rights, you are looking to see them respected and I believe that those rights were not respected." He says if the Chagnon family was determined to sell their company, they should have offered the shares around to various bidders—such as Pierre Karl Péladeau. "That would morally oblige you to find other buyers—to start a process, rather than decide on one day or one evening or a Sunday night at eleven o'clock that you decide to sell to Rogers." He contrasted the Chagnons' behaviour with what Quebecor did when it sold its controlling stake in the forestry company, Donahue, in April, 2000. According to Pierre Karl, he shopped the Donahue stake around before finding the highest bidder in Abitibi-Consolidated, another Montreal company, which bought Donahue in a $5.8 billion gulp.

The Caisse's response to the Chagnon-Rogers accord, he says, was entirely understandable, given the lack of consultation, in spite of a shareholder's agreement. "If someone is telling you you're a piece of shit, and then is hurting you, so do you continue? No, I think that you have the right to make your right respected." According to Pierre Karl, that lack of proper process explains why the Caisse went to court, got the injunction and held Rogers off until a new bid could develop.

In August, Pierre Karl raised the ante, teaming up with the Caisse's subsidiary, Capital Communications, to launch a new $5.4 billion all-cash deal for the shares in Vidéotron that the two partners didn't already own. Ted Rogers in Toronto was considering his options, and the Toronto business press went wild with accusations of political meddling by the Caisse. Among the allegations was that Quebecor was fronting a plan for Quebec's Parti Québécois government to nationalize the cable company.

Pierre Karl explained himself in an August 21 article in *The Globe and Mail's Report on Business*. "To those who allege that this transaction is motivated by politics, I say bluntly: No way. Our takeover bid is motivated by business logic—not politics or some dark politico-economic plot to nationalize Vidéotron."

Pierre Karl, like many of the new convergence gurus, had caught the spirit of the new math: "By merging Vidéotron's Internet access capabilities with Quebecor, we will be building a company that will be much more than the sum of its parts." He spoke of plans to roll out Vidéotron's holdings into a new company, Quebecor Media, which would be 55 percent owned by Quebecor and the rest by the Caisse.

After huddling with his brain trust, Ted Rogers finally threw in the towel on September 11, 2000, and Vidéotron's board accepted the Quebecor offer. After a seven-month battle, the cable company belonged to Pierre Karl, subject to regulatory approval. But it was a pyrrhic victory, coming with a debt load that would hobble Quebecor, perhaps for years to come. It came near the top of a stock market cycle, a cycle that would soon see the price of Quebecor shares plunge into a downward spiral. The debt and the recession would force PKP into radical measures to cut costs and hold the line, as well as nurturing a bunker mentality that would leave the young CEO on the defensive.

As with all the media takeovers in the year 2000, there was an admission that the price was high, but it was the going price. "It was easy to say we overpaid, but it was a competitive environment," Pierre Karl would say later. "If we were not to pay that, we were not going to be able to have those assets. What was the price to pay for those assets? Was the price unreasonable? I don't think so." Whenever there is a takeover, there is going to be a hefty premium on market value, as there was in Quebecor's purchase of the Sun papers. "Yes, we paid a premium of the market because it was a takeover bid and that's the way it works." By buying at the top of the market, Vidéotron's timing was abysmal. "It was easy to say the timing was bad but it was bad for everyone," he shrugs.

Still, Pierre Karl had collected a group of assets that, in their breadth of activity, constitute the Canadian equivalent of AOL Time Warner. He had all the tools for a vertically integrated content and carriage machine—print content through his newspapers, from Sun Media to *Le Journal de Montréal*, Quebec's highest-circulation paper; a Quebec-dominant television network in TVA; valuable on-line properties, led by Canoe; and the massive pipes of Vidéotron's extensive cable network. There was also retail, through Archambault music stores and though Vidéotron outlets, which sell cable subscriptions, digital set-top boxes and cable modems. Such ubiquity meant he could put together packages of advertising that would deliver almost the entire Quebec population to clients. It was, however, with the exception of the Sun papers and Canoe, a Fortress Quebec model. "There is no doubt that Quebecor has the vertical convergence model, which is the pipes and the content. It is the AOL Time Warner model," says no less an authority than CanWest president Leonard Asper.

But the losers certainly looked like they were winners too. André Chagnon walked away with a huge cash payment, which he used to establish a $1.4 billion family foundation, the country's biggest, which is dedicated to breaking the cycle of poverty and to combatting illness by concentrating on obesity and cancer. Ted Rogers emerged with his balance sheet still intact, and with the $241 million breakup fee that had been negotiated with the Chagnons, which would allow him to fight again. As Quebecor was preparing to take over Vidéotron, John Tory Jr., the president of Rogers Cable, was wistfully dreaming of what might have been if Rogers had been able to buy Vidéotron. "We actually could have connected it into one network and done a lot of things of working together. Vidéotron had great expertise with telephony that we didn't have. We had a greater ability to market and penetrate cable prod-ucts into the marketplace. We had the synergies we could use with the wireless business, of using that to cross-promote cable."

Pierre Karl still faces constant allegations in English Canada that his Vidéotron deal has made him a mere instrument of the powerful Caisse de dépôt, whose decisions are driven by a blend of standard investing principles and ardent nationalism. It appears that Quebecor had become "a fig leaf for the Caisse de dépôt," in the words of media baron Conrad Black. Interviewed after the closing of the Vidéotron deal, Pierre Karl dismissed the charge that the deal was all about politics, about the Caisse keeping major Quebec entertainment assets out of the hands of a Toronto interloper—in fact, *the* Toronto interloper Ted Rogers. "I'm sure that is a story that walks itself like a dog!" Pierre Karl scoffed. "A story with legs, a story that's been walking for the last twelve to fourteen months in Toronto. I would say this is probably something that the Toronto audience would like to read, and in fact, journalists are giving them what they like to read." Instead, he argued, Quebecor and the Caisse have been doing deals like this for a decade—this is just a couple of old partners getting together on a highly leveraged but very manageable takeover. All that is needed is a rigorous attention to cutting Vidéotron's inflated cost base, bolstering the balance sheet and someday floating the media assets as a separate public company. "I'm not saying this is a no-brainer, but it's not really complicated either," Pierre Karl assured me. "It's a question of creating those savings."

Back in Toronto, Ted Rogers and his team were licking their wounds, but they didn't react when it was suggested that they were robbed by a politically motivated alliance of Quebecor and the Caisse. They felt the deal would have made perfect sense for Rogers Communications, which already controlled most of Ontario's cable systems and was about to strengthen its presence in the Toronto area and in Atlantic Canada through a swap with the Shaw family. This was not some airy-fairy concept of content-carriage convergence. It was about developing cable clusters, about building a seamless system across Eastern Canada, while leaving the West to the other major cable family, the Shaws. Ted Rogers, the aging warrior of Canada's wired wars, may be accused of doing a lot of mad, hubris-tinged deals in the past, but this one was rooted in reality, they argued.

What's more, the Rogers team still felt that Vidéotron would be theirs someday, if only because it just makes so much sense. Reports flowed out of Montreal that Quebecor was hard-pressed to keep its prize assets, as it struggled with its debt load. In the meantime, Rogers felt there might be opportunities for alliances. "The Caisse cleaned us out on Vidéotron, but we talk to them," Ted Rogers said, sitting in his big airy office in downtown Toronto. More explicit was Phil Lind, the Rogers vice-chairman: "There's a sense the Vidéotron deal will come back to us at some point."

"Good for him," Pierre Karl defiantly snapped, when he was told that the Ted Rogers team still believed it would get Vidéotron in the end. Pierre Karl was amused that Rogers, whose monopoly company is loathed by legions of Ontario cable subscribers, should suddenly be treated like a hero in the Toronto media for being "robbed" by the Caisse and Péladeau. "And now he's the emperor—that's so funny, eh?" Pierre Karl shook his head, as if he just couldn't win. "But now he's a great guy."

9 ROGERS AND ME

"THEY WON, WE LOST. NEXT!" THAT'S WHAT TED ROGERS was telling people the week after he had conceded the takeover battle for Vidéotron to Pierre Karl Péladeau. It was a phrase he had borrowed from U.S. media tycoon Barry Diller, and he clearly liked the sound of it. Six months later, he repeated it in an interview with me, referring this time to the long-distance telephone wars of the early nineties and his battles with Bell Canada. "One thing about Ted, he does not look back and second-guess himself," says John Tory Jr., his close family friend and president of Rogers Cable, the country's largest cable system. "He will talk about it, but he doesn't sit around and say, 'If only I had done this or that.' He does what he does and if it turns out to be a bad mistake, he moves on."

Ted Rogers, the happy warrior, was perversely proud that he had walked away from the Vidéotron battle, choosing not to make another deal-clinching bid—although some insiders say that the ultra-competitive Ted stepped away only reluctantly, that he had to be persuaded by members of his board. Backing way from battle seemed so un-Ted-like. "He is the best dealmaker I have ever seen," says Jim Sward, a former Global TV and Rogers media executive who has seen him operate up close. "He is tenacious beyond belief—he's just relentless," says another former senior executive. He is the most persistent, the most obsessive of takeover artists—he loves the deal, the pursuit and the victory. But now he was going cold turkey, or at least cool turkey.

"Ten years before, I would have gone after it, if we could have," Ted admits in his hearty, raucous way, explaining that the Vidéotron battle had come two years into his "1998 project." That was Ted's equivalent of the AA pledge—he made a public commitment in 1998 that he would deliver his company to investment grade status, that it would pay dividends and it would be the kind of company that cautious, prudent institutional investors would want in their portfolios. That meant refraining from bidding takeover targets up to impossible levels.

He has also had a nice consolation prize—the $241 million cheque that was the kill fee from the Quebec cable company. It was pocket change in the world of media megadeals, but handy seed money in Ted's own convergence pursuits. Ted had never considered Vidéotron a convergence play—it was just another stage in the constant consolidation of the cable industry. But he did have another card up his sleeve and it was all about sports. While the Vidéotron battle was unfolding, Ted was edging towards a deal to buy the Toronto Blue Jays, a baseball team that had won the World Series in two glorious seasons in the early nineties but had since fallen into a mid-range limbo—not good enough to win anything, not bad enough to prevent ardent fans from being teased with illusions of victory each spring, only to see their hopes dashed each fall.

Interbrew, the Belgian beer giant that controlled Canada's Labatt Brewing Company, had put the team up for sale and rumours persisted through 2000 that Ted was looking at it. Ted had someone in mind to run the ball club: Paul Godfrey, the former Sun Media president and a powerful ex–city politician, a superb schmoozer with the gift of making any new acquaintance feel like a lifelong friend. Godfrey, who had left Sun Media with a lot of money courtesy of the Quebecor takeover, was minding his own business in early summer when Ted phoned him up and said, "I want you to run the Blue Jays when I buy it." Godfrey, who had long dreamed of bringing the National Football League to Toronto, was puzzled at first because Ted is not your sports-watching kind of guy, but he soon began to buy into Rogers's plan. So it was no great surprise when Rogers clinched the deal in September, buying control of the ball team from Interbrew for $171 million, which was not even breaking a sweat for the guy who had just been turned back in a $5 billion bid for Vidéotron.

Let it be said from the start that Ted Rogers is the least likely billionaire to buy a sports franchise. He is not the type of rich guy who likes to rub shoulders with athletes, to hang around dressing rooms basking in the reflected glory of sharp-shooting basketball guards or power-hitting first basemen. Rogers doesn't even play golf, like his arch rival Jean Monty. He tries to swim every day for his health, he is a disciplined treadmill walker, but he couldn't care less about spectator sports. Ted has never had time for sports, hasn't thought about much besides business and his family, and perhaps the Conservative Party—in that order. He simply works harder than anyone else alive. He lives his life in bulging briefcases he carries around with him, to the cottage, on the boat in the Bahamas, on his private plane. He is the nerd as mogul, a total square, dweebish and obsessive.

But Ted Rogers became a Blue Jays fan for one compelling reason: he was concerned about the future of mass-audience television and the advertising model on which it was based. In this uncertain future, live sports were something a lot of people still wanted to watch, and they wanted it in real time, not taped for a later showing. So maybe the Blue Jays weren't the most attractive franchise in Canada's biggest market— that was clearly the Toronto Maple Leafs, the iconic hockey club, but the Leafs weren't available, at least at that moment. But Ted could see the synergies—the Blue Jays were irreplaceable content, to help fill up the television channels and radio sports and talk shows. Not only that, but the opportunities for cross-promotion were endless, especially in Rogers' core Toronto market. Ted Rogers, the non-jock, was having a convergence vision.

But the Blue Jays were just part of the equation—Ted had to own his own sports broadcasting vehicles to carry this live, unpredictable programming. Specifically, Ted wanted a sports TV channel, and one had conveniently become available. The purchase of TSN by CTV in 1999 meant that its controlling interest in rival CTV Sportsnet was on the market. The CRTC, predictably, ruled that CTV could not control two specialty sports channels. Ted already owned a 29 percent minority chunk of Sportsnet—in fact, Rogers Communications had been a co-founder—and held right of first refusal for CTV's 40 percent controlling stake, and was aggressively angling for it. In addition, Ted moved into the radio sports-talk slot, buying the FAN 590, a Toronto all-sports station, and its affiliates. In the words of one Rogers executive, "Ted very much wanted to own a sports network, because it was a valuable asset and the premium content going forward is live sports, fast-breaking business news and live news."

Once Ted zeroed in on Sportsnet, the Blue Jays were a natural complement. Says Tony Viner, the executive who runs Rogers Media: "The most compelling form of broadcasting in our view will be news and sports; our broadcasting companies are focusing on those two. If you look at the Jays as part of that chain, they're the program creators: Every time those guys trot on the field, they produce two and a half to three hours of copyright programming." Then he adds, "Sometimes it's a comedy, I think you'll agree."

There were suspicions that the shrewd Paul Godfrey was pulling the strings of Ted Rogers's conversion to sports, but Godfrey seemed as surprised as anyone that Ted wanted the Jays. Tony Viner agrees it may have to do with marketing as much as anything. "Ted is a brilliant man in many ways, a great salesman, and he thought it would be a great opportunity to build the image of Rogers in a community that was very important to us." It may not be the big bonanza of other Rogers deals, Viner admits, but "those of us who work with Ted accept that he sees things that we don't."

The deeper motivation behind Ted's sports obsession was, as usual, technological—in this case, a machine that could render television programming and advertising obsolete. New ultra-efficient personal video recorders, known by brand names such as TiVo and Replay, had begun to allow viewers to zap the ads from programs with uncommon ease, much more simply than they could program their old VCRs. This meant that my daughter could now watch *Buffy the Vampire Slayer* at the same time as her buddies, but could avoid all the credits, the lead-ins, and, most important, those intrusive ads. With a couple of timing adjustments, she could still call her friends the moment her ad-free show ended, to compare the sensations when Angel kissed Buffy, or Willow kicked the stuffing out of Spike. In time, she could program the device to continually scan for the kind of vampire-butt-kicking shows she might like, and automatically record them without her specific command, presenting her with a customized television channel, the personal channel of Katie, the Buffy Watcher. Like many people in the industry, Ted had my daughter Katie in mind, or at least people like her. He worried about the end of mass programming as he knew it, and for the commercials that were the revenue base of the television industry. "We believe the personal video recorder is just starting," he told me, adding that he wasn't talking about the crude old VCR. "That means that the programming that is live for advertisers will be much more valuable than programming that is capable of being recorded. Who wants to record the hockey game? Who wants it the next day? But you'll record a movie." Indeed, live sports viewers were the people Ted could depend on, who would likely to continue sitting through the games and the commercials because they couldn't afford to miss the spectacle—it was too unpredictable. Ted understood that, and, as with so many things in his life, he was willing to bet on this vision—not really big money but not chicken feed either.

John Tory Jr. *is* a big sports fan—he was once commissioner of the Canadian Football League. Tory was impressed by an article in *The New York Times Magazine* that stated that 80 percent of TiVo users were deleting the commercials, except for the commercials in live sports and hard news. With sports, he says, "You don't want to delete anything because you don't want to miss anything. You don't know if they're going to come back and say something is going on. The commercial might be pre-empted because something is happening. You just want to watch it live. You don't want to watch the football game four hours later because you've already heard the score on the radio. You don't want to watch it knowing what the outcome is, because it spoils all the fun."

In a world of fragmenting viewer tastes, sports content was becoming more valuable because it showed an ability to hold a mass audience, and a growing global audience—witness young people in China sporting Michael Jordan T-shirts. *New York Times* sports columnist Harvey Araton, writing in *The New York Times Magazine* in 1998, said the universal appeal of spectator sports was irresistible to communications moguls who were hungry for must-have content to stuff into their pipes. "The world has become a playground for the media conglomerates as they pursue live unscripted programming that is more valuable than ever on an increasingly crowded TV dial," Araton wrote.

Ted was closely watching the New York cable company Cablevision, which owns a controlling interest in Madison Square Garden as well as hockey's New York Rangers and basketball's New York Knicks. AOL Time Warner, through Time Warner's acquisition of Ted Turner's media empire, now owns the Atlanta Braves baseball team, the Atlanta Hawks basketball team and the Atlanta Thrashers hockey team. Tribune Company owns the beloved losers, the Chicago Cubs, a relationship that has done nothing for the Cubs' charming futility when it comes to reaching the World Series. Walt Disney Company aimed for the ultimate convergence when it acquired a hockey franchise it called the Anaheim Mighty Ducks, from the series of Disney movies about a sad sack team of kids coached by Emilio Estevez, and, of course, the arena was called the Pond. Disney also had about a quarter interest in the Anaheim Angels baseball team, who play not far from Disneyland. But the most ambitious sports owner among the mogul class is Rupert Murdoch, the Australian-American owner of News Corporation, parent of the Fox network and other properties, who bought the Los Angeles Dodgers baseball team in 1997 for US$311 million—a franchise that had only recently been valued in the press for $180 million. But his most audacious play was a run at Britain's revered Manchester United football team, in a $1 billion offer that was turned down by British competition authorities. His dream was to deliver the games of this cult-like football team exclusively over his BSkyB satellite service. For Murdoch, sports is the "battering ram" to break into markets for his pay-for-view satellite services. And Ted, too, was looking ahead to the potential of video-on-demand.

But the success of all these sports-media convergence models is far from proven. Disney, in particular, has been pulling back, and Murdoch has taken a beating on some of his sports broadcast investments, writing down his programming assets by $1 billion in early 2002. It seemed that the TV sports market could become saturated. And the choice of franchise is crucial. To qualify as valuable content, a sports team has to capture the affection of viewers (Chicago Cubs), be a traditional winner (Atlanta Braves) or constitute a religion (Manchester United). The big attraction of the Blue Jays would seem to have been that they were available, put on the market by longtime owner Labatt, the Canadian beer giant. Labatt's ardour for the Jays had cooled in recent years as baseball salaries soared, audiences fell from the levels of the euphoric World Series years and the ownership of Labatt shifted to a remote Belgian company with the remote name of Interbrew.

And these are, after all, just the Blue Jays, not the legendary Dodgers, the team of Koufax, Drysdale and, going back to their Brooklyn days, of Jackie Robinson and Duke Snider. Canadian sports teams are a dodgy business at best, and baseball is particularly dodgy as player salaries have skyrocketed to out-of-control proportions and the core of the fan base has becomes progressively older. The Blue Jays represent the worst possible business equation—revenues in weak Canadian dollars, and the major costs in U.S. dollars, and those costs of player talent are being bid up by ego-driven owners, such as New York Yankees' George Steinbrenner and Tom Hicks, who controls the Dallas Stars hockey team and baseball's Texas Rangers. The player auction hit absurd heights leading up to the 2001 season, when the Rangers contracted to pay shortstop Alex Rodriguez US$252 million over ten years to sign with them. Even Jays first baseman Carlos Delgado managed to extract $68 million over four years. This salary crisis in baseball has already driven the Montreal Expos, Canada's other baseball team, to the brink of extinction. Ted's move is essentially a bet that baseball's economics are going to return to sanity, that small-market teams can have a place in all this and that, just maybe, the Canadian dollar will find some strength. Meanwhile, Paul Godfrey has to meet the conflicting demands of financial restraint and putting a winning team on the field that will attract eyeballs for Ted Rogers's sports media properties.

Not that he has to worry that Ted will be the Toronto version of meddling George Steinbrenner. Indeed, in the first season he owned the Jays, Ted went to only a couple of games, where he sat patiently and did his cheering thing. He is clearly awkward in his sports team owner role, showing up at the SkyDome on opening day 2002 with a team jacket over his blue suit and a maple-leaf flag sticking out of his lapel, and admitting to reporters that he is "the village idiot." His lack of interest in the sport itself is vast. One Rogers executive joked that if someone said Tie Domi, the enforcer for the Maple Leafs, would be playing second base for the Jays' next season, Ted would absent-mindedly say, "Yeah, sure, okay." In fact, Paul Godfrey may have the most operating independence of any senior manager in the Rogers group, even though he has had to operate under a do-more-with-less approach to player salaries.

If Rogers's sport strategy is going to work in Canada, the best city is certainly Toronto, the country's strongest, most populous sports market, and the epicentre of Ted's vast cable and wireless operations. The opportunities for cross-promotion are endless—witness the barrage of Rogers commercial messages at the Blue Jays' home in the cavernous SkyDome, and the campaigns to sell Blue Jay tickets through the cable and media properties. But the ideal sports asset would be the hallowed Leafs, and there are constant rumours that the financially stressed majority owner Steve Stavro would be interested in selling. Leafs minority owner Larry Tanenbaum, the steel and construction heir, would probably be a bidder, as might the Thomson family, with BCE, who could add the hockey team to their own growing collection of sports content assets, including TSN.

The other problem with sports content is to find the real synergies: In theory, Paul Godfrey would surely not want to make low-ball sweetheart deals for Jays' broadcast rights with Rogers' own TV and radio stations, if he wants to maximize his own earnings potential and keep his other shareholders happy. Similarly, Rogers' sports stations would surely want to air the best programming possible, not necessarily the Blue Jays, particularly if they are twenty-five games out of first place on September 1. The key, of course, is to make the Blue Jays a winning must-see franchise. In the end, sports franchises and sports broadcasting assets may each become more valuable, but not necessarily because the two will neatly "converge" with each other. But in this convergence world, the marketplace would be further muddied by the fact that the two major TV specialty sports channels would be owned by two fiercely competitive conglomerates with a long and bitter history of battling each other. BCE had TSN, and Rogers wanted Sportsnet, which would complicate the bargaining for Blue Jays rights.

For Ted, buying Sportsnet was a task that took far longer, and was far more trouble, than he had hoped. One complication was the CRTC's reluctance to let cable companies own analog specialty channels, the so-called beachfront property on the television dial. The commission had frowned on the system's powerful gatekeepers being able to own the restricted supply of sixty analog channels, cognizant of the danger that they would show preference for their own channels over independent broadcasters' products. The cable companies hit the roof when BCE, which owned the competing ExpressVu satellite service, was allowed to buy CTV, with its raft of specialty channels, including the powerful TSN. The commission accepted CTV's argument that it needed a strong, well-funded parent company if it was to survive, and to continue to fund original Canadian programming. Besides, Bell ExpressVu, while growing quickly at great cost to its bottom line, did not qualify as the dominant form of content distribution that cable certainly was.

The CRTC had announced that it was reviewing its policy regarding the cable ownership of specialty channels when I caught up with Ted Rogers in mid 2001. Given the tension between BCE and Rogers, negotiations were going nowhere with rival CTV and the trustee who was overseeing the sale of the Sportsnet channel. Rogers at one point alleged that it had reached an agreement to buy the station earlier, before BCE bought CTV, but that the deal had been overruled by the network's new masters. CTV denied it. Some industry people said that CTV was "ragging the puck," waiting for the CRTC ruling and hoping the cable industry's hopes would be dashed.

The right of a cable company to own analog channels was "absolutely vital," thundered Ted, who viewed the whole debate as a replay of earlier battles with his nemesis BCE, in which he felt the cards had always been stacked against him. In this instance, Ted's words were hardly mellow: "We don't intend to lose on this. If that happened, if we could buy guns and start a war, we would. The idea of BCE being able to own half a dozen or a dozen specialty channels on analog, and we're not allowed to own one—it's outrageous. I mean, that's what causes revolutions. You know, it's just unbelievable the advantages that Bell gets from the regulators, I could cite you fifty examples. And we're fed up with it."

The CRTC, a group of men and women drawn from across the country, was clearly divided on this issue, an issue that became a test of the commission's conflicted mandate in the early days of the twenty-first century. The commission was supposed to preserve fairness and diversity, allowing all broadcasters equal access to the distribution systems of cable and satellite. Yet it wanted to encourage the creation of strong, well-funded companies that could invest in Canadian production, just as the global media industry was evolving into larger converged entities with names such as Viacom and Bertelsmann.

The Shaw family, owners of the country's other major cable company, were also watching the CRTC's deliberations closely, because their own expansion dreams were predicated on being able to buy more specialty channels. John Cassaday, the president of the Shaws' media company, Corus Entertainment, couldn't understand why there was such a fuss over cable ownership when there were already specific rules to prevent the cable firms from showing "undue preference" to their own television stations. Cassaday thought the CRTC's ambivalence on this issue reflected concern, particularly among the broadcasters, such as CHUM and Alliance Atlantis, about one particular cable owner who might become too powerful, and might then exploit his advantage. "It's all about this deep-rooted animosity, a fear of Ted," Cassaday said.

In the end, Ted didn't have to reach for his pistols. In June, 2001, the CRTC ruled that cable operators could now own specialty and pay channels, a ruling that eliminated any regulatory barriers to Ted's sports strategy. The decision reflected the regulators' belief that fair dealing could be ensured by the broadcast rules, without the need for any overarching ban. A month later Rogers bought CTV's 40 percent interest in Sportsnet for $120 million, taking over a property that was the third highest revenue generator among specialty channels in Canada, with 2000 sales of $67 million. But its revenues were less than half those of TSN.

Ted's sports model had many detractors, but one person was taking his vision very seriously. Jean Monty could actually see what Rogers was trying to do. His concern was that Ted would wrap up all the prime sports franchises in Southern Ontario, including the Jays, the Leafs and the Raptors basketball team and recreate the Madison Square Garden model of sports-media integration. In sports, he said, the real fear was that a single owner, with prime media properties, would be the only broadcast source of a must-have sports vehicle. "If ever that happens, and you think sports is the key thing, what the hell do you do? TSN is a very important property for us, the leading sports channel in Canada. Obviously when Ted bought Sportsnet, the price he paid had to be strategic," Monty said. "It's got to be that he is talking to the Leafs and Raptors and putting together Madison Square Garden North. So if he does that and keeps a good piece of that, it undermines our sports-information capability. And so we're going to be conscious of that."

Monty emphasized that there is really only one sports group in Canada that's making it and that's Maple Leaf Sports & Entertainment, the owner of the Leafs, the Raptors and the Air Canada Centre. "They've got a good business model because they've got Toronto. It's location, location, location." But Maple Leaf Sports president Richard Peddie has his own media aspirations, and in 2001 he launched digital TV channels for both the Leafs and the Raptors. Peddie argued that sports teams in the future will have to become much more proprietary about their own content, as they seek to extract more dollars from broadcasting rights, as opposed to the people who fill their parks and arenas. Currently about 40 percent of the revenues generated by professional sports teams comes from game tickets, compared with 20 percent from broadcasting. That latter figure must rise, Peddie argues, and it will force sports teams to take more control over their content. They will move more of it away from free conventional broadcasting, and into digital, subscriber-funded and pay-for-view media.

Ivan Fecan, president of Bell Globemedia, suggested that Rogers's purchase of the Blue Jays was "a very brave thing to do. Was it smart? Who knows? Was that the right team to buy, did he buy at the right time? I don't know, but I'm glad he did, because it helped me get a price for Sportsnet. It worked out fine for us."

Fecan said success on the field is what really matters in establishing the value of sports content. The one exception may be the Leafs, who were able to draw huge crowds even through the dry years of the 1970s and 1980s. "But typically, if the team does well, everyone wants a piece of it. If it doesn't do well, you can't give it away. There are plenty of examples of people who went and bought teams. They've got to be in A-markets and Toronto is the A-market of Canada." By spring 2002, Ted's sports-media strategy was falling into place: Sportsnet would be carrying 90 of the Jays' 162 games that season, and the FAN 590 would be airing the games on radio. Now all he needed was a winner. Meanwhile, Ted's chief financial officer, Alan Horn, was ominously warning that Rogers Communications would look for "other alternatives," if it could not fix the Jays' financial losses, which were costing the parent company more than $50 million Canadian a year.

Of course, the sports thing isn't the only convergence Ted is pushing—he's also an advocate of something subtler and less sexy, which he calls marketing or branding convergence. It means bundling all of

Rogers' products under the same brand names, the same billing systems, the same call centres, so that one service rep can talk about everything Rogers offers and can cross-sell like mad. The uniform branding meets with some resistance inside the Rogers organization, particularly among some of the strong media brands (think *Chatelaine* or *Maclean's* magazine.) "Convergence has everything to do with branding, in my view," Ted says, "a desire for people to make life a little simpler, easier. If you've got five different services with five different brands, the cost of marketing is extraordinarily high, you're mailing out a bill for a single customer and there is customer service set up for a single product." He admits that Bell, too, is pushing hard in this area of branding convergence. "What goes with that is eventually the opportunity to have billing for all the products, and one-stop shopping; you can make one call and they can look after all of your needs. I think that's probably convergence."

What is not convergence, he argues, is traditional cross-promotion— "you rub my back, I'll rub yours. In other words, if you have a newspaper and television station, they promote each other. I don't think that's convergence." For one thing, he says, you don't need to own the two cross-promoting media—he could do what they call "a contra deal" with, for example, *The Toronto Star* to advertise each other's next big series or project. In fact, Ted is already doing cross-promotion and multimedia ad packages with Izzy Asper, and there are hints about an even closer relationship, although probably not to the extent of exchanging shares. Ted and Izzy need each other—Ted has the pipes, Izzy has the content and they share a common enemy: the ubiquitous BCE. In fact, Jean Monty expected he might eventually face a combined force of the cable companies and CanWest. The irrepressible Ted nearly gave the Aspers a heart attack in 2001, when at a press conference in Winnipeg he joked that the two organizations would probably merge. Then he laughed and talked about vague co-operation and sharing of resources.

Ted points to his campaign to bundle everything the company has under the Rogers name—remember Cantel? It's now Rogers AT&T Wireless. "I think it has everything to do with branding.

That's why we changed our name to one." Because of Rogers' financial and customer-relations fiascoes of the mid-nineties, the company debated whether it should actually promote the Rogers name—it was saddled with a lot of bad freight from the negative option billing fracas. But Ted prevailed and "Rogers" is now the universal brand name. He contrasts this with Shaw, for example, which has cable operations called Shaw and a satellite service called Star Choice. But, he adds mischievously, it makes a lot of sense for them because they're going to sell Star Choice someday—probably to Bell.

Ted admits that his branding convergence is very difficult to pull off because of the traditional separation of corporate divisions. "Everybody says, 'Ted, you hired us to run X, we're working our butt off to run X, and I know Charlie over there with product Y—great fellow but it's not part of my bonus with his returns. So I want to help and he wants to help me but we've got our own jobs to do.' That's the problem." One Rogers officer agrees that he is not motivated to do much on convergence because his own paycheque is still predicated on success in his particular unit. That's the quandary for many of the media convergers—getting employee rewards in sync with corporate objectives that seem vague and illusory.

Outside live sports, Rogers is extremely skeptical of the idea of a cable company—or any distributor—owning exclusive media content. It just wouldn't work for any company that wants to maximize its reach and its revenue. "If we owned the *Sun* still, would we want to put all the *Sun* content just on our Web site and not on others? Do we do that with *Maclean's* magazine, do we have it just on ours? No, because it's in the interest of *Maclean's* that it be widespread. It's in the interest of the media to have the widest distribution possible."

In fact, except for sports, Ted Rogers seems a bit jaded by the idea of media convergence sweeping the world at the turn of the twenty-first century. Perhaps it's old hat to him. He has been a convergence player for years. He has owned broadcasting and cable assets for almost four decades. He invested in wireless telephones in their infancy. He has played with cross-promotion through his magazines and broadcasting. He has owned the Sun newspapers and sold them to pay down debt—and regrets it now, because the Sun papers would play well with his sports strategy. The BCEs and CanWests and Quebecors are the new kids; Ted has been playing this game for years, and nothing much surprises him.

If Ted has a dream, it is the merging of wireless and cable with long-distance and local telephone service into one system, on one bill, all brought to you under the Rogers brand name. He has been frustrated so far on the telephone side, seemingly trumped by his traditional rival BCE. But as long as he lives, he will probably push for this dream. Ted is like the crazy captain of the yacht who is zipping madly among the shoals and the sandbars, and we—his customers, regulators and executives—are just along for the scary ride, shouting all the time about how we were going to crash. But the engine and the waves are so noisy—and the ride is so much fun—that Ted can't hear us, maybe chooses not to hear us. We don't want to be on the boat, but dammit, Ted will take us there anyway.

10 A CORUS LINE

IT WAS MARCH, 1996, AND THE WORLD FIGURE SKATING Championships were in full swing in Edmonton. It was a bad week for the host country—a fifteen-year-old American phenom named Michelle Kwan glided her way to the women's title, while another American skater, Todd Eldredge, stole the men's championship. Canada's pride and joy Elvis Stojko ended up in a disappointing fourth place after a disastrous long program. The action off the ice was much more satisfying for Edmonton's JR Shaw, the owner of the largest cable TV operation in the West and patriarch of a burgeoning media dynasty. The Edmonton event drew huge television audiences, and it also gave Shaw a chance to size up John Cassaday, the president of the host television network, CTV, and one of Canada's smartest media managers. This was not some idle chit-chat about double lutzes and triple salchows—it was a big step towards JR Shaw's methodical construction of a Canadian media powerhouse. "John Cassaday's a tough guy to hire. It took me a year and a half or so to do it," JR said later.

The two men had met before—Cassaday, an urbane marketing man with an easy humour, had spoken at some cable industry events. From those meetings and from the skating championships, JR decided that he wanted to know the younger man better. It was a critical time for JR Shaw, a solidly built man with expressive eyes, who had already amassed great wealth since leaving his native Ontario more than thirty years earlier. Now, he was about to embark on a new chapter in one of Western Canada's most impressive business stories.

JR had moved west in the sixties to establish his family's pipeline coating business in Regina and Edmonton—and to get a little breathing room from his family. He landed the first cable licence in Edmonton in 1970, and, from that seed, built Shaw Communications into one of the best-run cable companies in North America. He was one of several entrepreneurs, along with Ted Rogers and André Chagnon, who had consolidated the country's cable TV industry. The Shaws, who were also on the verge of getting a direct-to-home satellite licence, controlled about about 25 percent of the country's cable market. But nobody in Eastern Canada knew who they were, with the exception of Ted Rogers, who had spun a few mutually profitable deals with the family.

But these days JR, with four children in the company, had some things on his mind besides cable. Shaw Communications had a fast-growing stable of media enterprises, which now consisted of eight radio stations and interests in specialty TV channels, including the popular kids' channel YTV, the second biggest revenue earner among all the specialty channels. JR was determined to expand this side of his business a lot more. He could see that content was going to become the hot property, the stuff to put in the pipes that he and other cable operators owned. Also, the broadcasting industry was consolidating in Canada and in the United States, with more properties in the hands of fewer owners. Just as in cable TV, JR was determined he was going to be one of the eaters, not one of the eaten.

But the most important reason for wooing John Cassaday was, ironically, to advance the careers and prospects of his own family. His two oldest children, Jim Jr. and Heather, were deeply involved in the business and clearly wanted to carry it on. "I want the kids involved in the business but I don't want them working for each other," JR said. He knew the pitfalls from his own experience of working in the family pipeline construction company with his older brother, Les. It was natural that his rambunctious older son, Jim, would want to run the cable side. Jim, a stocky, goateed guy more comfortable astride a Harley than behind a desk, was taking a stronger leadership role and had worked beside his father on the family's big cable deals of the nineties. Heather, a thoughtful woman with an M.B.A. from University of Western

Ontario, had managed some of the media properties. But Heather also yearned to be an active mother with her two daughters, and working as a fulltime CEO was not what she wanted. That opened the door for an outsider to run the media business day-to-day, and who better than John Cassaday, who was already commanding the biggest private television network in the country?

There was another issue lurking in the background: the CRTC was opposed to cable companies owning the analog specialty and pay television channels that had staked out much of the TV dial. The regulator was concerned that the cable kings could exert their influence to favour their own channels, while elbowing out those of rival broadcasters—or consigning them to the nosebleed sections of the TV dial. At the same time, the CRTC was selectively approving some cable-analog purchases, while rejecting others. After all, the Shaws did own YTV, one of the plums of the specialty world. Expansion into specialty channels was a big part of the Shaws' expansion plans. As JR Shaw and his family planned their big push in media, this had become a crucial issue, and they were looking for guidance. In 1995, as the CRTC developed its policy prohibiting cable ownership of specialty channels, Heather Shaw says the family asked the Liberal government for advice on how to expand the media side of the business. The message came back: Have separate and distinct structures for each side of the business. "We said, 'OK, if that's what it takes,'" Heather recalls.

So that's why the crafty, charming JR Shaw ended up relentlessly wooing John Cassaday through most of 1996–97. One day Cassaday received a call from one of JR's executives, who said the cable baron would like to visit CTV. It was a small organization, and Cassaday walked JR around it, talking to the people. JR was impressed with the younger man's easy manner. "You go to the places where people work, you find out how they work with people," JR explains. "What do we do without people? We can't do it all ourselves." JR contrasts this with the working style of his Toronto counterpart, Ted Rogers. "Ted does a lot himself. Ted works the hardest of anybody in the industry. Whether he works smart or clever, it's his company and it's his style." This is a typical JR statement because, in the end, it is all about him and Ted. The Shaws are obsessed with Ted Rogers, what he thinks, how he manages, what he owns and doesn't own. Ted was now a player in media, so JR would be, too, but he would do it in a bigger way.

John Cassaday's background certainly qualified him for a top media job, as well as a sensitive role in a family company. Starting out as a journalism major at the University of Western Ontario, he saw the error of his ways and quickly transferred to business studies, where he showed an unusual aptitude for marketing. He graduated to a job with General Foods in Toronto, where he shortly moved from a production to a marketing role with the packaged goods giant. He then joined Campbell's Soup, and in a meteoric rise, at the outrageously young age of thirty-four, became president of Campbell's Soup in Canada. Under the guidance of Gordon McGovern, the president of the Campbell's Soup Company of Camden, N.J., he was then sent to England to help sort out the company's troubles there. While he was in England, McGovern left the company, leaving his protégé, Cassaday, high and dry. The timing was right for a Toronto headhunter to come along with an invitation to apply for the job of CTV president.

It was a case of jumping out of the frying pan into the fire, as Cassaday moved to a high-profile but impossibly difficult job. He soon learned that CTV was not a real company but a co-operative of warring factions, each with an effective veto on major decisions. It may have been the most dysfunctional corporate entity in Canadian history, but because of its cultural importance, it could not be allowed to fail. The CRTC wouldn't let it. Some of the co-op members were, on their own, fairly significant companies—Maclean Hunter and Baton Broadcasting, both of Toronto, WIC of Vancouver, Electrohome of Kitchener, Montreal's CFCF, all giants of Canadian private broadcasting. As Cassaday tried to strengthen the network, every initiative got bogged down in power struggles between Toronto-based Baton, controlled by the Bassett and Eaton families, and WIC, controlled by Vancouver's

Griffiths family. The situation was so nasty that the various partners were actually competing against each other, and ultimately the network, for prime U.S. programming. Meanwhile, a well-financed and united Global TV, now wholly owned by Izzy Asper's CanWest, was able to swoop in and snap up the best shows.

"CTV was a very difficult environment—it was a microcosm of Canada, rich and poor, big and small, French and English," Cassaday recalls. "Probably the biggest lesson for me was managing a troubled business without cash. Survival was really Job 1 for four years." The second big lesson he learned was conflict management, and he came to the conclusion it was all about process. "Basically, people are not mean-spirited, they just look at things from their own interests." Cassaday learned this from a Boston consultant named Roger Fisher, who wrote the book on conflict management and came to work with Cassaday on the CTV impasse. "One of expressions that he used was 'Essentially conflict is all about people looking at the world from different angles of the bell tower.' We can look at the world as full of sunshine but if you're in the shade, you have a different perspective. But they are both right, they both think they're right. Roger taught me to really focus on interests, not positions."

He tried to tell the CTV warriors that their position might be that they had to get control of CTV, but their real interest was to make sure they could participate in decision making, to have a say in what programming went on the air, to help select the president. "If we can focus on your interests and not your position, perhaps we can find some room to negotiate. That was a powerful lesson to me because I began to realize if you and I disagree, you can't just overpower the other person."

That kind of thinking helped save the network from utter collapse. Cassaday and Fisher brought CTV's warring tribes together in a mediation session, which spawned a new shareholders' agreement at CTV. No more vetos, no more paralysis. At least, that was the thinking. Baton Broadcasting, the Toronto company that had always wanted to own the network, decided to step back and become just an affiliate owner. But the situation was unstable and Cassaday's agreement came unravelled, at the ultimate cost of his own position in the network. Baton Broadcasting got its own hot-shot president, Ivan Fecan, who led the company on a consolidation drive that ended only when Baton took effective control of CTV in 1997.

As these battles were rumbling in the background, JR Shaw and Cassaday met over dinners and talked about the industry, and both could see massive consolidation coming. "It didn't take a lot of imagination to realize we were sitting at a point of time where the next three to five years were going to be very, very pivotal," Cassaday recalls. "But JR had a feeling he could build something." When it became clear Baton was taking control of CTV and Fecan was in the driver's seat, he didn't want to be a lame duck. "I phoned JR in July [1997] and said, 'We've talked, do you want to do something?'" JR invited him aboard. On Friday, August 31, 1997, he left CTV; he started at Shaw the following week in Toronto.

When Cassaday joined Shaw, he was not thinking necessarily of a separate public company—the assumption was that he would be the boss of a media division inside Shaw Communications. The Shaws figured that they were on-side with the CRTC's thinking, because they had just won approval to own large shares in the kids' specialty channels Teletoon and Treehouse TV. They had also applied to buy a minority stake in Headline Sports, another specialty operation. The company assumed it was a slam dunk—the channel was already controlled by another cable operator, and the Shaws were replacing an existing financial investor. But the CRTC denied that application, which shocked JR Shaw. The denial raised the broader issue of whether the family would be able to build the media powerhouse that they wanted so much.

Another risk for Cassaday was that he was entering a family company as a non-family executive. There was the chance he wouldn't fit in, and there would be a probationary period when both sides had to establish a comfort level. What made it even riskier was that Shaw Communications was going through its own succession, as JR stepped aside for Jim Jr. to become chief executive in December, 1998. The transfer of authority happened more quickly than Cassaday expected, Suddenly the man who hired him was not the guy in charge.

The succession at Shaw also triggered a change in style. JR is charmingly low-key and disarming, qualities that have served him well in romancing partners, would-be sellers of cable systems and, of course, the CRTC, the industry's regulator. It worked well during the Shaws' frenetic growth years of the nineties. But Jim was a different kettle of fish, a guy with a zest for jokey confrontation, a bit in-your-face. "I think we're a little more sales-driven than we used to be," Jim says of the change from his father's era. "We're not as conservative as we were, just a little edgier, and it comes from me. The environment is a little rougher, people are asking more of us that way, and we're pushing a little harder."

Jim says the family talked about how Cassaday would work out. "We said, 'Let's see how he does first, you know, coming into a family situation, a very senior guy.' He came in and worked for me for a while, then the family had to evaluate him and said, 'Yeah, we like him, he's the right style for us.'" There is speculation that, at times, the well-tailored Cassaday was trying almost too hard to fit in. At one point, he started growing a goatee, in the desperado style of Jim Shaw, but it was later discarded, after he endured merciless kidding from his friends.

Cassaday says Toronto media types were generally surprised at his decision to join the Shaws because the family was not well known in the East; it was still viewed as a little Edmonton cable company, a bit player and not a star on the national scene. The stock had been languishing for some time. Yet Cassaday says that in JR Shaw, "I saw an individual who was deeply committed to growth, who had the financial capability to do it, was well-liked by the regulators and we both shared the view that there were great growth opportunities."

Eventually, the Shaw media strategy began to take shape. The family decided that the best opportunity lay in spinning off a separate public company, with its own identity, its own balance sheet and its own access to capital markets. The television and radio properties would be unencumbered by the capital spending and heavy debt loads of the cable company. The idea was to increase shareholder value by having two pure plays, with their own bank lines of credit and ultimately their own takeover currency in the form of their own stock.

JR insists the primary rationale was not to get around the CRTC's resistance to cable-specialty ownership. Splitting the company into media and cable operations wouldn't protect the Shaw interests. "They're going to be family controlled, both of them, because you can't do it otherwise. So if they're going to hit Shaw Communications, they're going to hit the media company. It doesn't matter if it's the left punch or the right punch, it's all hitting the same group of assets." JR says the split was primarily contemplated because the public, mainly the stock market, likes pure plays, companies that do one specific thing or another, not conglomerates of different assets. Also, he wanted his top executives to be thinking about one thing only. "We wanted Heather and John, when they got up in the morning, to think about specialty services and programming or broadcasting, And when Jim gets up, he's thinking about cable."

Another piece of the puzzle was to dramatically expand the number of radio and TV properties the Shaws owned. JR had that figured out too, but it was proving far more difficult than he had expected. Shaw Communications had become embroiled in a messy, prolonged battle for WIC, pitted against another Western-based company that was going through generational change—CanWest, led by the Aspers of Winnipeg. It was an excruciating period for Cassaday, who knew that the addition of the WIC radio stations and specialty channels was the crucial building block for the content company he would eventually run. He was basically parked in the corner until the WIC deal was done.

That strategy began to play itself out. In summer, 1998, the WIC deal was finally completed in principle, with the Shaws getting the specialty and radio assets and CanWest getting WIC's nine conventional TV stations and half of ROB-TV, a joint venture for a business TV service with *The Globe and Mail.* The Shaws were able to unveil their media plans in the fall of 1998 at a glitzy press conference at Toronto's News Theatre. The new company was just called Media Company until they could come up with a better name. But it was already a big machine: 23 large- and medium-market radio stations; ownership of a band of specialty channels, including YTV, Treehouse TV, CMT (Country Music Television) and stakes in four others; and the WIC collection of specialty or pay channels, Viewer's Choice, Superchannel, Movie Max and the Family Channel. JR did not show up for the press conference—he was enjoying a vacation in a rented hillside villa in Tuscany while his team met the press. The irrepressible Jim Shaw shared the platform with John Cassaday, and tweaked him gently: "John's position depends on his performance here today."

Despite the upbeat mood, the Shaws were not quite ready to break out the champagne yet. They had to wait another year for the final WIC agreement, while the tax implications were being worked out. Cassaday, in a supreme understatement, told the press that "it was a long, arduous process." And it was not until summer, 2000, that the CRTC approved the splitting-up of WIC.

There was another important stepping stone in the Shaws' rise. After heavy lobbying by the broadcast industry, the CRTC in 1999 introduced a policy change that allowed a single company to own as many as four radio stations in the same local market, instead of being restricted to one station, as in the past. Multiple-station ownership would allow companies like Shaw to come at the same market with a bunch of formats—you want country music, you want adult contemporary, you want news or sports talk, we'll do it all, and we can sell this to advertisers in one neatly wrapped package. The WIC purchase strengthened the Shaws' radio presence in some of Canada's biggest markets, enabling them to become the first Canadian broadcast operators to make use of this multi-station ownership opportunity.

The new rules firmed up the Shaws' game plan. They were now determined to build the leading entertainment company in Canada on the strong specialty TV assets and growing radio network. But the

Canadian market was constrained in size. So the Shaws and John Cassaday had a grander idea yet—to develop a core expertise in kids' and music programming, which would be the vehicles that they would ride into the international markets. Cassaday made it clear that once it built an efficient mass of operations in Canada, the new company was going global in a big way.

That theme was driven home in September of 1999, when the company took its new name, Corus Entertainment, and went public, with its new stock issued as dividends to existing Shaw shareholders. That very same day, it announced it was buying the choice radio assets of the Blackburn family in London, Ontario. In the crazy stock market of the time, Corus's market capitalization, which was originally $400 million, was quickly bid up to about $2 billion, making the Shaw family even richer. The world now knew who JR Shaw was, and his generational game plan was clicking into place. He went to Corus's first annual meeting in 2000 and had trouble controlling his emotions. "I made the first motion; it was to install Heather as chairman and it just about broke me up. For a second there, I could have almost lost it—in making the first nomination for this company. I've seen it come from the first radio station we bought in Red Deer [Alberta] years ago and to see where it is today—I love it."

Cassaday set up shop in offices in the downtown Toronto office tower BCE Place, in a breezy colourful open area where visitors are greeted by a big mural showing the Pied Piper leading a group of frolicking children—or perhaps the Corus shareholders on their way to a market killing. A copy of that same mural was hoisted as a banner over the atrium in the Shaw Communications building in Calgary, where Heather Shaw maintained her office. Her plan was to fly down to Toronto once every three weeks, to take part in the big decisions, but to let John Cassaday run the daily operations. It was a perfect synergy, a smart professional manager teamed up with an active owner.

Of course, the Shaws weren't writing an original script at Corus. In taking the media company public, Heather says the family was much influenced by their management mentor, John Malone, the U.S. cable consolidator and builder of Tele-Communications Inc. (TCI), which had spun out Liberty Media as a separate content investment company. Malone is a brilliant, intimidating entrepreneur, who, like the Shaws, often gets labelled a cowboy and was once referred to by Al Gore as "Darth Vader." The family had watched how Malone's TCI had spun out Liberty Media and then taken it back into the fold. "We saw the shareholder value that was created by rearranging or reshuffling the assets," Heather says. "We watched with interest what they did, and we dividended out the Corus shares to existing Shaw holders." It was no great surprise that Liberty Media ended up owning about 20 percent of the new Corus.

Corus exploited its rising stock value to go on one of the biggest acquisition sprees in Canadian media history, using its newly minted shares as currency in seven transactions costing almost $1.5 billion in its first two years. The largest and most important was the $540 million takeover, announced in September, 2000, of Nelvana, a Toronto animation company that had developed a reputation for its children's production, with such titles as *Babar* and *Little Bear*, and the cartoon show based on the hit series of Canadian books *Franklin the Turtle*. Most important, it had a growing library of at least seven hundred hours of animated programming, a valuable commodity in an age when content was golden.

The Shaws had been eyeing Nelvana for some time as a natural fit with its children's programming thrust. But the animation company had raised eyebrows when it purchased Klutz, a children's book company in Los Angeles, for which it needed an injection of financing. The firm's managers had embarked on an investment road show in the United States, but they were finding it was a tough sell. Michael Hirsh, Nelvana's president and co-founder, called Cassaday one weekend and asked for help. The Corus president was receptive, but Cassaday suggested that the market was telling Nelvana that it just wasn't big enough to do all the things it wanted to do. Cassaday agreed to talk about financing as long as they could sit down and explore the prospects of doing a bigger deal. As Cassaday talked to Hirsh and his partners, one thing led to another, and the deal was done: Nelvana became part of Corus.

Corus was also moving rapidly on its other front—it wanted to become the largest radio broadcaster in the country. A number of medium-sized players, such as Telemedia of Montreal, were retreating from the market, leaving it open to the onrushing trio of Corus, Rogers Media and Standard Broadcasting, the Slaight family company, with its CFRB cornerstone in Toronto. Corus was an eager buyer of many of these suddenly available stations. It also launched some new radio concepts, including its MOJO Radio format, known for its motto "Talk Radio for Guys" and for a commercial of a scantily clad woman wielding power tools. The concept seemed to involve a bunch of guys sitting around being obsessed about sex and sports. But for Heather Shaw, the world was unfolding as it should: by mid-2001, the radio holdings had grown to forty-nine stations. Being a separate company, she said, "allows us access to our own cash flow and our own debt capital that we can grow on the radio and television side. If we were still part of Shaw, there would not be forty-nine radio stations but we would still be in the twenties."

In the heady days of 2000, the Nelvana deal was welcomed by the markets. It was, of course, a convergence play—Nelvana's cartoons could feed nicely into Corus's stable of children's programming. Corus's TV division could help underwrite Nelvana's most promising projects, providing valuable early funding that would, ideally, allow a project to be paid for before it even hit the international market. "The business all starts with the fact that somebody's got to trigger broadcasting, so that's where the magic works for us," Cassaday said. He noted that Nelvana, despite a stellar reputation, has never really scored an international megahit, along the lines of Rugrats or Pokemon.

"It's like major league baseball," said Cassaday, a big baseball fan who had recently been reading a new biography of Joe DiMaggio. "The more times you swing the bat, the more likely it is you're going to hit it out of the park. Nelvana will hit a home run at some point."

To maximize those swings, Cassaday was putting the Nelvana people together with Corus television officials in an integration team to look at synergies and new products.

Cassaday acknowledged that working through these relationships would be a tricky process. Exclusive deals don't work for either side. Nelvana can't sell programming just to Corus's TV channels, and Corus's TV outlets can't buy only Nelvana products. Each side has to make it on its own terms, or the company and its shareholders suffer. Still, Cassaday would have to start by erring on the side of helping Nelvana out. He talked about what happened when Disney bought the ABC network, which had been one of its biggest customers. After the purchase, Disney found it couldn't sell as many series to ABC as it did before, because no one at the network wanted to appear to be in Disney's hip pocket. In the end, ABC devoted an entire time slot to Disney and they got the synergy they wanted, but it took years.

Cassaday realizes the biggest tool he has to drive the convergence between Corus and Nelvana is the stock options that Corus issues to its television programming vice-president. Still, "we can't tell them what to put on the air because at the end of the day if our ratings go down, we're going to lose ad revenue and we're going to lose subscribers, so there's always this balance."

Cassaday joked at an industry conference that the first example of convergence was the merging of the veterinarian and the taxidermist. "The good thing is that no matter what happens, you get your dog back," he said. That sums up what he's doing at Corus—trying things, spreading his bets, hoping something works. He's convinced convergence can work, if only in terms of the radio advertising packages he can now assemble in local markets. But he also believes that a media company has to be big simply to get the attention of advertising buying shops. If you're sitting alone with just one channel, by the time a big advertiser gets around to noticing you, all you get are the scraps. When advertisers sit down to plan a $60 million media buy, they ask first who the big players are, and then they move on. But what happens when, say,

TV and newspapers are offered together? That still isn't clear to Cassaday. He wants to see the creation of single source advertising research that can establish the effectiveness of these combination media buys.

In the hyped-up atmosphere of buoyant stock markets and convergence mania, Cassaday tried to keep things in perspective. Companies such as Corus or Shaw Communications or Bell Globemedia were coasting along on the media business's narcissistic fascination with itself. More column inches were being devoted to Corus's moves than to the rampaging consolidation in Canada's oil patch. "If we were consolidating the shoe business, it wouldn't get the same attention," he laughed. Cassaday knew that the positive-hype bandwagon could easily reverse itself and head the other way—and it did. His acquisition spree would be less admired later on, when the economy slumped, Corus's advertising revenue took a beating and the problems of integrating Nelvana became more prominent.

Like Ted Rogers, Cassaday was intensely interested in the outcome of the CRTC's review of its ban on cable companies owning specialty channels. As he awaited the verdict, Cassaday was unsure what would happen. He figured the split on the CRTC was fifty-fifty, with the free-market-oriented interim chairman, David Colville, holding the balance. Cassaday expressed concern that the Canadian government was sending out mixed messages—on the one hand encouraging the establishment of big strong Canadian media players, but on the other hand hobbling companies that wanted to become more significant forces at home and abroad. "We are so obsessed with maintaining our cultural sovereignty," he pointed out. Whenever Canada goes to trading negotiations, everything's on the table—cars, wheat, dairy, mining—except one area, culture, and that is untouchable. "On the other hand, we are concerned about Canadian media companies getting too strong." In his view, Canadian media companies have to be allowed to get big—it is indispensable for survival in a global media industry.

Meanwhile, Cassaday was able to make light of all the speculation about the Shaw family's role in Corus. At a cable TV convention,

Cassaday told the audience a story about one hectic morning when both the Pope and JR Shaw were in his reception area waiting to see him at exactly the same time. A frantic assistant asked Cassaday which one to bring in first, and the Corus president replied, "The Pope, because I only have to kiss his ring."

When the CRTC finally approved the right of cable companies to own analog channels, Cassaday was exultant. "A significant piece of uncertainty surrounding our ability to be a dynamic growth company has been removed," he said. At the same time, independent broadcasters were crestfallen when they heard the decisions. "The commission doesn't understand the leverage that cable companies have," one executive told *The Globe and Mail.*

But for Cassaday to pull it off, Nelvana had to score some worldwide hits, the advertising market had to come back with force and Corus had to show it was more than an acquisition machine—Cassaday had to demonstrate that he could blend this strong collection of assets profitably. The market had generally applauded the quality of the acquisitions, even though they were considered a bit pricey, all purchased in a seller's market. But now, in the cooler climate of the post-dot-com crash, he had to deliver the results.

Corus's strategy was also evolving, as it refined its target markets. It still saw children's entertainment as a key focus, but it also wanted to "own" two other groups—young men aged eighteen to thirty-five (see MOJO Radio) and women aged thirty-five to forty-nine. One of Corus's most controversial moves was the purchase of WTN, the Women's Television Network, from Moffat Communications, which itself had just been bought by Corus's sister company Shaw Communications. It was the kind of cozy deal that raised eyebrows, especially at a hefty price of $205 million. To reduce costs, Corus shut down WTN's Winnipeg base, cut fifty jobs, consolidated operations in Toronto and prepared to relaunch the channel as simply W. The outcry was loud, particularly in Winnipeg, but also among women who feared a dumbing-down of the old WTN. Now that the applause of a receptive stock market has faded,

John Cassaday and the Shaw family are facing a more critical audience.

Still, JR was pleased with what he had wrought, even though he wasn't sure exactly what was driving this great acquisition machine. Family was a big motivation, the desire to build something that would endure, but success was creating its own pounding momentum. "I don't think it's greed, but it's adrenaline, in my view. If it's greed, I guess that I'd want something that someone else has, that they don't want to sell— and that does come into play every now and then. But now that adrenaline gets going, and Jim's got it and Heather's got it.

PART 3 THE FUTURE

11 OKAY, WHO'S LEFT?

ROBERT PRICHARD, LOOKING WAN AND HAGGARD, AGREES that it's been a rough week.

Prichard is gamely participating in a panel discussion at an advertising conference, only two days after the CRTC torpedoed the convergence strategy of Torstar, the company where he would become chief executive officer within three weeks. Torstar, the publisher of the country's biggest circulation newspaper, *The Toronto Star*, has lost its bid to launch three southern Ontario conventional television stations, beaten by a Western Canadian upstart, Craig Broadcast Systems, and by Rogers Communications, which has won a licence for a multicultural station. Prichard, Torstar's chief operating officer and a former university president, is dealing with the disappointment as best he can—by extolling the virtues of the newspaper as an advertising medium. "It's always there with you," he tells the conference. "You can't buy around it." He quips that he had also prepared notes on the virtues of local television, but he had set them aside for forty-five days—the deadline for appeals to the federal cabinet on the new licence award.

Prichard, who had joined Torstar only nine months earlier, insists that despite the rejection of its television application in early April, 2002, nothing much has changed for Torstar, which remains a Southern Ontario print powerhouse. But, in fact, the CRTC loss has to be a bitter pill to swallow, and some members of the Torstar family are far less temperate than Prichard in expressing their feelings. Antonia Zerbisias, the acerbic television columnist for the *Star*, has written a ferocious column, dismissing Craig Broadcast, which runs TV stations in Winnipeg, Edmonton and Calgary, as "a financially insecure Alberta broadcaster who, as everybody in the industry knows, has been standing under a streetlamp offering itself up to anybody with the cash to get it through the night." She argues that the real winners from the decision are U.S. programming distributors, who will now enjoy another bidder for their wares, while the ultimate losers are the people of Southern Ontario, who will fail to benefit from Torstar's promised 85 percent Canadian content on the three stations it planned—in Toronto, Kitchener-Waterloo and Hamilton. Zerbisias, who insists her comments are not the sour grapes of a loyal employee, points out that while Torstar promised $87.1 million to fund independent production, Craig was only prepared to spend $15.4 million over the seven-year term of the licence. She quotes an unnamed TV industry player: "This is the worst decision in the history of the CRTC."

Indeed, Torstar has to climb down from some high expectations. Prichard and David Galloway, the outgoing CEO, had been pitching the new TV stations as a relatively low-cost, rational way for the company to enter the convergence game, without blowing its brains out. Only a year earlier, the soft-voiced, buttoned-down Galloway had explained at the annual meeting why the company had sat on the sidelines in the merger craze that had stalked the communications industry in 2000. Torstar did believe in convergence, Galloway assured the meeting, but not at the price that CanWest had paid for the Southam newspapers, or what BCE had forked over for CTV.

"We believe convergence can create value through operational synergies, repurposing of content, cross promotion and cross-selling. There are benefits, but the issue is, at what price?" he said, playing the role of the last rational man left in a world gone mad. "Has Torstar stood still? Of course not. Are there any dance partners left? There are, and we're dancing," Galloway proclaimed in the ballroom of Toronto's King Edward Hotel, as he pointed to a strategic alliance he had forged with the CBC that would "give us many of the benefits of convergence without a dollar being spent."

Indeed, *The Toronto Star,* the newspaper, remained a powerful franchise, with 450,000 copies sold every weekday and, 680,000 on Saturdays, a force in its core Southern Ontario market. Torstar's weekly newspaper chain, Metroland, dominated its suburban markets and Torstar owned strong regional newspapers in *The Hamilton Spectator*, *Kitchener-Waterloo Record* and *Cambridge Reporter*. But Galloway faced a chorus of detractors who insisted that Torstar was not capitalizing on its strength, that it had been left behind in the cross-media merger sweepstakes, that it was confined to its Southern Ontario island, however rich that island might be. While its rivals had been linking up, it had missed the boat, critics say.

It also faced difficult times in its core newspaper business, caught in a torrid market share war that erupted with the arrival of the *National Post,* and then in an economic slowdown that hit newspaper advertising hard. It had made a bad investment in children's publishing and was being hit with losses in its on-line properties. The jewel was its Harlequin Enterprises book division, which continued to make nice profits from its factory of romance yarns. But rumours abounded that Torstar might spin it off as a separate company or sell it for big bucks.

The future of Torstar was a matter of intense speculation, because it was one of a handful of important companies that were still independent after the great merger mania of 2000. The betting was that one or all of these companies would depart the scene over the next few years. This group of players owned strong franchises, but some were too small to survive on their own or, like Torstar, they had not found a cross-media partner or strategy. They were family businesses or founder owned, which meant they were by nature both stable and unstable. They had a longer-term perspective than widely held companies but their prospects could change in a second, with changing alliances, the death of a patriarch or the shifting financial priorities of partners or family members.

Besides Torstar, the closely watched companies included CHUM, the Toronto broadcasting company controlled by the secretive Waters family; Alliance Atlantis, a broadcaster and movie producer-distributor, still in the grip of its forty-something founders; Astral Media, a

Montreal TV and radio company controlled by the Greenberg family; and, to some extent, Craig Broadcast Systems, a family-owned TV station operator. There were other interesting players—Cogeco, a Quebec-Ontario cable company owned by the Audet family, and GTC Transcontinental of Montreal, controlled by Rémi Marcoux, which had become a force in magazine publishing and community newspapers. In the aftermath of the big 2000 deals, the rumour mill was working overtime: Torstar was merging with CHUM; Corus was buying Astral; CHUM was buying Craig; Rogers and CanWest were buying anyone, everyone, maybe even merging with each other. And Jean Monty hovered over this scene like a large purring jungle cat, ready to spring with his billions of dollars in a CTV-style raid.

At Torstar, much of the speculation was riveted on the well-dressed group of men and women seated in the first couple of rows at the annual meeting—the directors who represented the five families, the descendants of earlier *Toronto Star* managers, who control the company's voting shares through an elaborate trust. They seemed on good terms, but the word on the street was that behind closed doors these families were feuding over the future direction of the company. The Honderichs are squared off against the Thalls; the Campbell and Hindmarsh families are backing the Honderichs; and the Atkinsons are behind the Thalls. The network of alliances made European politics on the eve of the First World War look straightforward. The Honderichs—whose current standard bearer, John, is *The Toronto Star*'s publisher—were reported to have made a takeover offer for the company and been rejected. They were also the instigators of a merger offer for CHUM, with its strong bevy of TV stations in Ontario, but the offer had fallen apart over issues of control. Ted Rogers was interested in doing a deal, and this had Galloway's support. There are continuing reports that Izzy Asper, part-owner of the *National Post*, would like to own the lower-brow *Toronto Star* and downsize the money-losing *Post* into a financial daily, or even a financial section within the *Star*.

Galloway, in his pleasant way, toyed with the reporters' questions after the meeting: "I haven't talked to Ted in some time," he said of the cable baron, although he joked that Rogers had urged him to buy some Blue Jays tickets. Torstar was also not in discussions at the moment with CHUM and its octogenarian owner, Waters. "The last time I looked CHUM wasn't for sale—they have an ownership structure similar to ours." Galloway, of course, was being slightly disingenuous— CHUM had a single controlling shareholder, but Torstar had five controlling owners who could not agree on the future of their prize asset. Indeed, family companies always find it hard to change direction when they move into the second or third generation. That's because the interests of succeeding generations become so varied, as the brothers, sisters and cousins proliferate—some want dividends, some want growth, some want to carry on their family management of the sacred trust. So imagine the complexity when there are five families involved. The potential for conflict and confusion expands exponentially.

The seeds of this impasse can be traced to the legacy of Joseph Atkinson—known as Holy Joe—a crusading newspaperman and fervent Methodist from Newcastle, Ontario, who joined what was then the *Evening Star* in 1899 and took over majority ownership of the paper just before the First World War. Atkinson proceeded to shape the newspaper in his image: prohibitionist, pacifist and politically liberal—sometimes even socialist. He also nurtured, along with his editor, Harry Hindmarsh, a style of entertaining, enterprising journalism in which *Star* reporters would climb mountains, rescue fliers or find German tarts who had been sleeping with Soviet spies and Canadian cabinet ministers. It was for decades a successful stew of moral high road and hokey sensationalism. Atkinson died in 1948 at the age of eighty-two, and left his shares to the Atkinson Charitable Foundation, thus freeing the paper to continue its important work as the liberal (Liberal?) conscience of Canada. But the Ontario government, run by the Tories, introduced legislation to make it illegal for a charity to own more than 10 percent of a business. Fortunately, a sympathetic buyer emerged, in the form of a consortium of the trustees of the foundation, people with close ties to *The*

Toronto Star and its beliefs. In 1958, the five families, all sprung from *Star* editors and managers, bought the paper, and when they did, they swore an oath in the Supreme Court of Ontario that they would run the paper according to Holy Joe's beliefs.

These principles are contained in Atkinson's will, which decreed that the profit motive must be relegated to secondary importance behind the *Star's* community and social role. For many years, the *Star's* crusades for multiculturalism, the role of women, a strong government and, of course, the Liberal Party aligned nicely with growing profits. But in recent years, Torstar, the company, had drifted a bit, and its stock market value had languished behind that of other media companies. It had lost out on acquisition targets—the Sun Media chain—or walked away from pricey assets, such as CTV. Now, in an age of convergence, its political principles seemed incompatible with many would-be buyers—Ted Rogers, a Conservative Party loyalist, or even Izzy Asper, who at least supported the same political party as the newspaper. Rumours were also floating that takeover king Gerry Schwartz, Asper's former partner and another heavyweight Liberal, would like to take a flutter on the media and the *Star* would be his favoured vehicle.

To make matters more complicated, David Galloway and John Honderich were uneasy colleagues who often found themselves on opposite sides of the debate over the *Star's* future. Galloway pushed for a convergence deal, preferably with Rogers. The bow-tied, effervescent Honderich had wanted the CHUM deal, and when he didn't get it, gave up his role on the Torstar board, and as president of its media division. No matter how socially progressive the paper's editorial policy, the corporate infighting was just as nasty as in any other company, perhaps nastier.

Yet at Torstar's headquarters at One Yonge Street in Toronto, there was a stubborn pride in being the last of the independents, a newspaper company that was not part of a conglomerate, nor yet the tool of an opinionated entrepreneur or family fiefdom. So what if there were, in fact, five families unable to decide on the company's direction?

Galloway, a hired hand who was not from the warring families, seemed weary of all the speculation about Torstar's future, but insisted his stand-pat philosophy is not just face-saving from his inability to clinch a deal. It is about price, he maintained. As for the reports of a company hamstrung by its internecine squabbling, he threw cold water on the speculating: "I think there's much more written about it than is going on in reality."

At fifty-eight, after thirteen years in the CEO's job, Galloway wanted to go off and do some things for himself. He helped the board recruit a successor in Prichard, the former University of Toronto president, who was inexperienced in the media but skilled at schmoozing and a quick learner. "Rob is very connected to the media and newspapers and the value system of the *Star*. If you can manage University of Toronto, you can manage anything," said Galloway, who was also not a newspaperman when he became CEO of Torstar. He had been a co-founder of Canada Consulting Group, a rare Canadian entry into big-league strategic management consulting. He joined Torstar in 1981, helped the company make a big purchase of weekly newspapers, then ran Harlequin for eight years, before moving back into the parent company as a co-CEO with his friend David Jolley. Any situation where the CEO job is shared is inherently unstable, and Galloway eventually took over the full job and Jolley left the company.

As the end of his Torstar tenure grew close, Galloway argued that Torstar had, in fact, found a convergence play that made sense for it. It applied for new television licences in three cities in Southern Ontario. Torstar had a clear Southern Ontario strategy that would blend the clout of the *Star*, the *Spectator* and the *Record* with the opportunity for massive cross promotion on new TV stations in Hamilton, Kitchener and Toronto. Galloway admitted there would be no home runs with this strategy, even though "we could drive the broadcasting viewership in those markets to a greater extent than anyone else could." Despite huge commitments for local programming, this venture wouldn't break the bank, because Torstar would not have to pay a big premium for acquiring an existing broadcast company.

As a convergence advocate, Galloway liked the strategy of cross-promotion best, even though it isn't a huge revenue earner. He agreed that strong content could be spread across different media, though he was skeptical of the talk of combining news operations in more than one medium. But Galloway also liked the potential rewards from an AOL Time Warner kind of deal. He admired Steve Case for locking in the stock market value of America Online when it shot through the roof during the dot-com craze. But more than that, Galloway saw AOL Time Warner as a subscriber gold mine. Time Warner would bring in the magazine and cable subscriptions, and AOL the huge Internet subscription base. In this converged world, you could take three groups of subscribers, put them together in a massive database and cross-promote and cross-sell like mad. Imagine the synergies, too, if you put Harlequin Romances or a book club together with the subscription base of a cable company. The possibilities were phenomenal, Galloway figured.

Although he wouldn't come out and say it, David Galloway would have embraced a deal that would put a newspaper like the *Star* together with a cable and wireless giant, such as Rogers, or a cable and satellite operator, such as Shaw. The combination of newspaper and cable subscribers would be powerful, whether through an alliance or through ownership. Press reports indicated that Galloway pressed hard for the Rogers deal, though in public interviews he remained coy about his role.

At the television licence hearings in late 2001, Torstar was up against applications from Alliance Atlantis, CanWest Global, Rogers and Craig—in addition to the intervention of CHUM, which opposed the granting of any new licences in the tough conventional TV market of Southern Ontario. Led by Prichard, the new public face of Torstar, the company made an impressive pitch for its Hometown Television, promising a cross-promotion juggernaut that would sweep over Southern Ontario. "We believe we can use the promotional power of our daily newspapers, which have an extraordinary reach in terms of people in Southern Ontario—two and a half million people a week read one of our newspapers," Prichard boasted.

But it was all for naught, as Torstar was turned down. In a tight three-to-two decision, the CRTC panel indicated that it felt the company had promised too much, and that it wouldn't be able to deliver on its generous local and Canadian content commitment. Also, the majority said it preferred to strengthen established broadcasters rather than welcome a new TV player, even one as well-heeled as Torstar. It was a striking demonstration of how the broadcast regulator can, with one decision, create great value for one company and deny it for others. So as David Galloway prepared to leave his job, he had positioned the company as best as he could, but it still lacked a convergence strategy. Torstar would go on, but its form would depend on the peculiar dynamics of the five fractious families that shape its governance.

A man and a woman are making passionate love on a motel room bed, their bodies writhing towards ecstasy. Suddenly, at the moment of ultimate pleasure, a pleasant-looking bespectacled man steps out of the closet and walks past the startled lovers as they scramble to cover their private parts. "Hi, I'm Ian Greenberg, president of Astral Media," the intruder says, seemingly oblivious to the now furious love-makers. As the audience to this clever video erupts in hysterical laughter, Greenberg proceeds to describe Astral Media, a large Montreal-based TV and radio broadcaster, and welcome moviegoers to the Toronto International Film Festival.

As this sexy little video plays on a big screen in Toronto's Roy Thomson Hall, fifty-nine-year-old Ian Greenberg is sitting in the audience, tickled pink at the audience's appreciation of his little thespian contribution to the opening night gala, which Astral is sponsoring. It is still a light-hearted audience on this evening a few days before the September 11 terrorist attacks in the United States. The ribald clip is an appropriate lead-in to the movie *Last Wedding*, filmmaker Bruce Sweeney's examination of love, sex and betrayal among Vancouver's Gen-X crowd. Astral is a regular gala sponsor at the Toronto film festival, and Greenberg, through these promotional videos, loves to insert himself as a character. For weeks before the festival he has urged people to watch the screen very closely—there will be something neat to see.

Through these actorly turns, the outgoing Greenberg displays his puppy-dog eagerness to put his own imprint on his company and his industry. Astral is now unmistakably his, in style and character, six years after he became president on the death from pancreatic cancer of the formidable Harold Greenberg, his brother and the dominant force in the company for its first thirty-five years. Ian is the younger brother who has come out from under the shadow of a larger-than-life sibling. Now he is proclaiming to the audience that this is not Harold's company, this is his company.

Investors and analysts have no trouble grasping who is in charge. Ian has brought focus to the rambling collection of businesses that Harold Greenberg had assembled. This is no reflection on Harold, a visionary who longed to be Canada's movie mogul, and who loved producing films, even though he only had one success, the adolescent teenage schlock comedy *Porky's*. "Thank God we had one winner; everybody forgets the twenty losers we had," Ian says. "People say, 'You did *Porky's*—didn't you find that successful?' Let me tell you something, when we did *Porky's* we were this close to being in serious trouble. It was dog after dog after dog, and dogs are expensive."

Ian, by focusing narrowly on media properties, and not chasing after diversions like film production, has made the company financially strong and a stock market darling. Astral bills itself as Canada's largest operator of pay-TV, pay-for-view and specialty TV channels, with a line-up that ranges across such services as the Family Channel and its French equivalent Canal Famille, as well as the Movie Network, Viewer's Choice and Moviepix. In addition, it owns a bunch of radio stations and is a major billboard advertiser.

But Astral's success has created a perverse problem for Ian Greenberg—because Astral is so desirable, he constantly has to tell people that the family-controlled company is not for sale. Astral is seen as the ideal programming and content provider for a number of the giant companies, but Ian, somewhat exasperated, insists that selling is never at the top of his mind. "When that day happens, we'll address it. But right now, I only know of one strategy, and that is the strategy to grow," he tells me, repeating his lines for the umpteenth time.

The transformation of Astral began even before Harold Greenberg's death in 1996. The family had already begun to discard parts of its scattered collection of outfits—such as its photo shops, film labs, film distribution and other film services—and concentrate on its core media businesses—television, radio and billboards. Ian said Harold certainly bought the idea of increased focus, but "I don't think Harold on his own would have gone to the extreme I did in making it a pure play."

The path may have been clear to Ian but it was wrenching for the Greenberg family, for it meant surrendering parts of a cherished family legacy. As young men, Harold, Sidney, Ian and Harvey Greenberg went into business together in 1961, just after their mother had died, and not long after their father's passing. "We were just sitting around talking— our mother was sort of the glue in the family, an absolute angel and inspiration," Ian recalls. "We were thinking: In her memory, shouldn't we try to do something together to keep together as a family unit?" The brothers, who had four sisters, stirred up a little financing and went into business running photo shops in Montreal's Miracle Mart supermarkets, owned by the Steinberg family. As the photo business flourished, the company diversified, moving into film and television under Harold, who became the driving force.

In 1980, Harold led an application to offer pay-TV in Canada, in the first round of such licences to be offered. But instead, the CRTC issued regional approvals to relatively small players. But when the winning licensees quickly got into financial trouble, the Greenbergs returned to the fray and, along with the Allard family of Edmonton, scooped up the bankrupt pay-TV services in Canada. With financial support from Edward and Peter Bronfman, they developed First Choice into a viable pay-TV operation for Eastern Canada. But

Harold had to abandon his great love, film production, because of the potential conflict of interest, although the family still distributed movies. André Bureau, Harold's old friend and now Astral's chairman, says the portly Harold "always looked like he was a mogul. So when we say he was the biggest producer in Canada, we mean it in both number of movies and his weight."

The bailout of First Choice moved the Greenbergs into television broadcasting, which was to become one of their foundation businesses. Another of Harold's smart moves was recruiting the courtly, meticulous Bureau, a lawyer from Trois-Rivières who had one of the deepest résumés in the Canadian communications industry. He had worked for Paul Desmarais in the newspaper business and had served as president of Telemedia, the vehicle of Montreal entrepreneur Philippe de Gaspé Beaubien, before becoming chairman of the CRTC in the eighties. He was controversial because of his strong industry orientation, but no one doubted his shrewdness. After Bureau left the commission, Harold hired him as a senior executive in the growing broadcasting division. Bureau was a great plus, both as a canny lobbyist to the commission and for his mediating skills. "It was not always easy between the brothers but because of my relationship, I became a kind of intermediary between them," Bureau says. "Even in times that were pretty tense in the family, I was the guy who could continue the day-to-day operations without problems."

So when Harold died, Astral already had a succession plan in place, as Harold's younger brother Ian and his old friend André Bureau took over. "People thought it was the strangest combination in the world," Ian says. "It works absolutely marvellously because we complement each other in many ways. André is very good as far as vision and strategy, and he's very adept at being sort of the fatherly figure, the diplomat. He's complemented by myself, whose strengths are in finance, in discipline, in driving the company forward in meeting all its objectives."

The transition from a diverse conglomerate to a single-focus media company was tough, Ian says, because there were strong family links to the businesses that were sold. All in all, there were twelve Greenbergs working in the company, including a number of cousins and children of the brothers. Some relatives ended up leaving the company, including Harold's son Stephen, who joined the new owner of Astral's former film distribution business. Stephen, who has since moved on to run his own company—in partnership with André Bureau's son, Jean—has come to terms with the changes in Astral, but it was hard at first. "When you mix business and family dynamics, there is always an emotional factor," he says.

Over time, the family's opposition has been tempered by the fact that Astral's stock price has risen smartly. One reason was that Astral was on everyone's lips as a takeover target. The company is 57 percent voting-controlled by the family, and Ian Greenberg sounds exasperated as he explains, yet again, that Astral will be an acquirer, not a seller. Still, analysts are closely watching the moves of Corus Entertainment, the media vehicle of the Shaw family. Astral would be a good fit for Corus's suite of specialty channels and radio stations.

The question remains, What does it do next? Ian will not be CEO forever, and he says the board will soon start discussing a successor, who may or may not be a member of the family. More important, who will be the custodian of the family shareholdings from among the twenty-seven cousins who are the children of the eight Greenberg brothers and sisters? The lines of succession are still unclear. Will the next generation of the Greenberg family still want to own Astral after Ian passes the torch? That is something even Ian Greenberg cannot plan around.

It isn't just Astral Media that puts on the dog at the Toronto International Film Festival. One of the highlights is the annual party hosted by Alliance Atlantis Communications, a sumptuous affair held at the Royal Ontario Museum. The two companies are often lumped together, both Canadian, both owners of attractive specialty channels. Both have CEOs who insist they can do very well on their own, and do not need the welcoming arms of a huge conglomerate.

But while Astral is a company that has become intensely focused, Alliance Atlantis has branched out. It was originally a film production company, but has added movie distribution, then broadcasting, and even movie theatres to its mix. To the outsider, Alliance Atlantis is a chameleon, shifting shapes and colours. From one angle, it is a creative production shop, from another a distributor of Hollywood block-busters, such as *The Lord of the Rings*. It is a broadcasting risk-taker that is also hugely dependent on government funding for its culturally prized production work.

Its chief executive, Michael MacMillan, is himself a bit of a chameleon. He is the picture of Toronto Gaelic cool in contrast to Ian Greenberg's Montreal Jewish gusto. MacMillan is the tiny perfect mogul, with neatly trimmed beard, not a word or a pound in excess, a runner who keeps himself in splendid shape. But privately, there is a madcap MacMillan, a party animal who might toss buns at boring dinner speakers or go skinny-dipping at the Cannes Film Festival.

While Alliance Atlantis is now a fairly large company, there is also a Micky Rooney–Judy Garland, let's-put-on-a-movie feel to its history. Part of the folklore involves three friends who meet at Queen's University in Kingston, Ontario, in the early 1970s and decide to start a film company together. Janice Platt, MacMillan's former business partner, recalls that she intended to be a teacher and librarian, took a film course for a lark and ended up in the same class as MacMillan, the son of an insurance salesman from Scarborough, and his friend Seaton McLean.

The three clicked, and after a brief temptation to go off together to film school in San Francisco, they all headed for Toronto, to a house on Church Street, where they made films on the ground floor and lived upstairs. The company, then known simply as Atlantis, was born. "We did it out of not knowing any better," says Platt, who now farms with her husband and home-schooled kids on the Bruce Peninsula northwest of Toronto. "Naïveté isn't such a bad thing."

"We were hands-on filmmakers living like church mice," MacMillan recalls. "Yet back when people asked us what do you want to be when you grow up, we'd say, 'Have you ever heard of company called Paramount?' That was our line. We said it with intended humour but what we really wanted to say was 'We don't know what's in front of us. We want to be of decent size. And we always wanted to create something that would last beyond us.'"

From 1975 to 1983, the partners paid themselves $100 a week each, which reflected their close-to-the-bone operating style as well as their long-term commitment. They felt they were going to be around long enough that they didn't need to make big bucks in the short term. The trio started out working on promotional films for the Ontario government, but in the mid-eighties made the shift into television drama, converting classic Canadian short stories into dramas for television. One of these was Margaret Laurence's *The Olden Days Coat*, which was financed by raising cash from family and friends. Once the Atlantis team saw how well it was doing, they contemplated a series of dramas, and found willing markets at the Canadian TV networks, including Global TV, which needed to boost its Canadian content. Also, there was a growing international market for serious drama that was not always American.

The breakthrough was *Boys and Girls*, the Alice Munro short story for Global that was nominated for an Academy Award and took the Atlantis team to Pasadena, California, for the Oscar ceremonies. What's more, they won, and there was Platt striding down the aisle of the Dorothy Chandler Pavilion to accept the award: "It was like another world—it didn't seem like me," she recalls. After the Oscars, the team received a slew of offers to move down to Hollywood and work on script development, but the Atlantis founders decided to stay home: "Why be a little fish in a huge pond? Why not a semi-sized fish in a small pond?" was how they saw it.

They all wrote and directed, but it was clear that the intense, perfectionist MacMillan was the deal-maker, and the guy with the big ideas. After a while, Platt became more detached, remaining close friends with the other founders but not sure she wanted to be part of a company that had became unrecognizable. "I couldn't see my mark anymore," she says.

She had also met a carpenter on one of the movie sets who shared her dream of returning to the country, and they married and started to raise a family. She announced her decision to leave in 1988 at a tearful dinner. The others were taken aback, but it was not the end of the relationship. When Atlantis decided to launch Home and Garden Television in the mid-1990s, Platt came back to Toronto to help do the spadework.

Then came the deal that propelled MacMillan and team into a bigger league. In 1999, in a deal heavily influenced by Bay Street investment bankers, the partners merged with Alliance, the movie production and distribution company run by Robert Lantos, one of the brightest stars in the Canadian film firmament. It was an odd pairing: Lantos owned the much bigger company, but it was MacMillan and team that took over the management of the merged business, which was exactly as Lantos wanted it. The personalities were a study in contrast: MacMillan is married to the same woman he met at Queen's University in the 1970s. Lantos's life is a parade of beautiful women and endless fodder for the gossip-mongers. Merging two entirely different cultures was challenging for McMillan, who complained that the outside world viewed him as some orange-juice drinking, granola-eating fitness freak who couldn't handle the pressure. At the same time, MacMillan is intensely ambitious and has a strong inner core that doesn't shrink from the task at hand.

Lantos, flush with $60 million from the sale of his shares, ended up with a new company, Serendipity Point Films, with an exclusive deal for Alliance Atlantis to distribute its original Canadian movies. Serendipity, housed in a spiffy new building in mid-town Toronto, is a mogul's dream world, decorated with posters of the seminal pictures of Lantos's life—the troubling *The Sweet Hereafter*, the juvenile *In Praise of Older Women* and the powerful *Sunshine*, the twentieth-century odyssey of a Hungarian Jewish family. As I waited for Lantos to see me—he was an hour late—Paul Gross, the director-star of the upcoming curling epic *Men with Brooms*, slipped out in the garden for a smoke, script in hand.

Lantos explained that he formed Alliance in 1985 because he wanted to have a company that was strong enough to finance its own work. To do this, he had to remove himself from hands-on production and become a financier and manager, but it was always his dream to go back to movie-making. "The moment came when I found a management team I thought was capable of taking over and continuing the company and running it effectively." That was when MacMillan and Lantos came up with the idea of merging the companies. But can Alliance Atlantis stay independent? Lantos says it's up to the four controlling owners—which include Ted Riley (another friend from the Queen's years) and Peter Sussman, besides McLean and MacMillan—and they won't tip their hands until the moment they decide to cash in.

As years have gone on, broadcasting has become a more important part of the Alliance Atlantis business, as it has gone through its own form of convergence. The stock market likes the higher-margin broadcasting business, with its strong stable of specialty channels, including History, Showcase and Home and Garden. Analysts are not as enthusiastic about the traditional production business, which is unpredictable and plagued by lower margins. Alliance Atlantis has been encumbered with a heavy debt load for a company its size. According to one fellow broadcaster, the problem with Alliance is they are not a pure play, and production is very tough place to make money. "It requires continuous funding. Look at every single production company—its debt increases every year. And so there is this need for money, which puts extra pressure on them."

Alliance Atlantis has stated an intention to reduce its exposure to production, but there is a feeling that the management team is unwilling to give it up. "Sometimes you rationalize your philosophy because of what you're stuck with," says Ian Greenberg, of Astral, who knows all about the challenges of shucking traditional businesses. "Michael is stuck with this infrastructure. He can't help it—his whole life has been there. Not only him, but his other three partners even today are all in production, not in broadcasting."

MacMillan isn't predicting a certain future, but he sees no reason to cash in his chips. He's only in his mid-forties, which is not the time to retire. "We think that our plans are not only smart and exciting, but we're not seventy years old and exhausted. We have lots of energy to carry out our plans. So we might buy more companies, we might merge with companies, we might get bought, we might do transactions that are so different you couldn't begin to describe them."

MacMillan and partners signalled their intention to be strategic buyers when in February, 2001, they acquired Salter Street Films, a Halifax company that produced such television shows as *This Hour Has 22 Minutes*, the raucous satirical comedy journal. The price was heavy—$71 million for a small production outfit—but also included were the rights to a new international film channel, part of the menu of digital channels to be unleashed that fall. It would belong to an impressive array of digital channels the company would launch, including joint ventures with National Geographic and British Broadcasting Corporation on a kids' channel and a Canadian news channel.

Alliance Atlantis seemed to be a company with a future—especially in broadcasting—but MacMillan knows how transitory such success is. Few of the significant companies of the 1980s are still around now. "The thing I've learned is never say never. It's a long life with lots of twists and turns," he says. "We've got some pretty good plans, we think our view of the world is quite reasoned and has a good chance of succeeding that of production companies that began in seventies and eighties, and we are the only ones to make the transition from manufacturing to distribution and to retailing. That's a huge journey, a gigantic one, and I think we've done a good job of it."

So good a job, in fact, that Alliance Atlantis may become the realization of someone else's media dreams. But don't count out the driven Michael MacMillan.

For the first time in living memory, the controlling shareholder of CHUM Ltd. has not spoken one word out loud during the entire annual meeting. So I approach Allan Waters and ask him, "Does this mean you are stepping aside?" Hard of hearing, with a noticeable tremor, the eighty-two-year-old chairman and chief executive officer seems bewildered by the question. Yes, he explains, he stepped aside to let his son Jim run the meeting. "No, I mean, are you going to leave your job to make way for your sons Jim and Ron?" One of Waters's board members, another elderly man, steps forward and emphatically points to Waters: "He's still CHUM. He comes in every day." Waters nods and chuckles.

Allan Waters is indeed still CHUM, almost fifty years after he bought a Toronto radio station at the 1050 spot on the AM dial and turned it into the voice of Toronto rock 'n' roll. The betting is that he will be CHUM to his dying day. There's a good chance that CHUM, the crown jewel of independent Canadian media, will not be sold until Allan Waters departs this world. Meanwhile, Waters's health and intentions are probed, discussed, speculated upon. There are reports that a merger with Torstar was very close but was turned down because Allan Waters wanted equal control, which the owners of the much larger newspaper company could not countenance. He has also talked a lot with his friend Ted Rogers, who makes no secret of the fact he would love to own the broadcasting company.

Usually Allan Waters sees the CHUM annual meeting as an occasion to try out some of his inexhaustible collection of corny jokes. This time, his fifty-something son, Jim, the spitting image of his father thirty years ago, handles the proceedings. Jim explains that the family just thought it was time for a change—although a public relations person says the family wanted to send a signal that Jim and Ron really are in charge these days. Jim Waters is also adamant that there is no change in the company's determination to stay independent. CHUM, the focus of constant speculation about its future, is not talking to anyone—not to Torstar, not to Corus, not to BCE and not to Rogers.

The CHUM meeting is a bizarre combination of a folksy family gathering and a hotshot media event, which sort of describes the company itself. Five Waterses grace the head table of directors: Allan, his wife, Marjorie, and their three children, Ron, Jim and daughter Sheryl

Bourne. Sprinkled through the audience are CHUM officials, including a man dressed in a striking black suit with a collarless white shirt—Moses Znaimer, the president of CITY-TV, the resident genius of Canadian television. Znaimer needs no other introduction—he is just Moses. He is the public face of CHUM–CITY-TV, and there are some people who think Moses Znaimer actually owns the company. He does not. Allan Waters does. Moses is a well-paid employee.

CHUM is in fact a collaboration of two broadcasting geniuses. In 1957, Allan Waters, a former ad salesman and hawker of patent medicines, converted his recently bought radio station to rock 'n' roll, a shift so shocking that it aroused protest from clergymen and parents. For years CHUM dominated rock 'n' roll radio in Toronto and made Waters and his family very rich. Its split personality was evident even then—off-the-wall DJs like Al Boliska and Jungle Jay Nelson, blending with the quiet, obsessively cost-controlling ownership of Allan Waters.

In the early 1970s, Znaimer was the boy genius of the Canadian media, the driving force behind one of Canada's most innovative television ideas—with Phyllis Switzer and some partners, he created CITY-TV, and a jumpy, edgy style of urban programming that connected with its young, hip audience. But CITY made money only one year in its first six, and faced a financial crunch. In 1978, Znaimer and his partners needed a cash injection, and along came fiscally prudent CHUM to create this combination of Znaimer's brio and Waters's measured opportunism.

Znaimer, cutting edge and Jewish, is given a long leash to play with his ideas and to trot out his Zen-like musings about the power of the image and the death of the word. Waters, strait-laced and Anglican, all ties and jackets, is rarely quoted. Waters owns three million CHUM common shares, almost 90 percent of the voting interest in the company. Znaimer is paid $1.8 million a year for his services, but owns no shares to speak of. Drew Craig, the Alberta broadcaster who buys a lot of CHUM's programming, is impressed: "What a partnership—this dressed-in-black dramatic character and the polar opposite is Allan Waters."

CHUM has flourished as an international player, as one of the few Canadian companies to export original media content, with its rock video MuchMusic format and its CITY concept of interactive local television. There is the Speaker's Corner, a forum of motor-mouth opinions, the Breakfast Television Show, the willingness to block off entire sections of Queen St. West for Britney Spears or the Backstreet Boys. Its specialty TV factory, going beyond MuchMusic and its spin-off MuchMoreMusic, has unleashed the Star! and Bravo! channels in analog format and new digital titles such as Book Television, Fashion Television, the Drive-In Classics and SexTV, as well as MuchLoud and MuchVibe. CHUM's great advantage is that these new channels represented incremental expansions of existing programming. It already had strong brand names in books, music, fashion and sex. In fact, much of CHUM–CITY's programming has always been about music, fashion and sex.

Through it all, the parent company CHUM exhibits a fetishistic attention to cost control, while allowing the dynamism to flow from CITY's Queen Street West playground, in a building that once housed a Methodist book publishing company. It has become the fourth force in Canadian broadcasting, now with TV stations from Ottawa to the West Coast, including new outlets in Victoria and Vancouver. Even in areas where CHUM is not a presence, it sells programming to independents, such as Craig Broadcast, operator of the A-channel mini-network in Alberta and Manitoba. The CHUM-Craig relationship is mutually advantageous, but also highly competitive. There is speculation that CHUM would buy Craig Broadcast if the conservative Waters would part with some cash or shares because it would strengthen CHUM as the clear fourth network. But feisty Drew Craig jibes that he might actually buy CHUM someday. Relations between the two firms deteriorated further when Craig, who manages his family's TV operations out of Calgary, acquired the new TV licence in Southern Ontario, where CHUM already has two stations and was concerned about the potential dilution of its base. Even more insulting to CHUM, Drew Craig made a deal with giant U.S. content player Viacom to bring in MTV, the U.S.

competitor to CHUM's MuchMusic, as a partner in two new digital channels. Viacom had an option to buy control of these channels if foreign ownership rules were relaxed.

Although a publicly traded company, closely held CHUM acts more like a private fiefdom and is loath to divulge much beyond the minimum required information to investors. Some analysts complain that CHUM doesn't command the best margins in the business, that it owns great assets but the assets are under-managed. For example, it has done a marvellous job of marketing its programming and concepts in foreign countries, but it hasn't truly exploited this advantage. Astral's Ian Greenberg is amazed that CHUM never uses stock options as an incentive to attract and keep good managers. "The Waterses are a very fine family, but Allan is paranoid about dilution—therefore, no options. He pays his people well, no argument there, but the fact is that from an employee point of view, the only way to accumulate any wealth is through options, because typically in most people's lives, the more you make the more you spend."

Yet Mark Rubinstein, an Alliance Atlantis executive who spent ten years at CHUM, insists that the Waterses' ownership is underestimated. In the seventies, the only way CITY could survive was if a company like CHUM could come in, bringing investment and business discipline. But he also believes that the owners were more daring than people give them credit for. He points to CHUM's involvement in specialty television in the eighties, at a time when few people grasped that there was future in this emerging TV category. "Those decisions were both supported and led by CHUM's owners," he says, while other conventional TV players, such as Global, were slow to move. He believes the Waterses understood the specialty trend in TV programming because they had seen their own radio industry become more narrowly focused on niche programming.

Indeed, the Waters radio franchise, especially its old AM stations, has been struggling with its niches. The entire AM band has been a challenge for broadcasting companies, as quality music programming has shifted to the stereo sound of the FM dial. That has left monaural AM with a motley collection of some music and a lot of talk and information shows in news, sports and sex. The Waterses themselves shifted 1050 CHUM AM, their cornerstone station, into an oldies format, and then into music of the 1960s. As ratings continued to slump, 1050 CHUM became an all-sports talk station, as part of a new CHUM network, called the TEAM. But the transition seemed unable to halt the station's ratings slide in Toronto.

CHUM, so radical in other ways, was always reluctant to pursue any kind of synergies between radio and TV, even though it owns both kinds of broadcasting assets in a number of cities. Allan Waters's view has been that the television and radio systems worked better if they were in competition, with radio ad salesmen fighting their TV counterparts and radio news guys jostling with TV camera crews. Competition was good for everybody. But that may be about to change. When it acquired a new building recently in Ottawa's Byward Market, CHUM used the ample space as an opportunity to bring together its Ottawa Valley CHRO television station with its four radio stations in the region, including the longtime ratings leader, CFRA. The physical convergence provided the opportunity for programming convergence, as well. The television breakfast show, for example, actually used people from CFRA as on-air commentators. For CHUM, this was way-out stuff, and if it worked, the concept might spread.

Things were changing in other ways, too. The company was now being run by a troika: chairman and president Allan Waters and his two sons, who were both executive vice-presidents. Jim also doubled as the head of the radio division, while Ron ceded the television president's job to Jay Switzer, who combined management smarts with a strong programming background. Switzer, one of a new generation of CHUM managers, was also a link to the past—he is the son of the late Phyllis Switzer, who as Znaimer's partner was a co-founder of the original CITY-TV.

The big question remains: Will CHUM be sold? It is impossible to divine the thinking of the reclusive Waters clan, but TV boss Jay Switzer said the reasons for selling are not that compelling. First, he could see no fundamental change coming in CHUM's business that would force the owners to sell. Also, he could see continued commitment by the next generation of Waterses. CHUM enjoys the simplicity of not having a lot of cousins and nephews to appease—unlike Astral, he says pointedly. As for Allan Waters, he has humble tastes: He's living in the same house he's lived in since the fifties. In Switzer's admittedly biased view, there were none of the factors at work that would make you think that the Waterses would sell out soon. In fact, he argued that CHUM would be the last of the five big independent properties that might undergo a change in ownership.

But there remains the fact that "the boys," as these two middle-aged sons are called, remain pretty much a mystery, essentially because they have been given so little free rein. When Allan passes from the scene, they may in fact decide to take their billion or so dollars and do something else—or they may hang in. Jim Shaw, the CEO of Shaw Communications, whose family is a potential buyer of CHUM, believes the sons are not as committed as their father: "They're country club guys—you see them hanging around golfing, doing their thing. Nice assets there. They'll go for a lot of money someday."

12 LIFE AFTER TED?

IT IS A NIGHT OF TRIUMPH FOR TED ROGERS, A NIGHT TO be fêted and fed by the cream of the Toronto business establishment. Rogers is the Toronto Board of Trade's Business Leader of the Year, honoured at a black tie dinner at the Westin Harbour Castle Hotel. The head table is huge, with a hundred people scattered across the stage. Guests are treated to ribbon-waving rhythmic gymnasts and the leaden jokes of Premier Mike Harris, who quips that with all the media convergence going on, "I expect to wake up one morning to discover I work for Ted Rogers too." Huge laughter erupts. The acceptance speech is vintage Ted, embellished with tributes to his late father and mother, to his beloved Loretta, to John Tory Sr. and his stepfather, John Graham, leading up to his trademark signoff: "And the best is yet to come."

But it is not the best of times for the communications executive. Ted is moved by the tributes, but he is terrified that he won't be able to get through his prepared speech. Rogers has sight in only one eye, and that "good" eye is not functioning well. Ted has recently undergone surgery for skin cancer on his face, one of a series of afflictions that he has borne throughout his life with a cheerful forbearance. In removing the cancer, doctors cut into a muscle around his eye, causing his eyelid to droop, making tears flood constantly into his eye. He is struggling with the fuzzy vision, trying to keep up with his prodigious reading load. But on this night, he doesn't know whether he can read the words in front of him. "I sure don't want to wing it, not with a crowd like that," he is thinking. To the audience the talk is funny, disarming, Ted being Ted, but it is painful to deliver. Even in triumph, nothing is simple for Ted Rogers.

Yet the night of January 22, 2001, caps off a successful run for Ted Rogers. He battled for Vidéotron, and lost—but he walked away with a huge breakup fee, and bought control of the Blue Jays from the Belgian brewer Interbrew. He has swapped cable systems with the Shaws, giving up Vancouver—a big blow to his old friend Phil Lind—but getting places like Richmond Hill and Scarborough, both Toronto suburbs, as well as New Brunswick and Northern Ontario, which strengthened his cluster domination of much of Eastern Canada. Ted pushed to buy the Blue Jays because he feels live sports is a great investment, but it also made him a home-town hero, now that the baseball team is back in the hands of a local owner. There have also been generous donations to the University of Toronto and to Ryerson University. In Toronto, it has never been easy to avoid Ted Rogers, and now it is harder than ever.

In fact, Ted has engineered one of the great comebacks in recent Canadian business history. Just as his own health declined in the mid-nineties, Rogers Communications went through a near-death experience. It was mired in debt, and in some circles, the company was written off as a no-hope basket case. The Maclean Hunter purchase, while strengthening the cable empire, piled on debt, and Rogers' investment in the long-distance telephone company Unitel was a disaster. Rogers limped away with nothing, at a cost of $500 million. The Rogers people insist the deck was stacked against them, but even Ted admits he handled it badly in managing relationships with his partners.

The darkest hour was in February, 1998, when Rogers share price sank to about $5, as debt hovered at a dangerous $5 billion. The company, which hadn't made a profit in more than a decade, was in danger of having to scale back the capital spending that is so essential for continued expansion of its cellular telephone system and upgrades to its cable networks. Ted seemed unwilling to sell assets to pay down debt, and he was reluctant to issue new equity, because it would dilute his family's ownership. He was lagging behind other companies in issuing stock options to senior managers. Never considered an employer for life, Ted churned through executives with uncommon rapidity. Colin

Watson, a longtime loyalist, was lured away by the opportunity to run his own company, Spar Aerospace. But the unkindest cut may have been the resignation of Graham Savage, his chief financial officer, who had joined him in the late seventies and left after a boardroom tiff, and whose relationship with Ted had never been repaired. Savage had seemed concerned with the financial plight of the various Rogers companies', and once, in response to a reporter's question about Rogers' financial strategy, cracked in his laconic way, "We are sacrificing short-term gains for long-term losses." Savage was clearly burned out, but Bay Street observers wondered if the CFO had also questioned the company's financial viability. In the middle of it, Phil Lind, Ted's longest-serving lieutenant, suffered a massive stroke on the Canada Day weekend in 1998. Gritty and loyal, Lind came back to the company eleven months later, but his right arm was disabled. In addition, the company was still sinking in the popularity ratings as a result of its disastrous experiment in negative option billing. It was a public relations nightmare, from which Rogers, never a popular organization, was not able to recover.

Worse than that, there was the growing feeling that Ted's business vision was becoming blurred. He seemed to be scrambling from one opportunity to another, or more recently from one disaster to another. Once famous for being a step ahead, he had become the one who reacted to technological change. Burdened with debt, he was not able to take advantage of opportunities as they arose. Despite all the innovation over the years, Rogers was not as successful a company as it should have been. Perhaps it was the debt, or the one-man-band approach, or maybe, heaven forbid, he was losing his touch. One executive recalls that Ted had to be pushed into offering Internet access on his cable lines. It hadn't happened like that before. Usually, it was Ted leading his executives into the future.

In the middle of this, Ted was being treated for a variety of ailments—double bypass surgery, and a series of aneurysms, the very condition that had killed his father sixty years earlier. He kept going through the careful ministrations of his Toronto doctor and through regular visits to the Mayo Clinic in Minneapolis. During one checkup trip to the Mayo Clinic, the specialists detected a nearly blocked carotid artery in his neck, which if allowed to persist might have killed him within weeks. They operated, saved his life and Ted was bustling around the office in no time at all. But he learned to be careful about his health, swam regularly in his various pools and hit the treadmill every morning. One new Rogers recruit wondered who this older guy was that carried a Tupperware tub to work every day, filled with healthy food such as carrots and celery. It was Ted, of course.

As he approached a speech in May, 1998, to the Canadian Club in the Royal York Hotel in Toronto, Ted was thinking about his mortality: He was getting older, he wanted to pass on the company to his children, who were in their twenties and thirties. The speech carried all the Ted flourishes, but included a pledge that shocked even his closest colleagues—he was going to turn his companies into the kind that conservative pension funds and insurance companies would want to include in their portfolios. "Mark my words—if the Lord allows me to finish my final five years as CEO of the Rogers Companies, we will by then be investment grade and paying dividends!" Ted told the blue rinse and pin-striped crowd at the Canadian Club.

"I did it because I was getting older, I wanted to protect the company for the family, and for the shareholders and the employees," he said later. "I didn't want harum-scarum. If something happened to me and we were so deeply in debt, that would really scare people." Rogers insiders said there was always the shadow of his beloved father, who died so suddenly, leaving the family with no option but to sell CFRB and the Rogers Majestic factory.

In the middle of this, Ted reached back, and as he had done many times before, he grabbed on to a lifeline. Ivan Fecan, the president of rival Bell Globemedia, calls him "the bionic man," a phrase that could apply to his repaired body or his often-restructured companies. Ted's survival strategy lay in his ability to develop a network of contacts in the United States and abroad who see him as a leader, a visionary, as someone they want to invest in. Just when things looked darkest, Ted was able to swing a 1999 deal in which phone giants American Telephone & Telegraph and British Telecom paid more than $1.4 billion for a 33 percent interest in Rogers AT&T Wireless, the cellphone subsidiary. The deal cemented Ted's continuing partnership with AT&T, while allowing him to keep control of the operations. In addition, the software giant Microsoft invested US$400 million in exchange for preferred shares and a stake in the cable business. The two deals reduced Ted's debt and put him, if not into investment grade territory, at least on the road to it. The Microsoft deal was the ultimate case of Rogers flexing his friendships, for he is personally close to Microsoft chairman Bill Gates, another dweebish guy whose vision far outstrips that of his peers, but who rarely evokes warm feelings among his customers. Ted is proud of his Gates relationship, and has been known to invite his senior managers into his office to hear his phone conversations with the richest man in the world.

Ted also demonstrated a willingness to sell off prized assets, a concept he has not always embraced. In this case, he got very lucky. Against the advice of managers, Ted had invested about $25 million initially in something called Rogers Network Services, which provided high-speed private telecommunications links for corporations. It was a small operation with revenues of about $50 million, but as the market began to consolidate. Ted was able to sell the unit, nicknamed RNETS, to a fast-rising telecommunications company called Metronet for $1 billion in 1998, which netted a $700 million pre-tax gain. He took back some shares as payment, which became an even bigger windfall when Metronet itself was sold to AT&T Canada. A tiny investment suddenly ballooned into a bonanza for Ted.

Not that life had changed entirely. The day he announced the RNETS deal, Ted walked into the office of Rogers Cable boss Jos Wintermans and fired him—an event that got little attention that day amid the market's excitement over the RNETS sale. After all, a little financial security couldn't stop the revolving door from swinging: Rogers Cable went through four presidents in two years before Ted

236 KINGS OF CONVERGENCE

persuaded his family friend John Tory Jr. to take over the job.

But Ted had accomplished a lot, and three years after his Canadian Club speech, Rogers claimed to be moving towards that investment grade status—although the consolidated debt levels would never shrink to the point where many investors would feel comfortable. Still, Ted was getting a kick out of the apparent paradox. "People just about split a gut laughing because Rogers had been in debt all his life, almost gone under four or five times. He must have been drinking or was on something. So we have now reached the point where we are just on the swing—we have some of the rating agencies calling us investment grade and others want to wait another year to see how we're doing."

The new investment partners and the spectacular deal with Metronet cemented a new image for Ted. He may not be as much fun, but he's less likely to bring down the company. It was this rehabilitation that allowed him to bid for Vidéotron—a move that made sense in terms of cable clustering—and to buy the Blue Jays. It was why the black tie crowd was singing his praises in January, 2001, instead of lamenting what might have been the outcome—the collapse or breakup of Rogers Communications.

The word on the street is that Ted has mellowed as a manager and a person, although not in terms of his obsessions. Tony Viner, the personable president of Rogers Media, said in late 2001 that "he goes out of his way to be non-confrontational, but he is as relentless as ever on what he considers to be the operational priorities. While he has not mellowed that way, he has mellowed on the personal side—the way he comports himself is different. It's partly health, partly age and he's trying to communicate a certain identity. I think with his health issue, he's always been a bit concerned with his mortality, after his father's early demise. I think it's related to his health and his aneurysms, but I think over the past eighteen months he's made a real effort to change himself."

Ted's work habits are still obsessive, and there are still the ubiquitous bulging briefcases even when he's flying down to the Bahamas on the Rogers jet, or when he's out on his boats—at Lake Rosseau in Muskoka or in the Bahamas. Often he is focusing on a particular aspect of the Rogers operations, and the relevant managers are sure to get a call from on board. Because Ted is most passionately interested in cable, John Tory Jr. is often on the receiving end.

"When we go into the office on Sunday, Ted's very often there," Tony Viner says. "So that's what you do at Rogers—you carry a phone with you, and he'll call. He's less intrusive—he doesn't call at three in the morning. Still, he calls when it occurs to him he needs to know something and he's happy to phone anyone in the organization because he wants an answer to the question." One former senior manager at Rogers remembers telling a lunch partner that he had to leave the restaurant early: "I've got to get back to the office. I have twenty-five e-mails from Ted to ignore." In his view, the problem was that Ted was always right, and how could you argue—he had built the company. Yet even this Rogers critic liked the man—he just knew there would be conflicts and that he would always lose.

I met Ted in his sprawling office, on the tenth floor of the Rogers building, on Toronto's Bloor Street East. Formerly the home of a bankrupt life insurance company, it was being moulded to fit Ted's ego and his needs. He had opened up the balcony, and Loretta had designed the space to include a small two-by-four-foot island of turf, so that their ancient golden retriever, afflicted with cancer, had someplace to pee when she came to the office.

Ted was in a great mood the day after the showing of a Global television show called *The Media Titans*, in which Ted had been grouped with an august group that included Izzy Asper and Conrad Black. The interview was wide-ranging and candid—he talked of convergence, was open about his health, took jabs at his enemies—mainly BCE—but with none of the bitterness he might have displayed in the past. He insisted there will be no more holy wars, just intense competition. He liked Jean Monty, whom he described as a "fierce, fierce, fierce competitor, one of the most competent men in North America." The

BCE boss's wife, Jocelyne, was "charming and very, very thoughtful." He pointed out that Loretta and Ivan Fecan's wife, Sandra Faire, are both involved in Sheena's Place, a support centre for young women with eating disorders. The connection is important to Ted and Loretta, for there have been eating disorders in their own family.

Of course, the talk inevitably turned to his succession, which was not yet resolved. The issue has been much discussed in the industry for a number of reasons—Ted's dominance of his company, the continual turnover of promising managers and the uncertain prospects for his own children. Ted had been saying he would leave the CEO's post on December 31, 2003, at age seventy. But if you would mentioned that deadline, inside and outside Rogers, people smiled and rolled their eyes. Even if Ted vacates the CEO's slot, they said, he won't leave the building. And how would you like to be the person who replaces him, with Ted looking over your shoulder and breathing down your neck? (Their skepticism may be justified: Rogers would later announce that he was extending his CEO contract by three years, to the end of 2006, although he could terminate the agreement with six months' notice.)

The children were still young and no one had stepped forward as a natural successor. Ted would like to see Edward Jr. seize the nettle, probably even ahead of Melinda, the child he describes as being most like him. (Melinda observes that her father always adds, "in a good way and a bad way.") It is hard being the children of Ted Rogers—there is a greater burden of expectation. When a single man touches so many areas of the company, he cannot be truly replaced. As Ted looked around him, he could see many of his communications peers who had stepped aside, at least officially, in favour of their children. He has been close to the Roberts family of Philadelphia, which owns U.S. cable giant Comcast— where Edward spent two years working and where Brian Roberts quickly rose to replace his father as CEO. Izzy Asper had picked Leonard as his successor, and Ted's alter ego, JR Shaw, had stepped aside for his son Jim and his daughter Heather.

The Rogers children were younger than the offspring in some of these families and they were as yet unproven. Lisa, the oldest, used to work at Rogers Communications in product development, but now was kept busy in writing and charitable activity, although her husband, David Purdy, was a well-regarded Rogers manager. The youngest child, Martha, was active in the holistic health area. The succession debate focused then on Edward, the thirty-two-year-old senior vice-president of planning and strategy, and Melinda, thirty, the vice-president for venture investments.

Asked if the Rogers kids have the same kind of intense work ethic as their father, Tony Viner said, "No, I don't think so, but the short answer is, who does? I think they're hard-working and industrious, but I don't know anyone who works like him." Viner added, "Nothing would make Ted happier than if one of his children succeeded him, but I think he believes there would have to be somebody in between."

Colin Watson is convinced that even though Ted may change his title, he'll be doing what he's doing until he's dead or incapacitated. "I don't think Ted Rogers, as long as he keeps his mental faculties, will ever stop doing what he's doing because it's his life. The logical conclusion is no one will succeed him until he's incapable of doing what he's doing. He may do a Bill Gates and just become the owner, and someone keeps the title [of CEO]."

In Ted's mind there were two distinct but related succession issues—who succeeds him as CEO and who gets to vote the family's shares in the company. The choice of CEO will be up to the board—although he will no doubt have a lot to say about who is a candidate. "If I was hit by a truck tomorrow, there would be a board committee and a search committee and they'd hire professional advisers, and within thirty-six months they'd have a CEO. Until then, there would probably be an acting CEO."

In terms of planning for a scheduled retirement, he said, "There should be somebody appointed chief operating officer before then, say a year ahead, so you begin to get Ted out of the details." The negative side is that when that happens, and people in the operating companies starting reporting to that person and not to Ted, some people will leave. And of course, if the COO doesn't get the job of CEO, that person will leave, too, and the result could be utter chaos.

Is it John Tory Jr.'s job to lose? Ted agreed that Tory is a strong candidate. "John's an extremely competent guy; he's keen, he's Canadian," he said, pointing out that a number of the Rogers Wireless bosses have come from the United States. The Torys and the Rogerses go back a long way. "I got a job with his grandfather. We've had a long association. I wouldn't be here without his father's help over the years."

John Tory Jr. is often called Ted's unofficial nephew—even his second son—even though they are not related. Tory, the son of Ted's most trusted adviser, has known Ted since he was six years old, but they became very close as Tory in his early teens developed an interest in Conservative party politics. The rising young entrepreneur and the bright teenager would correspond and talk on the phone about politics. When John Tory was seventeen, he got a job driving then prime minister John Diefenbaker around Toronto to give one of his patented tub-thumping speeches. "Ted was at the luncheon—he wouldn't miss a Diefenbaker speech—and it lasted about ninety minutes." At the end of the speech, Ted asked young Tory what he was doing for the summer. So Tory went to work that summer as a gofer at the Rogers radio station CHFI and graduated to reporter. He continued to work there summers for eight years until he got called to the bar. "I used to run into Ted when I'd come into work at three-thirty or four in the morning. I was working the morning shift and he was leaving the office. Coming down the elevator, he'd be carrying two briefcases at four in the morning."

Tory became a lawyer at the family firm but shifted into politics, where for many years he was the capable right hand of Ontario premier William Davis. After the Davis years ended in the early 1980s, he went back to law and worked with Ted as a legal adviser and on some of his boards. Ted kept trying to recruit him for the Rogers team, and Tory kept refusing because he didn't want to damage the special friendship. "I didn't want that to come to an end, because I was some executive that would be thrown off the tenth floor balcony on a bad afternoon." Tory finally joined the company in 1995, and, according to some insiders, he was at first appalled by the way "Uncle Ted" treated some of the senior managers. But he stayed and he formed a working relationship with the man he respects so much. "The first thing you have to do is make sure you stand up for yourself. If you let him roll over you because he's Ted Rogers—he's very smart and he's hugely successful—then it becomes very difficult to do your job properly."

But Tory's intentions are not crystal clear. People who know him well says he is a politician at heart and his dream is to be premier of Ontario. He did launch a trial balloon for a bid for the provincial Conservative leadership in fall 2001, after Mike Harris announced he was retiring from the post. But Tory quickly deflated the balloon, raising speculation about whether he really meant it—or whether it was a message to Ted.

Tory himself deflected the speculation, insisting that his job as president and CEO of Rogers Cable is challenging enough, especially given Ted's continuing interest in that side of his sprawling empire. "I think cable is his favourite business. He lavishes most of his attention on it because it's a business he knows inside out. He started it from nothing and I have my hands full doing what I'm doing now."

Other names popped up as potential successors, too. Chief financial officer Alan Horn had become a powerful presence in the new RCI, where bottom line is such a concern. But he had no experience in operations. Garfield Emerson was an old friend, much valued because of his work on poison pills in the Maclean Hunter takeover, but a corporate lawyer nonetheless. Nadir Mohammed, a bright young executive recruited from Telus, ran Rogers AT&T Wireless. But all these names paled beside that of John Tory Jr,

So it won't be someone named Rogers? Ted admitted that every time he suggests it might not be a family member who immediately succeeds him, "I get shit from the kids." He explained to them—Melinda and Edward, specifically—that he was talking about succession in 2004, and not 2014, when they would be old enough to serve as

CEO. The children asked him how old Brian Roberts of Comcast was when his father designated him to become CEO. And how old was Jim Shaw? "Jim Shaw was probably forty, Roberts was in his early thirties, but he's an extraordinary person." By the time of Ted's planned retirement at seventy, Edward Rogers will be thirty-four, "and in his mind, that's old enough." Still, at the 2002 annual meeting, Ted reaffirmed that there would be a "period of professional management" before any of the children might be ready for the CEO job.

Edward Rogers Jr. has made no effort to hide his ambitions. "I personally don't have aspirations to sit on the beach and just show up at board meetings. I like to be as involved as I can, and if I can reach the level of CEO, that's what I'd like to do." He agreed that he was probably too young to take over soon, but feels he has lots of time to grow into a bigger job.

Edward is a sincere young man, with a slight stammer and an office full of beguiling photographs of his daughter Chloe, who was turning five and is her father's joy. His manner is totally unlike Ted's—and he looks nothing like his father. He is stocky, with a hint of a paunch, his dark hair styled into a wave at the front of his head. He is well liked in the organization, but few see him as a future CEO, although it's unlikely they saw that in Ted, either. Like all the Rogers kids, he attended the University of Western Ontario, where he got a political science degree. Then he went off to Comcast, the Roberts company, where he worked in a couple of regional offices, in Baltimore and Philadelphia, before moving into head office. He says his strength is he knows the Rogers company inside out, having worked in a lot of mundane jobs. Insiders say he is not a natural in managing operations but thinks a lot about strategy. It has been a hard road for Edward. In a 2000 interview with *The Financial Post*, Ted said Edward showed "excellent judgment" but his son could be "a jerk sometimes, by being stubborn."

Melinda, Ted agrees, is the most like him, and most people concur: She is smart, hot-tempered, outgoing, a slim young woman with great determination. One former executive says there is a feeling in the organization that she would be a strong candidate for CEO someday—if only, in the executive's words, "she had balls." She went to the University of Western Ontario, studied at a European business school and took a master's of business administration at the University of Toronto's Rotman School of Business. Then she spent two years in California's Silicon Valley, working with Excite@Home, the ill-fated Internet company. That set her up for her next job, looking at investments for Rogers Communications, but also left a bit of a taint, given @Home's sad fate. Does she want to be CEO? Although her answer is cautiously worded, it leaves no doubt about her interest: "I would never rule anything out in terms of what I want. I think shutting doors is one of the worst things you can do in your life."

Rogers managers say Melinda, like Ted, works very hard at being well briefed. Not long ago, she appeared before an Ontario legislative committee as a director of a provincial corporation. Rogers managers say that she was the best informed director who testified. Does being Ted's daughter put pressure on her to be better? "I have a very competitive nature anyway, so I don't think being his daughter has changed anything. I wanted to make sure I knew what I was talking about."

But Ted insists that there is too much speculation about the CEO's job, and that's not the critical issue. You can always hire a CEO. The problem is how you do the succession in the family. "Who's going to vote the controlling shares? Who's going to be the owner in the next generation?" Ted watched closely how Ken Thomson, Canada's richest person, managed his succession. Ken's father, Roy Thomson, had designated his son to hold the owner role in his generation, even though he had two sisters. Ken seemed to be doing the same with his own three children, designating his son David as this generation's leader.

Ted agreed that there should be one Rogers leader, but the decision should be reviewed annually. So he set up a mechanism to do this, based on advice from his advisers, former TD Bank chief Dick Thomson and John Tory Sr. On his death, the shares go to a control trust, and he has named one of his children as his preferred choice as the leader and voting shareholder. But he also gave his board of advisers the power to change that person if they deem it necessary.

Ted won't say whose name he has submitted initially, but Edward did not deny that he was that person. "If it is me, we're still very much a family team," he insisted. But all of Ted's children are now at least thirty years old, which means any of them could be considered for that role under the review process. "It could be any of the children or it could be John A. Tory or Gar Emerson," Ted said. "The kids might not be up to it. Do you think I want to screw up everything I've worked for?"

Ted acknowledged that the company might yet be split up, particularly if foreign ownership rules are relaxed, allowing new injections of capital. The federal government has indicated it plans to review these rules, perhaps allowing foreign companies to take majority stakes in carriage companies, such as Rogers Cable, Telus and Bell Canada. According to Ted, AT&T might also take a higher stake in the wireless operations, but he questions why they would need to as long as they have confidence in the Rogers stewardship. Under this scenario, media companies would still require a strong majority of Canadian ownership, and Ted has talked from time to time of spinning out the television, magazine and other content properties as a separate public company. So much for convergence.

What does Ted do after he leaves the CEO's job? He will likely vacate his big office for another one close by, "because you don't want to stay in the same office." But even if he leaves, surely he will still be bursting into the CEO's office all the time? "Oh, I don't know, I'll certainly be dealing with his direct reports," he says, then cracks a smile to say "I'm just teasing." He says he has to start phasing out the idea that Ted Rogers is Rogers Communications. He doesn't go out on the investment road shows anymore, selling stock and bond issues. Despite the view that he's monomaniacal, he does indeed have other interests, such as helping to save the Canadian health care system.

When he moves out of the Rogers CEO slot, he will lead the charge towards increased private health care in the country. He insists he doesn't want to see rich people given unfair advantage by being able to jump the queue. But he is convinced there is not enough money in government coffers to provide the proper level of care. He thinks the answer is to have the government step back, take more of a regulatory role and allow private people to be owners and operators. He would insist on rules to ensure that good doctors would not be allowed to work only in the private sector, and that the health of ordinary Canadians would not be allowed to suffer. The idea, he says, is that "we're going to have rules that everybody will follow, whether it's the government or Ted Rogers wanting to open a hospital. And what's wrong with Ted Rogers opening a hospital?"

Some will say he just wants to make profits on the medical system. "Well, the last I heard there's nothing wrong with a profit," says Ted, although detractors will say Ted has much more experience in running a non-profit organization, known as Rogers Communications. But Ted promises that he would be innovative, provide all the necessary services and he would have to follow every rule.

For the moment, at least, Ted plans to still be the owner of Rogers Communications and to keep an eye on the business, perhaps moving over to vice-chairman or some other kind of role. His job will be to maintain the important relationships with the company's partners such as AT&T and Microsoft, although he intends to get Edward more involved in this. Ted would also like to take more time off, although he can't claim much success in pulling back so far. He insists he is still a valuable asset if only for his uncanny agility with numbers. "I'm not good on names but I remember numbers."

He tells of a conversation with Leonard and Izzy Asper over an ethnic television station in Montreal that he wanted to buy from them. The Aspers said they had just had the rules changed to allow a higher percentage of English-language content, but Ted challenged the Aspers, insisting they were wrong. The debate raged back and forth, until Leonard Asper said, "That's not right, Ted. What are you telling me my business for?" About a week later, Leonard called to admit that Ted was right all along.

Ted loves the story. "I enjoy debating and numbers. I've got a good memory." Is he a techie? "I got an expensive education, I surround myself with the engineers. And most people think I'm very engineering oriented, but I'm not into engineering like my dad." There is a group of Rogers engineers that meets four or five times a year for dinner and just to talk about ideas. Ted attends those dinners. "We've done this for twenty years; many people say the real decision-making is done after a number of bottles of wine being consumed at those engineering dinners, and there's a certain degree of truth to that. I'm very influenced by them. I tend to be the champion of the engineers."

Ted Rogers isn't done dreaming. He has one more convergence card to play—and it may be the most important one of his life. Despite his kind words about Jean Monty, he knows that he still can't offer the full product range of services that Bell Canada does. Like his friend and would-be partner André Chagnon, he figures there's only one way to accomplish that—to smoke BCE out of its effective monopoly on local phone service. If he can't do that, BCE will continue to be able to amass huge profits in that near-monopoly of local telephone service, giving it the flexibility to lower prices on wireless, high-speed access, satellite and all the products where they are competing with Rogers.

In Ted's thinking, Rogers simply has to get into local telephone service, but the business has to make technological sense and it has to make money. Ted has a vision, shared by cable operators such as Chagnon and Cogeco's Louis Audet, to offer local phone service through the cable industry's Internet capability, using the nascent technology of Internet telephony. It's not as expensive as standard telephone circuit switching, but, he admits, it is not developed yet. There's a technical challenge with IP telephony, the kind that Ted relishes.

When the power goes off in the house, the Bell phone still works, and the consumer can still call the doctor or the 911 emergency number. But the Internet telephone would be cut off. "I have a very simple solution, so simple it must be stupid, and it's this," he says, pointing to his cellphone. He suggests giving every household a cellphone, putting it in a charger in the house. "And if the power goes off, this will run for maybe six days, with the kind of batteries we have now." Ted says he can't wait till he starts working on "this simple little solution" with his engineers. "I'm now determined to get it done. I don't know when, but it's important."

Phil Lind hears Ted obsess on Internet telephony and it both worries and excites him. He's been there with Ted before. Lind believes that Rogers' convergence strategy in the long term means combining wireless, long-distance and local telephone and cable TV. Rogers is still missing the middle two pieces. But to offer telephone service, it has to be sensible from a cost point of view. Lind worries about a repeat of the experiment with long distance, when Rogers went into it knowing it was too costly but assumed that the system would eventually correct itself. "But I didn't know at the time there were no limits to the power of the [telephone companies'] inertia. They've been at this game a long time, they're not going to change, and they're not going to let go of anything without a fight."

He says the power of the Bell lobby is so strong that it will never allow itself to be beaten on anything. "Bell is the giant of all giants in this country, and now they're into the broadcast business as well—and in the sports business and in the newspaper business. They're [in] everything. In your wildest dreams in the United States, you could never imagine the power that Bell has in Canada being there in the States. It just couldn't possibly exist. I don't know if they manage things well, but they're surrounding us." For Lind, the issue is always the power of Bell. It is the eternal battle and Rogers keeps fighting it, even if Ted insists he is more tolerant towards the "evil empire." Ted admits that "there are ways in which Bell and Rogers could work together and should; it's a little country and we're stupid to have holy wars. That's my approach; I'm not full of emotion, I know they're a real competitor, and they're coming at us; I know what they're doing engineering-wise and I fear them, respect them."

Ted's greatest regrets are personal more than business-related: "I wish

I could have spent more time with the children when they were younger, the usual. There are the businessman's regrets about wife and kids." He admits that Rogers has missed opportunities, namely selling the *Sun* chain of newspapers. "We wished we hadn't, and we did other things, but you still can't do everything in life." But the uncertainty of succession must still be a regret. Does Ted look at JR Shaw enviously, and how he has passed the torch? No, Ted insists, he has made his choices. And besides, entrepreneurs are not jealous of other entrepreneurs. "We're goddamn lucky to be where we are and I'm goddamn lucky to be alive. Because I've had a heart attack, quadruple bypass, a single aneurysm, a quadruple aneurysm, a carotid artery here that was 95 to 98 percent blocked. In another week I would have died. So the Shaws have done better than us in some ways; Bell is much bigger than us in every way. I'm lucky we have what we have. We're trying to give a little bit back to the community, as you know. . . .

"We're doing it our way, as Sinatra used to say."

13 THE RIVER HEIGHTS KIDS

"I CAN TELL YOU'RE A HOCKEY PLAYER—YOU HAVE A hockey face," a woman once told Leonard Asper and he tells the story with obvious delight. Yes, Leonard acknowledges, it is a face shaped by confrontations with sticks, pucks and errant elbows—a broken nose, a long scar on the chin, various nicks and scrapes. It signals a love of the game that persists at thirty-seven years old in Saturday games played with a bunch of lawyer friends around Winnipeg for a team called the Pitblado Pistols, named for the law firm where he used to work. Hockey also leaves an imprint on Leonard's approach to life—the energy and openness, combined with an aggressive, in-your-face zest for confrontation.

Leonard Asper likes going into the corners like Mark Messier, one of his idols, but he doesn't carry a grudge. He has his father's quick tongue and love of a good fight. People who have watched say he is a very good hockey player, extremely fast, the kind of player who can shoot on the move without setting up, without giving the goaltender a chance to get ready. He is a jock but a jock with depth, a jock who reads. (The day after Mordecai Richler's death, he recalls the pleasure he found in reading *Solomon Gursky Was Here.*) Yet he admits he is not a big content guy—that's his brother David's role. "David really watches the product; I don't watch a lot of TV. I'd rather read a shareholder's agreement. I'd rather make sure for the shareholders that we have got the right goddamn clauses in them."

This dark-haired earnest kid who loves shareholders' agreements controls the biggest chunk of Canada's media: the second-largest private TV broadcaster, and the largest publisher of daily newspapers. Izzy is slipping into the background—somewhat reluctantly at times—and it will be Leonard's job to win or lose the media wars of the twenty-first century. He is now Canada's most important media executive, because, unlike his rivals at BCE and Bell Globemedia, Leonard actually owns the shop—or at least, he will someday.

The interviewer suggests that CanWest is taking a big bet with convergence, but the feisty Leonard will have none of that. It is no bet, he says, but "a strategy for accelerated growth." He is quick to point out, as does his father, that all his businesses—television, newspapers, on-line— are good assets on their own. "If not one dollar of convergence occurs, television is a good business, newspapers are a good business, on-line is a good business." Convergence is just the gravy, he says. It is partly a defensive strategy to protect against the increasing fragmentation of the audience, but also an offensive thrust that could pay off big-time in huge increases in ad revenue.

Leonard calls it a horizontal integration strategy, in which you develop advertising and content across a number of media—call them platforms—print, television, on-line, radio and billboards. In Canada, he admits, he still has to add the billboards, which he owns in Australia, and he still needs the radio. He also could strengthen his complement of specialty TV channels, which are still weak compared with those of rival CTV. Despite a choking debt load, CanWest is always looking for things to buy. That's why, a week after the $3.2 billion Hollinger deal, Izzy was out there trying to buy radio stations from Allan Slaight.

Leonard doesn't see any need to own the pipes—the cable lines or the satellites. It's not his business, he doesn't want to bet on the technology, and you can always do alliances to get what he wants. Leonard feels that if he has enough good content, no one is going to deny him access to the pipes. They wouldn't dare. "Pipes would always be helpful to our strategy but the real driver over the short term is the ability to sell across multiple media, and create these [advertising] packages, which we are doing daily." He insists the advertising rates in these packages are not discounted, because CanWest is creating entirely new products for clients and "we create special promotions for them that met that client's specific needs."

More than any company in North America, CanWest can offer a combined print-TV advertising buy, based on a countrywide chain of papers and a national TV network. Still, there are some real challenges with this ambitious strategy. One problem is that it swims against traditional practice. The media buying industry has always operated on a product-by-product basis—someone at an agency would buy radio ads, someone else would buy print ads. The two groups operated essentially as silos. For companies such as CanWest and Bell Globemedia, it means a dual challenge—they need to educate their own people and pull them together to offer multi-media sales or to build full-time convergence teams. But it also means educating the advertising industry and, of course, its clients. In some cases, the media companies have to act like ad agencies themselves, presenting clients with a concept—often, a package with distinct, original content. Of course, there would be no advantage if the clients tried to use these big packages to wring volume discounts. The deals have to add top-line revenues or the big takeovers were for no effect.

One problem in Canada is that there are relatively few advertising dollars available. Canadian ad spending is much lower than in the United States, even on a per capita basis, because of the constant spillover of ads from the U.S. media. Canadian media companies have to be inventive. But not every client in Canada is going to be interested in a national converged advertising project. According to Hugh Dow, a veteran media buyer and president of M2 Universal Communications Management, of Toronto, the national convergence market consists of only twenty-five to thirty large clients, which both CanWest and Bell Globemedia are targeting, each with some positive results. (Bell Globemedia was working with the Cadillac division of General Motors, CanWest with the Royal Bank.) But the the dollars were still small and the jury was still out on long-term impact. For some, the new deals were a threat to the sacred separation of advertising and editorial functions. Journalists were concerned about the potential control of editorial content by advertisers in these new convergence projects, in which a single advertiser was paying the full freight. Also, most of the early convergence buys did not consist of new money being spent. It was existing ad spending that was being taken away from somewhere else. These projects were coming to market at a time when advertising spending was languishing in the wake of the dot-com collapse, and then along came the September 11 terrorist attacks in the United States.

Izzy, however, was confident that the ad industry would ultimately see the value in these cross-media campaigns— for their pure efficiency, if nothing else. "It will take time to teach the agencies the benefit of convergence, but we are seeing some minor evidence right now. For example, if I walk in to see you, Mercedes Daimler, and you're going to launch a car, I can give you for your campaign the television, the billboard, the print side. That's one-stop shopping. Okay, you've got to do some filling in, but at least you've cracked 62 percent of your target market in that one conversation, which makes you more efficient."

At the same time, a company like CanWest, which derives more than 80 percent of its revenue from advertising, is extremely vulnerable to an ad recession, such as the one that gripped the industry in the latter part of 2001. One of Leonard's goals is to raise the percentage of non-advertising revenue, and he sees a number of ways—through merchandise sales, by selling more programs generated by Fireworks, CanWest's production subsidiary; and through higher subscription fees from specialty channels. CanWest is also pressing the regulators for something more revolutionary: to make the cable companies pay Global for the inclusion of its conventional network on their packages, just as they do with specialty channels.

Leonard and Izzy have their role models, including Viacom, the giant U.S. media company, which distributes and produces content through such properties as Paramount Pictures, the CBS television network, the Nickelodeon channel and MTV, the fabulously successful rock music cable channel. They admire Rupert Murdoch's News Corporation and the Tribune Company, publisher of the *Chicago Tribune* and *Los Angeles Times* and the owner of television stations. "If you merged Viacom with Tribune, now you've got the perfect play," Leonard says. "I think Viacom is the closest to us, but they don't own newspapers, and newspapers can give you such strength in local advertising."

Leonard boasts that under his direction, CanWest will someday rival those big U.S. companies in size. He does not blush when he says that his goal is for CanWest to be one of the world's top five media companies in the next decade, a truly global giant run from Winnipeg. "He's not just blowing smoke," Izzy says in agreement. "I say both regretfully and excitedly that we're on the low row of a ladder that's much taller yet. I don't think it will take another twenty-five years."

Leonard Asper is relaxing in his office, on the thirty-first floor of the Toronto-Dominion Centre at the corner of Portage and Main in downtown Winnipeg. It is a once-prosperous business area gone to seed, with closed stores, empty old office buildings, vagrants and panhandlers on the street. But from Leonard's office, you see none of that, only the city of Winnipeg and the flat prairie rolling out beyond it, the Red River snaking through the centre of the city and CanWest Field, the ballpark of the Winnipeg Goldeyes of the independent Northern League, where Leonard and one of his two young daughters will be attending a game tonight. It is early July, and he is dressed casually, in a grey collarless shirt and black pants.

It's been a tough time, he admits. When he dreamed of taking over CanWest, he wasn't thinking of running a company this big. It is hard on his wife, Susan, and he sees his family less than he would like. "My wife and I, we didn't plan this out. I don't think she expected this kind of thing, but she has been really adaptable." On a typical morning, Leonard enters the office at eight-thirty or nine, gets home at seven and plays with the kids until nine. Then he usually retires to his home office, where he works from nine-thirty to about 1:00 A.M. That's where he gets the reading and quiet stuff done, the preparation. In the winter, he'll go into the office on Saturday for three or four hours.

During the negotiations with Conrad Black, he realized that he had never anticipated the challenges of trying to integrate two large companies, including a newspaper unit with a heavy human resources component. "My regret is I just can't seem to be able to do it fast enough. Maybe I'm too impatient, but people keep bothering me with little things." He goes through a long list of things he needs to deal with: not enough computers, the hardware is old, the servers are obsolete, the software is inadequate, people have to be hired, and union contracts are expiring. "Now this manager doesn't get along with that manager, and in Calgary or whatever city, the local TV and newspaper convergence aren't working." There are seven thousand things that can go wrong, he admits, adding that seventy-five thousand things may go right, but when you get into details, it's never as easy as it looked on paper.

Izzy sees his son's obsession with details and it worries him. "I wish Leonard would spring himself for more thinking time," the father tells me, adding that he seems to be the only one in the company who has the time to plan. He is encouraged that Leonard has hired a full-time tax manager, a human resources expert, a finance chief and is bringing in an R&D component. "He's got to get away from micro stuff, but he is reluctant to delegate." (In June 2002, CanWest would hire a chief operating officer who would take some of the load—and some hands-on authority—away from Leonard.)

Despite the workaholic schedule, Leonard realizes he will never be Izzy—nobody will be Izzy. "It's like at the Edmonton Oilers, they've won Stanley Cups with Gretzky and they won with Messier, and I always come back to hockey analogies. I'll win but I'll win a different way. I always figure that Gretzky has more finesse than Messier, and there's no doubt my dad has more finesse than me. You can't compare yourself with Izzy Asper. You just say, 'Look, I'm going to try to do the best I can and I'm just going to try to be me, not Izzy Asper, because that would be counterproductive.'"

He says he talks to his father just about every day, but Izzy gives him a wide berth in running day-to-day operations. As chairman, the father remains very active where he's best, in strategy development. In fact,

Gail, David, Izzy and Leonard meet often. "I am really the family representative running it in a way. David and I live beside each other and share a driveway—it's a curb, actually. A lot of business gets done that way. It's still very much a family business, it's not the Leonard Asper show, but on the other hand, I've got my [duties]."

Those duties weigh heavily on him. The night before I interviewed the Aspers, David, now chairman of the Blue Bombers football team, was at the game in Calgary, and Leonard was in the office, watching it on TV and finishing up a bit of work. The two brothers managed to celebrate the Bombers' victory together by phone. It's like that for the Asper brothers. Leonard has the big corporate job, David is the big man in the Winnipeg community. But there they were, on the phone after the game, revelling in another victory.

I had already met David, the burly open-faced older son, in the office of the real estate company that he runs with Leonard and Gail, many floors down in the same TD bank tower in Winnipeg. At one point in the interview, David asked me to transmit a message to Leonard: "Tell Leonard that Khari Jones says hi." Khari Jones is the name of the current Blue Bombers quarterback. Perplexed, I slip it in during my interview with Leonard: "David says Khari Jones says hi." Leonard breaks into a grin. He explains that when they were kids, his older brother spent some time at the Winnipeg Blue Bombers' training camp. When David came home, he would tell his kid brother, "Don Jonas says hi," referring to the then star quarterback of the Canadian Football League team. Ever since then, it's been a running joke between the brothers. David continues to pass on the message, invoking the name of the current Blue Bombers' star.

The message sums up the relationship of the Asper kids, from the time they were growing up in River Heights, the comfortable area of Winnipeg, far from the boarded windows and drunks of Main Street. The family is close, a tribute to the implicit partnership of Izzy and Babs, that while he was conquering the world, she was raising the kids. They all have a bit of Izzy—David and Leonard are quick to take offence, to leap to the attack, but they are also quick to pull back. All are lovers of the one-liner, the quick quip, the shot across the bow. Gail, who is very family oriented, is a motor-mouth of enthusiasm and warm, funny tangents. She warns a reporter to edit her quotes because she talks in endless run-on sentences. You can imagine dinners at the Asper home with the bursts of jokes and asides. Says one media executive who has worked in several places, "Of all of the moguls, Izzy is most blessed, in my opinion; three good kids, not perfect, but basically good kids, and they've got a sense of humour, a great tolerance for their dad, and they're fairly practical."

Gail says her mother Babs was always laid-back, able to remove herself from the stress of business life. "Mom could sit on a couch with foam exploding from the pillows and if she's got a good cup of coffee—not too hot—and a good book, she'd be very happy. And if my dad had more time to go out for walks and movies and go out for a bite to eat, like all her friends are doing, I think she'd be in heaven. But she knew what she was getting into—she had choices, her own marital choices, and she chose Izzy Asper, who was always a firecracker."

Izzy never forced the kids into the business—in fact, he was quite adamant that they should not join him at CanWest. He had seen too many botched successions as a tax and estate lawyer to count on any kind of multi-generation family business. As the children were starting out in life, there was really no family business at all. But he wanted them all to be lawyers so that whatever happened, they had a skill that was transferable to many situations.

Gail had been interested in the arts, particularly drama, but her father nudged her towards business law, which she took at the University of Manitoba. She married a fisheries scientist, Michael Paterson, and moved east to Halifax while he attended graduate school at Dalhousie University. Gail practised law and loved the easy-going life in the Maritimes. But she wanted to raise her family back closer to her mother and father. After a rush of big deals, her Halifax practice was becoming mundane and she was feeling frustrated. She started talking to her father about coming back. Her husband, too, was looking at a job in Manitoba. And Izzy was at the stage where he clearly could use some help. The business was growing, as CanWest kept adding stations and Global became more successful. He had a number of severe health problems, and was starting to think about what would happen if he wasn't around anymore.

At first, it was thought that Gail might practice with a Winnipeg law firm that handled a lot of CanWest's business, but instead she came into CanWest as an in-house counsel. For a while she even served as Izzy's executive assistant, but that didn't last long. One of her jobs was to move Izzy through a room at a public gathering, providing him with information about whom he was meeting, and why he should know that person. "Dad and I are both hopeless at that. I have a very bad ability with names and faces, so we'd be stranded in a room and Dad would be saying, 'He knows me, we ate at Sal's last year, who is he?' and I'd be saying, 'I have no idea.' We had to get out of there because we had no idea who anybody was."

Once Gail was inside CanWest, Leonard, who was in law school, and David, who was in private practice, began to agitate about coming into the company too. "The fences were down," Izzy recalls. "I never considered that Gail was coming into the business, I considered that she was going to be our in-house lawyer. But as soon as that happened, Leonard said, 'What about this nobody-in-the-business rule?' and I said, 'She's not in the business,' and on and on. Anyway the wall had been broken and Leonard came in. And David said, 'Okay, all bets are off, we're all in.' So I became director of a child care centre."

Leonard took easily to corporate life, even though he had to make sacrifices with his love of hockey and rock 'n' roll. Friends remember him as a nice guy, a pianist who would tickle the ivories at school parties. Paul Muchnik, a Toronto lawyer who played hockey for the same Winnipeg teams as Leonard, says "Lennie" "wasn't just out there for a skate, he was out there to play. He's a very good hockey player, he has good hockey sense, and he's tenacious, but in a positive way, gentlemanly." Leonard went to university at Brandeis in Boston, took law at the University of Toronto—with a heavy corporate and commercial emphasis—and worked at Global TV for a few years in Toronto, before coming home to Winnipeg.

David was a bit of a rebel, a good-time guy, famous hard-partier, known for bombing around Falcon Lake in his boat. Although he acceded to his father's wishes and attended law school—at California Western Law School in San Diego—David quietly resisted Izzy's preference for corporate and tax law, and instead was attracted to advocacy and litigation work. After law school, he spent a summer clerking at a New York law firm doing corporate work, and had a great time. But when he came back to Winnipeg to his father's old law firm and tried corporate commercial work, he left midway through his articling to go into criminal work.

On joining a smaller Winnipeg firm, he told the senior partner Hersh Wolch that he liked the action of criminal law, but he also wanted to make a mark for himself, not to go through life as just the son of Izzy Asper. Wolch remembers David's enthusiasm as he took on his first serious case, to defend a man charged with the murder of a Mountie. When David walked into the RCMP station, the officer in charge, on hearing David's name, immediately asked: "Are you Izzy's son?" When he heard those words, David's face fell, Wolch recalls. "Here he was, finally doing what he wanted to do, and I felt so badly for him. He was doing this just to get away from that very thing."

David Asper's profile soared in 1986 when his law firm took on the pro bono assignment of defending a young Winnipeg man who had been convicted of murder many years earlier but whose family was convinced the evidence was mishandled. In 1969, David Milgaard was a sixteen-year-old flower child, bombing around the prairies with a group of friends. The police concluded that he was the murderer of Gail Miller, a nurse's aid in Saskatoon. Convicted of murder, Milgaard had been in prison for almost seventeen years when his mother, Joyce, approached Hersh Wolch about taking on the case. Wolch enlisted junior lawyer David Asper to help him out on the file. The Milgaard case became a legal marathon as authorities put roadblock after roadblock in front of the team. While Wolch took on the case burden, David Asper handled the media—a very important part of the team's strategy—and worked with the family. "I think the fact he bonded with the Milgaard family says a lot for him. He bonded with them when they were in trouble, before anybody else was believing in them," Wolch says.

"At times I felt he was doing that and giving me time to work on the case. He freed up a lot of my time to work on legal aspects while he did some of the time-consuming work keeping things under control."

It was crucial for the Milgaard team to have the media on-side, because it was a way to keep pressure on the federal government, which was resisting any re-opening of the case. Wolch and Asper had an open-door policy—the media had free access to the defence team's files, could call the team twenty-four hours a day and there were no secrets. It was a winning strategy, because reporters would go out and dig up important facts for the Milgaard team. David Asper thrived in this pressure-cooker.

The Milgaard case was all-absorbing, as Wolch and Asper took it to the Supreme Court of Canada in Ottawa. That involved months of preparation, and a twenty-one-day marathon session before the court itself. Six years after his mother had first approached Hersh Wolch, David Milgaard walked out of Stony Mountain Penitentiary a free man after twenty-three years behind bars. Another man, Larry Fisher, was later tried and convicted of the murder.

In 1992 David felt he had done about as much as he could in criminal law. Besides, everyone was coming into the family fold at CanWest. Hersh Wolch felt that David had always intended to join the family business someday, after he had made his mark in the world. David Asper left the law firm well before the Wolch team had won a $10 million compensation package for Milgaard from the federal government.

But David Asper did get his reward. While Milgaard was at Stony Mountain in the late eighties, Asper would ride up to visit him on his puny Yamaha motorbike. "He'd look at my helmet and say 'Dave, I tell you, you get me out of here and I'm guessing there will be a little bit of money for me. I'm going to help you upgrade your bike.'" More than a decade later, Milgaard gave Asper a Harley Davidson motorcycle, a $25,000 bike, which Asper still has and cherishes. The licence plate reads DM2DA—David Milgaard to David Asper.

When David Asper became a lightning rod for the media as a CanWest executive—particularly as he led the family's editorial policy initiatives—Hersh Wolch felt he could deal with the challenge: "He's not fearful of being in the limelight." Wolch adds, "He can handle himself, but he can be less cautious than some people, which I think is one of the good things about him. I think his lack of caution was one of the good things in the Milgaard case. He wasn't afraid to stick his neck out."

When David went into CanWest, there were some immediate decisions to make. The three children had to sit down and decide, David says, "Is this worth carrying on and if so, can we carry it on collectively? Do Leonard, Gail and David want to work together? You have to look really meaningfully at each other and ask, 'Do I really want to spend the rest of my life with you?' We said yeah." At that point, the three siblings began a program of learning how to be owners and how business is done, with the idea that each would find a niche but one of them would emerge as the leader.

Gail continued to work as corporate secretary and got deeply involved in the Asper Foundation, the centrepiece of Izzy's wide-ranging philanthropic projects. This was no small job, because Izzy's vision is ambitious, both during and for after his lifetime. His goal has always been to grow his family foundation like the fourth Asper child, which on his death would receive at least a quarter of anything he has earned in his life. With that comes tax issues, agreements, legal stuff that Izzy felt needed an Asper touch. For Izzy, the giving is part of his identity as a human being, and he is passionate that it be done well. "I don't believe in an afterlife particularly, but I wouldn't want to be on my last legs with the prospect of feeling that my life's economic results were to be squandered. That would be an ugly picture to me and I want a pretty picture. That's what life is to me."

Leonard went from articling to working at Global Television for several years in Toronto and then moved back to Winnipeg as a vice-president. David lived a peripatetic existence, moving among jobs and going to where he was needed next—to New Zealand, to Britain, where he headed CanWest's abortive attempt to launch a Channel Five television network, and back to Regina, where he managed a CanWest television station.

David's reputation is that he is charismatic, emotional, immensely likeable, but a bit of a loose cannon, a guy subject to enthusiasms, a personality of extremes. One friend of David's says there is a tendency to dismiss him, but in fact he is quite smart, just restless. Like Izzy, he continually battles a smoking habit. His weight balloons and contracts almost at random. While Leonard takes the broad strategic view, David sees himself as passionate about operations, about getting his hands dirty with details. He likes to talk about the time he worked in Regina, where amid some very tough cost-cutting and layoffs, he tried to present himself as a hands-on, anti-hierarchical boss. "I showed up on day one on a Harley, and, you know, I walk into the place and they've been all corralled. I say 'Throw the gates open.' I say, 'Open the gates, everybody, and run free,' and we'd have Bible-thumping revival meetings in the studio and I'd go wild about competitiveness."

Izzy says he would have been happy with David and Leonard serving as co-CEOs but the children decided Leonard had the temperament and desire to be president and CEO. David, meanwhile, was the project guy, with a shorter attention span, who loved going off and focusing on something like the Milgaard case or the application for a TV licence in Britain.

Gail eliminated herself from the CEO stakes right from the beginning. She had done some work-related travelling and had seen the toll of business on family life. She now had two young sons and a yearning for a more normal existence. "I didn't want to be on the roller-coaster my brothers were on. I wanted to be on the carrousel, the steady ride." She jokes that her most important duty is contribute doughnuts every Thursday in CanWest's small Winnipeg corporate office. "One of my strengths is the Timbits." In fact, a former CanWest executive says Gail is the rock of the group, the one child who can stand up to Izzy, get him to behave and look after his health. Gail was partly drawn back to the company because she feared for her father's health if he did not have someone close to rely on.

Leonard, meanwhile, had all the training, plus a hunger for the big job. "It became clear that the kind of person who would have to lead CanWest is a person with that kind of corporate skill, a sort of natural inclination," David explains. "You have to feel comfortable in your own skin. I don't remember when we all sat around and said, 'Okay, Len's got to do it.'" But there were individual conversations that led to that conclusion. "It wasn't really much of a debate. It was more of 'Here you go, Len, here you go! Hey buddy, see you later.'"

The succession was established when Izzy stepped aside as president and CEO in 1998 to make way for Peter Viner, a respected veteran executive, who had joined Global even before CanWest owned it and was brought home from New Zealand to take the job. It was understood that this was a transitional appointment, and that Viner, whose brother Tony ran Rogers Media, would serve while Leonard was preparing for the job. But Izzy moved faster than expected, putting Leonard in the president's job in 1999, at the age of only thirty-five.

When CanWest applied for an Alberta licence in 1998, Drew Craig, who headed his own family's rival bid, had a front-row seat on the succession. CRTC hearings are often very ritualistic events, where the applying companies bring phalanxes of executives to the meeting in shows of force. The most important executives sit in the front row of the panel, close to the boss, the lesser lights in the rear row or in the first row of the audience. At the start of the hearing, Craig noticed, Leonard and David were in the back row, but at the end, they had moved into the front row. "Izzy had the boys up front, as if to say, 'Here are my guys, this is my team, this is the future.' They were getting their feet wet." If there was any doubt Leonard was the successor, it was eliminated during the WIC transaction, when he was Izzy's designated hitter in the tough negotiations.

David still likes to lead, but more from inside the company—and that's reflected in his controversial role as chairman of the Southam newspapers' publications committee, leading the charge on editorial issues. "I'm a shit disturber and I'm a bit of a dreamer and I probably focus too much. Whether it's a corporate issue or a corporate decision to be made, I'm thinking about how big a crew I'll need to do it. My mindset is operational." Meanwhile, Leonard has a feel for the corporate world, says David. "He moves smoothly in it, he speaks well, he knows the language, like the technical language, he took business courses which I never did. He's like Izzy, he really understands the technicality of corporate finance, and of legal relationships."

Besides, Leonard says he always wanted to do the CEO thing. "I've been quite consistent about that for ten years. If I wasn't doing it I would have started my own business and run that. David's role is more direct and hands-on and he's got a flair for it and he's good at all that stuff, at marketing. He's very populist in his approach to the world." It is that kind of non-elitist approach that, according to Leonard, is going to work for the Aspers in newspapers, just as it has worked in television. Leonard believes that CanWest and Southam can create the newspaper equivalent of what Fox TV has done with its television programming. It may be the dumbing-down of television, Leonard admits, but it is successful and it gets people talking. "Most people find Bart Simpson funny. He's not Masterpiece Theatre, but if you took the bell curve of people, that's where everybody is." The Aspers want to replicate in all their newspapers what Fox TV and the *National Post* are doing: not too high-brow, lots of sass and opinion, the ability to create hot public issues and ride them hard.

While the family line is that the two Asper brothers work happily together, there is clearly competition to get Dad's approval. While Leonard runs the company, David has worked hard on the community side, as the advocate for Winnipeg and the West. He is active with the Blue Bombers, and he was on the board of the Winnipeg Folk Festival, where he orchestrated a turnaround in the non-profit event's finances.

Some Asper watchers say he knows playing the local card is one sure way to get into Izzy's good graces. He is the one who most pushes Winnipeg over Toronto, and that is always popular with his father, the owner.

The East-West war is one of the ongoing subplots of the CanWest story and it continues in this new generation. It goes back to the Slaight era, when Izzy deposed the Eastern cabal, and to the Morton-Epstein period, when Izzy battled his Toronto partners for supremacy. The tension between head office in Winnipeg and Global Television in Toronto has continued ever since. There is always an uneasiness between holding companies and their operating subsidiaries, but in CanWest's case, it is exacerbated by geography and personality. The Winnipeg head office crowd could always win points by depicting Toronto as a den of over-spending, and there is no greater sin to Izzy than wasteful spending. "If you could Toronto-bash, that was political equity for you in Winnipeg," one former manager says.

Urged on by the head office staff, Izzy might turn down a Global TV expenditure proposal, but when the Toronto managers sat down with him face-to-face, and showed him why the expenditure made sense, Izzy might warm up and agree with it. It was even better when Izzy could visit Toronto, where he would see that the people there weren't dolts, weren't ripping him off, weren't spendthrifts. "But he very much counts people's loyalty on the basis of Winnipeg," one media executive says. "His model is Wal-Mart, because it can be run from a small community as a worldwide leader." The head office crowd, he says, "very strongly want the world to know that Winnipeg owns and runs this company."

Winnipeg may have a lot going for it as a place to live, but it is often hard to move senior television executives there. It is no longer a financial centre of much stature, and the air connections are more difficult than from Toronto. But David is at the forefront of a campaign to move more television, newspaper and convergence jobs to Winnipeg, now that the Aspers have so much job-making authority in their hands. I jokingly asked one senior executive if he'd managed to keep living in

Toronto rather than be transferred to Winnipeg. Yes, he had, but it was tough. So you talk about moving? "Every day," he said, with a comically deadpan look.

In his early forties, David Asper is now occupying positions where he can make a difference in the life of the city. "I'm not going to waste my time in this city, let this period of my life go by, without seizing the opportunity to make a change, make it better." With the takeover of Southam, he started moving positions to Winnipeg, including Murdoch Davis, the veteran journalist who became the vice-president of news. A major call centre was added in Winnipeg, and David insisted that was just the beginning. There is a master plan, he says, to move cable channels there, as well as the technical infrastructure for Global's national broadcast centre.

How long this enthusiasm for Winnipeg will last depends on how the family manages after Izzy departs from the scene. Asper watchers say that like any company founded by a hard-driving entrepreneur, CanWest will change dramatically when Izzy is not there to drive it forward. "I think the family is very torn. When Izzy goes, my sense is that the cracks will become chasms and they will become sellers," says a media executive who knows the family. David will no doubt stay in Winnipeg, but Leonard could end up in Toronto or New York, and Gail maybe on the East Coast, he says. For the Asper family, of course, those are fighting words.

In addition to pushing the cause of Winnipeg, David has led the family's controversial efforts to use their newspapers as a platform for its editorial views—while Leonard has kept largely out of the controversy. When I talked to Leonard in mid-2001, he denied that the family's ownership amounted to dangerous media concentration. There are just so many more media outlets now, plus the power of the Internet. Even within CanWest, there would be broad diversity, he insisted. All the papers had editors-in-chief who reflected local markets and local concerns. For example, the *Edmonton Journal* editor had told him that Edmonton, with its government and academic makeup, is a centre-left town, and Leonard agreed that the *Journal* would have to reflect that reality. "The key to making this work is don't destroy the brand. People read newspapers as much because newspapers agree with them—they get to have their soapbox. So you just can't mess with that."

But what about the fear that the Aspers will impose their own Liberal agenda? "This old Liberal crap is unbelievable," Leonard said bristling, adding that this view of the family went back to the early 1970s when his father was the Manitoba party leader. He said all the Aspers are "generally pretty centre people, fiscal conservative and social liberals." Indeed, David Asper said he had not voted Liberal in a long time, and from David's rhetoric, it was clear he found a lot to like in the Canadian Alliance policies. "I wouldn't be surprised to find there were some other non-Liberal votes in the family," he said. In describing the Aspers' politics, he used this example: When Paul Martin brought down his post-September 11 budget, it did not require the government going into deficit. While the Aspers found that laudable, at the same time they were asking, What occurred in that budget to make individuals freer from the weight of the state? "I think Gail might be a bit more Fabian [socialist] but Leonard and Izzy and I share that core philosophy," David said.

Interviewed in his Winnipeg office, David was bubbling with enthusiasm in his role as content guru. He had tons of ideas—such as making TV stars out of Southam newspaper reporters, and getting TV people contributing to Southam. In fact, the challenge was keeping him awake at night. "I'll look at all the content and try to maximize its use and it drives me nuts." David's role was to create a personality for the group, but without destroying the local character of the individual papers. "I'm the lava lamp guy in the group," he joked. "We now have this whole content engine. As a means to understanding how the papers work, how its content is generated and in shaping a view or editorial direction, one of us needs to be accountable for these businesses. They're important and they shape people's attitudes and perceptions and that's principally what I'm doing." He felt that the Southam organization will still be a lot of voices being heard, not just one central voice. Still, "we sort of want to start the conversation, and on a whole range of issues that you can't think of because they come up every day."

But as the Aspers started that conversation—through their allegedly hands-on approach to the papers' editorial policies—they stirred up a hornet's nest of controversy. Critics accused them of forcing their pro-Israel, pro-business and pro-Liberal views on their media outlets. Interviewed in the middle of that controversy—in January 2002—David was defiant in insisting the family was just trying to start a healthy debate. The charge that CanWest was centralizing viewpoints in its Southam papers is "one of the biggest piles of bullshit that has come out of this whole controversy." He added that CanWest would be issuing just one national editorial a week—most of the time. "That may go to three or it might be two or it might be none, depending on any given week," he said. If a local paper concluded it had some interest in commenting on an issue addressed in the CanWest editorial, it could do so. But why stifle opinions, such as by killing Stephen Kimber's column in the Halifax *Daily News*? "Sorry, but we're not going to publish opinions from people who say we're evil and bad," David said.

I asked David if I submitted a column that argued strongly that Palestinian leader Yasir Arafat is a freedom fighter, would he prevent it from being published? Probably yes, he said, "because factually and if the truth were being told, it is our view that Arafat is a terrorist, not a freedom fighter," David said. But then he added, "Now if you want to try to make the case that he is a freedom fighter, not a terrorist, we can have that debate." In the papers? "Sure, sure. We're quite happy to publish contrary points of view in a rational and accurate way and based on historical fact, but we are not going to publish uneducated rants." When I met Izzy, I also asked him if he would run the "Arafat as a freedom fighter" column. His answer: "Provided what you say is A. not propaganda; B. based on fact; and C. well reasoned, we'll run it, but we will not be a soapbox for our views or anyone else's that are contrived, that are propaganda."

Sadly, there would be more difficult times ahead in the relationship between the Aspers and the media industry, where they are now both insiders and outsiders. Yet the Aspers are not ogres—they are, in many ways, admirable owners for Canadian media—nationalistic, intellectually vibrant, lovers of the press and its rollicking give-and-take. Izzy is a man with some interesting things to say. But as Conrad Black, no shrinking violet on such matters, has pointed out, CanWest has mishandled its relations with its papers, its editors and the people who work for it. It could have avoided much of the rancor—and sparked the same debates—by submitting signed opinion pieces to its newspapers, instead of mandating unsigned editorials, Black said. The Aspers have been ham-handed, perhaps out of inexperience with the politics of newspapers or possibly from bad advice. They should have stated their intentions from the beginning and engaged in an open discussion, particularly with the people in their own newspapers. Instead, they issued edicts and editorials from on high, and when they met a negative reaction hunkered down and traded wild accusations with their critics. This botched strategy allowed their media rivals to seize the high ground on the censorship issue.

On the day of the January, 2002, annual general meeting in Vancouver, I talked a long time to Izzy Asper and Gail, Leonard and David, and they graciously, patiently, answered my questions. I got the impression that they wanted the controversy to end, they wanted to be understood, but they weren't sure how to do it while avoiding the impression of surrender. Izzy and his children, above all, are proud people and they do not surrender. At one point, Izzy realized that he hadn't made himself available to other reporters about the editorial issues. "I don't want to read a headline that says, 'Aspers duck reporters.' I'm not ducking them," he said, as he quickly left the hotel meeting room. No one would ever accuse the Aspers—father and children—of that.

Indeed, the issue refused to die, partly because the Aspers would not let it. In June, 2002, Izzy and David Asper fired Russell Mills, publisher of the *Ottawa Citizen*, over an editorial calling for the resignation of Prime Minister Chrétien. Mills said the Aspers complained that the

Citizen had failed to submit the editorial for approval to CanWest. Opposition politicians raised the spectre of direct political interference in a free press—and Mills was hailed as a martyr.

14 JR'S DYNASTY

THE FIRST TIME I SAW JIM SHAW, I WAS HAVING DINNER in the bar at Edmonton's MacDonald Hotel, a palace of an old railway hotel, perched above the North Saskatchewan River. A beefy guy with an ample gut, a tightly shaved goatee, casual dress and a prominent belt buckle, with the look of a housebroken biker sat down at the window table in front of me and ordered a drink. I kept thinking that I should know who it was—and then it dawned on me: This was Jim Shaw, the most important communications executive in Western Canada. Another man joined Shaw, and I could catch the vague drift of a conversation that was at once raucous, profane and gossipy, rising above the music and the banter of the hotel bar. The second man, a new recruit to the organization, was being guided through the inner workings of Shaw Communications—who was powerful, who was tough, whom you had to know. At one point, I could hear Jim complaining about how hard it was at the top, how he had to mediate the conflicting demands on his time and attention. His new colleague voiced his sincere sympathy: Indeed, it was tough being Jim Shaw, CEO.

Shaw had been in his CEO job for scarcely a year, and he was finding it harder than just being president. Still, he clearly loved the give and take, even if the job's demands consumed most of his waking hours. After all, he had served a long apprenticeship as he worked his way through the Shaw system under his dad. He knew what the job was all about—he had been building up to it for fifteen years. Now his father had moved off and was letting Jim run the place.

And he was pulling it off rather well, bringing what he considered a new aggressiveness to the organization. He had worked with JR on the difficult purchase of WIC, finally doing a deal with the battling Aspers; then in 2001 he had personally engineered the purchase of Moffat Communications, the Winnipeg cable and broadcasting company, in a $1.2 billion deal. He had pulled off a swap of assets with Rogers Communications that strengthened Ted Rogers's presence in Ontario and the Maritimes, while giving the Shaws control of the rich Vancouver cable market. Jim seemed to be an instinctive deal-maker like his father, although the style was less polished, more in-your-face, as if Jim were trying to tell the world, Hey, I'm not JR, I've got my own way of doing things.

The public image of Jim Shaw—and it's one he likes to cultivate—is the redneck, politically incorrect man of tell-it-like-it-is candour. "Jim does things differently, very casual, he's his own person," says the polite JR, who built his career on being disarming. There is a suspicion that beneath Jim's façade of boorish behaviour lies, well, a boor. But his defenders say it's all a ruse to deceive his rivals, that a keen, if unschooled, mind lies beneath that coarse veneer. Don't underestimate him, they say, or he'll clean your clock. "He has the outward appearance of a cowboy, but he's not a stupid hick. Boy, I tell you, he's made some sharp moves," says Allan Slaight, the owner of radio giant Standard Broadcasting. Izzy Asper sees himself as a prairie person, but in his mind, the Shaws are something more—they're Albertans, which suggests a crazier, fiercer mentality. It's easy to forget that Jim was born in Ontario and the family's Western roots are only about thirty-five years old.

The next time I saw Jim Shaw up close was about a year later, in his office at the Canadian art–filled Shaw headquarters in Calgary. On one wall, there's a Ken Danby print of a herd of pounding horses, called *Ahead of the Pace*, a gift from his mother when he became a CEO. A small model of a Harley motorcycle idles on his desk, reflecting his love of the open road. The view out the window is spectacular, mountains in the distance and the river sweeping through downtown Calgary. Jim is late for our meeting by several hours—he's been held up in Vancouver. When he gets to his office, he doesn't have much time to talk—he's flying down to

Phoenix on the Shaw jet that afternoon for a long weekend of golfing with some buddies. Jim clearly enjoys the perks of being CEO of Canada's second largest cable company.

Of course, he never worries about what people think of him—in fact, he's sure that they like "the character side of me. I'm traditionally a non-conformist, and the day I conform is the day I won't be here. I like to break the rules. I like to think about things different. My wife always says, 'You think you made the rules and you can break 'em.' I say that's the way I am, I like to push it to the end. . . . I do it in here, I like to do that. I make my own mould. You can tell me you like it or you don't."

Around Shaw Communications, most people seem to like Jim's ways, or at least that's what they tell an inquiring journalist. The management style is macho, boisterous, but the business side is very serious. The Shaws under JR and Jim are great operators, perhaps the best cable operators in Canada, maybe North America. They delegate, they give their people real responsibility. They pay attention to the consumer. And people don't leave the company. The epitome is Randy Elliott, in his mid-fifties and vice-president of technology, who started in the cable business when he was nineteen in Woodstock, Ontario, which was where he was working when JR took over that franchise. He followed JR to Edmonton in 1971 and later to Calgary, in a career that has spanned thirty-five years with the Shaw family. If you don't fit in to the Shaw culture, you might be fired, someone tells me; but if you do fit in, you'll probably stay forever.

A deep management team means Jim doesn't have to be a brain surgeon. He doesn't have to do the deep thinking. He can be Jim, the wacko public face of Shaw. Of course, he loves to shock, to zap someone with a sharp quip, such as "we really shook his peaches," the now famous line he used to pique Izzy Asper. Jim looks for killer lines like that, stuff from the movies and pop tunes that he files away in his mind as ammunition for the right moment. And sometimes he just likes to stir things up. With his rube persona as a shield, he can raise unpopular issues, particularly in the cable companies' battles with their broadcasting cousins over the content, marketing and placement of channels. Jim's outrageous comments leave people off balance and wondering, Does he mean it or is this just part of the act? There was the time, at the 2001 cable convention in Toronto, when he said that half the digital specialty channels being launched that year would fail. That comment elicited a fiery rejoinder from Michael MacMillan, head of digital and specialty broadcaster Alliance Atlantis, claiming Jim was all wet. "Jim must have been kidding," MacMillan told me a day later, struggling to contain his displeasure. Hurricane Jim also told the industry gathering that he was considering not showing PrideVision, the gay and lesbian channel, as part of the free three-month preview of digital television services, even though the CRTC had awarded it must-show status. He explained that some folks in his conservative viewing areas wouldn't cotton to having gay TV forced upon them. The industry people rolled their eyes, but some suggested Jim was simply expressing what was on a lot of people's minds. (Shaw Cable followed through with its threat by removing PrideVision from its free digital trial, until the CRTC forced the company to reverse its policy.)

Jim says he's never been sold on this convergence stuff—in fact, the Shaws could be called the anti-convergence convergence players. They are big owners of both content and carriage, the ideal combo, but they have purposely separated their cable and satellite assets from their media assets in Corus. "We don't think there's a lot of benefit to having them totally integrated, and we haven't seen anyone show us a path that says integration would be a superior way to go," Jim says, not even getting into the whole debate over whether cross-ownership should be allowed. "What Bell's doing I think is absolutely crazy"—he catches himself and says, "not crazy, but I don't think you have to have those pieces to be a leader." When they had both cable and media under one roof, he says, the Shaws felt they were jeopardizing both businesses. They were always making decisions that were compromises, that were not really best for the either the cable or the broadcasting side. These compromises were "kinda like a marriage, where you want to find a common middle. Well, here you don't want to find the common middle. You want the best for each."

During the massive takeovers in 2000, it would have been easy to get caught up in the feeding frenzy. People were always calling, trying to make deals, but the Shaws stuck to their knitting, although the knitting was getting rather large and complex. "We stayed on our focus, no newspapers, no other stuff; now just consolidate and just get it working right," Jim says. Sister Heather says the family did take a look at buying newspapers, but were concerned that the newspapers' most important brand names—mainly, the writers—were mobile assets that could easily walk out the door. That didn't seem to be the best foundation for a business.

Investors certainly like the Shaws' operating style, and while the company isn't well-known in Toronto, it's well regarded south of the border. About 60 percent of its shareholders are Americans, including Warren Buffett, the great value investor from Omaha, Nebraska. Buffet's company, Berkshire Hathaway, which has fashioned a fabulous investment track record by holding Old Economy stalwarts such as Coca-Cola and the *Washington Post*, owned about 22 million Shaw shares in March, 2002, worth about US$417 million, making Shaw the Omaha company's tenth largest holding. Jim told ROB-TV in early 2002 that he and JR had recently visited the Buffett people, who had left the impression that they "would never sell." Not that Shaw Communications is flawless—it took some heavy hits in technology investments under its Shaw Ventures arm, proving it wasn't immune to the fallout of dot-com fever. For example, in the fourth quarter of 2001, it managed to dump its shares in Vancouver's 360Networks, a notorious failure in the telecommunications business, for a total loss of $139 million. In the first half of 2002, Shaw's share price fell amid investor concern about debt, slowing Internet-subscriber growth and general uneasiness about accounting in the cable and telecom sectors.

Under Jim, the basic cable business hasn't changed a lot from JR's tenure, although the approach may be a bit more aggressive. The company isn't above running attack ads in the media, making fun of its competitors, such as Rogers and Telus, the Western telephone company, and Bell

Canada. At the 2001 annual meeting in Toronto, shareholders were treated to videos of rock bands smashing Bell ExpressVu satellite dishes instead of guitars, and shots of Jim tooling around Calgary in the role of a smirking mobster, the lead character in a TV series called *The Shawpranos.*

As power shifted from JR to Jim, the Shaws continued to display their smart operating instincts, particularly in their approach to high-speed Internet service. Like many cable operators in North America, Shaws joined up with Excite@Home, the California company that provided a network for high-speed subscribers. But while Ted Rogers was closely allied with the parent company, At Home, and its major investor, AT&T, the Shaws gradually moved away to build their own backbone network, called Big Pipe.

According to Jim, it was a seat-of-the-pants thing that he and the boys worked out on the Shaw plane one boozy day. "That's something we came up with after we'd had a couple of bottles of wine coming back after some transaction in Toronto, sitting on the plane and just talking, kind of kicking ideas around. We come up with lots of crazy ideas; some work and some don't. The big thing with us is we like to take the pieces, shake them up, throw them on the table and see how we can put them back a little bit different, a little bit better."

In no time at all, Jim and the boys were spending $50 million to build their own data centre and high-capacity network to carry bigger loads of Internet traffic. "The name of the game is high bandwidth and delivery to the home," Randy Elliott says, adding that if Shaw can do it all themselves, they can simply control their expenses better. Having their own network came in handy when Excite@Home's network began to experience serious problems in 2001, with Internet subscribers of many cable systems unable to gain access. Then the parent company declared bankruptcy and went out of the business, causing its cable-company allies to scramble for substitute service. It was a predicament that Shaw Communications was largely able to avoid.

The Shaws have also put a lot of emphasis on signing up high-speed customers—they made it a company project and have involved as many employees as they could. They called it the March for a Million campaign, and they've set aside $15 million in employee bonuses to make it work. It all happened because Jim Shaw read in the newspaper that Jean Monty was planning to double Sympatico's high-speed subscriber base in a year. Jim started asking how much it would cost for his company to get to a million subscribers, starting from 300,000. "That's a Shaw-type thing that no one else would do," Jim snorts. By April, 2002, they had taken the total to more than 700,000 high-speed subscribers.

The Shaw campaign was also hurting its regional phone company competitor, Telus, in terms of high-speed Internet subscribers. In an interview in late 2001, Telus president Darren Entwistle conceded that his competitor's agility was bothering him mightily. "If we had to do a list of the people we would least like to compete against, the top of the list is Shaw," Entwistle told me in a moment of candour that's rare for a chief executive officer. "If you asked me to evaluate on a global basis who I think is the most formidable cable modem deployer globally, I would say Shaw. We couldn't have picked a worse competitor. They're doing very well." At the same time, Entwistle conceded that his company had frittered away a first-mover advantage in the high-speed Internet business. One of its predecessor companies, B.C. Tel, was a world leader in the ADSL technology used by telephone companies. "We made some poor choices," he said, in terms of how Telus was spending its capital. "We didn't invest in ADSL technology—we sat on our hands—we did not build robust practices for volume deployment." Entwistle outlined a list of things the company had done poorly—managing supply relationships; building call centre systems; training people. "Unfortunately now we're in a situation where we are rectifying all of those shortcomings in the midst of a furious battle—I wish we could say let's call a halt to it and lets get all these things resolved and let's go back on the battlefield. But I can't afford to do that because I'm up against one hell of a formidable opponent—and in a battle, frankly, I cannot afford to lose."

But for someone who claims to be a cable guy, it took some time for Jim Shaw to figure out what he would ever do. After private school at Shawnigan Lake on Vancouver Island, he entered the University of Calgary, but left without graduating, and went into business with a couple of friends, doing landscaping, construction, demolition, selling Christmas trees, and assorted other diversions. He was always a diamond in the rough, loud, brash and underneath it all, a basically shy person who overcompensated. At twenty-one, he and his pals pretty much drank away most of what they made. "You don't need much to survive— just some burgers and some beers," Jim recalls. After resisting the family business for a while, he figured what the hell, and at twenty-three joined JR in Edmonton. JR remembers that as soon as Jim joined the company, he was always ambitious for a better job, always agitating to move up. But working in Edmonton was claustrophobic for father and son. Says Jim, "I told him I had to get away from him. 'You're driving me crazy,' I said. I was a young guy and you can't be too close to your father—he's your friend but you can't be running over each other."

So JR sent him out to work in a suburban Victoria system the Shaws had just bought. Jim liked the area—his private school had been nearby. He started on the bottom as a cable installer, putting down wires. After a while, it became clear Jim could do the job. Then the job of manager for the system became vacant, and JR decided it was time for Jim to get serious.

One weekend, his father paid Jim a visit at his bachelor's pad, and they went to a nice restaurant nearby. Sitting around the fireplace after dinner, JR said it was time for Jim to grasp the nettle. "I told him exactly how I got started in business and the opportunities my dad gave me, and that I somehow persevered. Finally at end of the night, I said, 'You've got an opportunity here—you could become manager. And you have to tell me in the morning if it's yes or no.'" JR had a nice deep sleep in Jim's apartment, and woke up to find his son had hardly slept a wink. JR figured that was a good sign. "'So what's your answer?' I asked. 'If you say yes and you succeed, I know where you're going. If you don't succeed, I don't know where the road goes. We'll cross those bridges when they come.' So he said yes and he got the job."

But family companies are more complex than they appear. When JR called the Vancouver regional office to announce Jim's appointment, the officials there gave him a lot of grief. The message from regional office was that Jim wasn't ready yet, and besides, they had somebody else in mind for the job. "So I said we can carry this conversation on for a long time, but I'm not in the mood," JR snorted. He left no doubt about who was in charge: "I didn't start this company and work all those years not to give my family an opportunity. I'm going to invite my kids into the business in jobs that have expertise and hopefully they can do the jobs and so I guess if you're going to take this attitude, I'm telling you right now that Jim is the new manager for the system and that's it. That was the message. I can tell you this, if the owner don't invite his family in, nobody else will." JR figured the real reason for the resistance was they didn't want to have a Shaw sniffing around the B.C. operation.

Jim did well in Victoria and then moved back to Edmonton as operations manager. In no time, he was doing deals beside his father. He was heavily involved in the Maclean Hunter carve-up with Ted Rogers and became quite close to Ted, who seems to find Jim's biker pose rather endearing. There is a lot of macho kidding between the veteran and the forty-two-year-old Jim. "Jim, of course, wants to dress differently to distinguish himself from his father," Ted cracks. "I can't think of another reason he'd want to look like that."

Cable industry insiders say that Ted admires the way Jim has risen to the top and replaced his father as the key decision maker. And Jim sees Ted as a mentor, just like his father. "Him and I are very good friends. We talk quite a bit, we compete and not compete," Jim says, in a remark that while not grammatically exemplary does sum up the relationship. Still, there is a palpable tension between the two companies. While they don't compete in cable because each company enjoys a geographic monopoly, the Shaws have their Star Choice satellite system that goes up against the Rogers cable systems, and they have rival radio stations in a number of markets. But they also compete in visibility, image and performance.

And the styles are entirely different, Jim says. "I would say that the one big difference between Shaw and Rogers would be that if the Shaw group came up with a recommendation and floated it all the way up to my office to do something, we would probably do it." On the other hand, if the idea floated all the way up the Rogers organization, "I'm not sure it would go through. A lot of times you'll see them wanting to do exactly what we're doing, but because it's kinda centrally controlled, they have a lot more problems trying to deal with just everyday cable issues."

The two also indulge in a long-running series of pranks that would make twelve-year-old schoolboys seem mature. A few years back, Shaw and Rogers had a sales competition where the two management teams agreed that after the competition, they would go out for dinner and pay for each other's meal. The winning team would get to eat steak and drink fine wine, while the losing team would have beans and beer. The Shaw team won the sales competition—"hands-down," says Jim—and got to eat the steak. The Rogers managers got the beans. But that was just Chapter One. A while later, Jim Shaw gave Ted Rogers an investment tip on a stock, and the stock paid off very nicely for the Toronto entrepreneur. Jim sent Ted a note saying he now owed him a steak. "So we sent him the whole live steer," Ted cackles.

A couple of weeks later, on a winter weekday night around six o'clock, a truck pulled up at Jim's residence in Calgary's posh Mount Royal area and the truck driver unloaded a live steer on the street. Jim recalls the scene: "This thing is jumping around, and it's all white out, and this thing is gassing out the back and blowing brown stuff everywhere, and I say, 'Oh great.' These guys are honking and this thing's getting more nervous." Eventually, the truck took the poor animal away, Ted ordered it butchered and processed, and it came back to Jim Shaw packed in a freezer. But the story wasn't over. Jim got a couple of his people to find a cut-out metal bull by sculptor Joe Fafard in the style of the buffalo at the Shaw Building's entrance in Calgary. He shipped it to John Tory with instructions to put it in the middle of Ted's office. "Thing weighs a ton," Jim says. "And we sent him a little note: 'You go to Calgary to get the beef, you come to Toronto to get the bull.'"

For Jim, his true testing ground was the big deal to acquire WIC's radio, specialty TV and satellite assets, when the Shaws faced the Aspers head-on—it was a dream match. Both were Western, both combative, both in the throes of succession. In fact, there was a kind of pairing off in face-to-face negotiations, as Jim took on Leonard Asper, Izzy's chosen successor, and JR took on Izzy. But Jim says that JR was out of the country most of the time and it was left to him to do most of the dealing.

In fact, deal making is one area where Jim seems to excel, even in comparison with his shrewd father. For some time, the Shaws had owned a 10 percent interest in Moffat Communications, a Winnipeg broadcaster with a big regional cable operation. As cable assets became more valuable, Jim kept asking Randy Moffat, the controlling shareholder in Winnipeg, if he was interested in selling. Moffat's nice collection of assets included the Women's Television Network, a once-struggling specialty channel that had emerged as a prize property in the television wars. Moffat, a second-generation owner with two daughters and a son, stated publicly that he'd never sell, but Jim kept a cordial conversation going.

As the market heated up, Moffat's resistance melted. In November 2000, Jim was in Lake Tahoe and Reno, Nevada, bidding on some cable operations when the call came from Randy Moffat. After some pleasantries, Moffat informed Shaw that he was ready to sell. Jim told him he was going to Toronto the next day, but would drop down in Winnipeg on his way home to Calgary. "So we rented a hotel room, came down and spent half the afternoon yakking." Shaw told Moffat that he didn't have the Winnipeg company's financial numbers but he could give him a ballpark price. Moffat, who was fifty-seven, had already contracted TD Securities to advise him. The two parties met the following week and the deal was done. At a total cost of $1.2 billion, it brought the Shaws 320,000 subscribers, cementing its number two position among cable companies, with 27 percent of the Canadian market, right behind Rogers's 28.5 percent.

For Jim, the Moffat deal was clear evidence that he was in the right game—making deals in cable. He admits he's not the right person to run broadcasting, unlike Heather or John Cassaday: "Nah, I think I'm too much of a cable guy. I bring the right kind of skill sets to what I do here. I understand cable real well, the competing, dealing with the telcos, network type stuff—I do that real well."

But with her M.B.A. and her good education, why isn't Heather Shaw the CEO of the cable outfit? Jim says he was probably the one who wanted it most, and who worked the hardest for the job. "It's not that other family members don't work hard, 'cause they do. But if you asked my sister if she wanted to be CEO of Corus, she'd say no. If you asked me what I wanted to be, I'd say I wanted to be CEO. Everybody in our family plays different roles."

Heather, of course, took a different route to the top. She was by nature more serious than Jim, but with an ironic touch. She is also the best educated of the kids. She admits that as a youngster she felt a lot of pressure to go into the family business because her siblings weren't interested. Jim was more interested in cattle and Christmas trees in his early sow-your-wild-oats days. Then her father eased the pressure by telling her she could do whatever she wanted to do. She was welcome to join the business but she didn't have to—there was no pressure. It took a big load off her mind and, in the end, she did decide to join her father at Shaw Communications.

For undergraduate studies, she went to a small Christian college in Iowa, then finished her degree in the business program at the University of Alberta. She worked awhile for the company and went back to school to take her M.B.A. at the Richard Ivey School of Business at the University of Western Ontario. "There were all these companies from the States recruiting at the school, and someone said, 'Why would you work in your family business when there are all these opportunities?' And I'm thinking, 'Why wouldn't I? Why not create wealth for myself, my family and shareholders, rather than make a wage while creating wealth for somebody else?' To me it was a no-brainer: why would you go outside when you have all these opportunities inside?"

Was it always destined that Jim would run the cable side because of his birth order and gender? Heather says she doesn't think so. "Jim showed the aptitude and the interest and he had the opportunity," she says. I ask JR why he divided the roles the way he did and he seems baffled by the question. Jim wanted to have his father's job from the moment he joined the company, JR says. "But did you ever ask Heather whether she wanted the presidency of the cable operation?" "No, not really," he says. According to the Shaws, it was just a natural flow of events.

Jim relishes the competitive side of the business, now that Bell ExpressVu is a tough rival as a satellite operator. "We like to compete, oh yeah, oh yeah," Jim hums. But he concedes that his inclination towards outrageous statements partly reflects the boring nature of the cable business. "We need a challenge to get us going; otherwise, it's just cable TV. It's a turn 'em on, turn 'em off type of business, pretty boring stuff—here's a bunch more wire, let's wire that house, uh-huh, uh-huh." He then lapses into one of his trademark narratives of how he unleashed another great line on a Bell ExpressVu executive when the satellite company first invaded Shaw's Alberta market. The guy, Jim says, "had such a big ego." Jim describes how he and the Bell executive were participating in a panel discussion, when, "at the end they asked me what I think, and I could only think of one thing to say: 'Big hat, no cattle.' I'm telling you, we just roared him with that—he was done."

But the most fun comes in the by-play between Rogers and Shaw, the allies-enemies of the industry. In 2000, in the wake of all the big convergence deals, Rogers and Shaw did a major swap of cable systems, which allowed Shaw to take Vancouver and Rogers to take parts of Ontario and Atlantic Canada, including New Brunswick. According to insiders, there is often a debate after these swaps—quite common between these two companies—about what was actually included in the deal. Insiders say that subscriber numbers tend to be a bit overblown, and the existing owner of the system has been known to strip the operations bare.

This time, the Rogers people were incensed with what they found, or didn't find, in New Brunswick after the Shaw team had finished with the offices. So John Tory sent a sink to Peter Bissonnette, Shaw's president, with the message that since Shaw had taken everything else, it might as well have the kitchen sink too. According to Jim, "It's like the old cable thing, where we've done so many deals with those guys, they're taking everything, we're taking everything. As soon as you sell them something, you strip it clean."

Jim admits there are aspects of his job he doesn't like. Echoing his conversation in the Edmonton bar, he says it's hard to find his own space and his own identity as he contends with everyone else's demands. Still, the transition to CEO was not hard because he'd grown up with the company. The difference was that in the old days, JR would do the deal and Jim would go in afterward to clean up, including getting rid of surplus people. He tried to make the firings as clean and quick as possible—he recalls, time after time, going into a room and telling everybody that they were all sacked.

Jim gives the impression that he will not be long for this business. "Father's way is okay but not the way for me," Jim admits, adding that he won't stay in the job any longer than ten years. He feels he's done a pretty good job of managing the company to this point, but he loves motorbikes and he misses not having enough time to hit the highway. "It's not a lifetime job, plus it eats you up a bit—it just consumes you, you're working all the time. I'm just saying there is a time after that when it's my time—I want to do things, I want to travel."

He has a place in the mountains, just a short hop away with the plane; he used to own a place in Phoenix, and would like to buy another one. "But that's only a week here and there. I'll go to France, read books and drink wine and eat cheese for a year. I could probably get my fill after a year." He has three young children, and it's not important to him that they eventually become part of the business. Besides, the company is getting too big now to depend on family management.

Heather Shaw believes her family has been spared the infighting that often goes on when strong-willed children compete for leadership in their generation. "The danger period in the third generation has passed for us. That's the point at which the companies and/or the families fall apart. We've got two great companies—and Jim's taking care of Shaw Communications, Brad's focusing on satellites, Julie's handling all the architectural needs, and I'm involved in Corus. Usually people fight over control, but here, there's lots to go around."

JR Shaw, who has become chairman of the big oil company Suncor, seems to have his estate planning in place. But that probably wasn't the only reason for splitting the cable and media companies. Industry speculation is that if the rules are changed to allow higher foreign ownership of cable companies, an opportunistic U.S. player, perhaps John Malone, would take a much bigger stake in Shaw Communications, and possibly buy out the Shaws entirely. That suspicion is reinforced by the sense that JR, Jim and Heather Shaw are above all pragmatists. They love the business, but they aren't married to it. In the long run, the Shaws will likely be sellers, and they will do very well for themselves.

15 THE PERILS OF PIERRE KARL

IT'S A LOW-KEY SPEECH FOR A CEO WHO IS LAUNCHING
one the most radical experiments in Canadian communications. Pierre
Karl Péladeau's address to the Quebecor annual meeting lays out no
grand vision of convergence. It is mostly about people, the specific
people on his team. Péladeau names more than twenty-five of his key
managers, methodically describing their contributions to the audience
in the darkened ballroom of the Marriott Montréal Château
Champlain. A Toronto investment banker who has flown into
Montreal for the meeting is disappointed. He has come to hear some
flashing insight into where Pierre Karl was taking this debt-laden company. But there was nothing in the speech that the banker could sink
his teeth into.

Yet the speech does seem designed to serve a purpose—to prove that
Quebecor is something more than Pierre Karl, and that he can attract and
keep a competent management team. News reports in the early months
of 2001 have left the impression that senior managers are leaving him in
droves. With this speech, and the painstaking naming of his key managers, PKP is telling his critics, Look at all these people who are working
hard for me, who share my dream. Quebecor is not a one-man band.

PKP will argue that all the reports of mass defections from
Quebecor—and particularly from its new Vidéotron cable acquisition—
are exaggerated by his enemies. Whenever there is a takeover, he says,
people naturally leave. Beyond the defections, he insists he will be vindicated for his expensive Vidéotron takeover. But to outsiders, he appears
to be a besieged young man, lurching from one crisis to another. The
English-Canadian press is still giving him grief over the price he paid for

Vidéotron, and his apparent supine fealty to the Caisse de dépôt. The consolidated debt of Quebecor and its printing and media businesses approaches a staggering $8 billion. The advertising and printing markets are in the sewer, and Quebecor stock has tanked. Speculation persists that Rogers will eventually end up with Vidéotron, perhaps in partnership with Cogeco, the second-largest Quebec cable company. What's more, PKP has found himself in a slanging match with the well-liked Chagnon family over his sharp cutbacks of costs and staff at Vidéotron. His aides say the cable system he bought is appallingly run, with horrendous customer service. Claude Chagnon, Vidéotron's former president, gives a newspaper interview in which he says that Quebecor's management style seems to be "fire all those who have experience."

As if that's not enough, Pierre Karl has had to back down from a nasty public feud with John Weaver, the hard-nosed American who is president of the world's largest newsprint maker, Abitibi-Consolidated, also of Montreal. Quebecor had become an 11 percent shareholder in the newsprint giant, the result of a $5.8 billion deal in April 2000, in which Pierre Karl arranged the sale of Quebecor-controlled Donahue to Abitibi. The deal symbolized Pierre Karl's shift of Quebecor's focus from his father's interests in printing and forestry into the exciting world of the new media. With his debt load rising, he was anxious to unload his Abitibi holdings, but the company's stock was weak.

So Péladeau tried to orchestrate a coup that would see Abitibi president Weaver replaced by the former Donahue president Michel Desbiens, a well-regarded manager of a well-run company before the sale to Abitibi. The hope was that the stock would pop when Desbiens took control, allowing Pierre Karl to unload his Abitibi stock for a nice bundle to pay down debt. The only problem was that Weaver had his backers, too, and they felt he was coping quite well in a tough newsprint market. The other major Abitibi investors refused to join in the coup. So the stubborn Weaver stayed put. Pierre Karl eventually had to call off the anti-Weaver campaign, and in June, 2001, he sold Quebecor's Abitibi stake for about $600 million, far less than he wanted. Again, it became part of the growing public image of a man losing control over the events in his life.

Not only that, but Pierre Karl had separated from his wife, Isabelle, and was being seen in the company of Julie Snyder, the sassy, late-night Quebec television host who had taken her act on the road, making a name for herself in Paris. La Snyder had been a superstar, drawing huge nighttime audiences on TVA with her zany tactics, such as querying political officials about their sex lives. She once interviewed French actress Catherine Deneuve with a brown paper bag over her head, and she talked chanteuse Céline Dion into singing parts of the Montreal phone directory. She persuaded the mayor of Montreal to jump—clothed—into a fountain with her.

But until October, 2001, her relationship with PKP had been mainly a matter of rumour in Montreal's close-knit media world. It suddenly became a public issue when the Quebecor boss was grilled about Snyder by the tough Paul Arcand, who hosts a talk show on Quebecor's own television network, TVA. The interview, much promoted in Quebecor's converged print and broadcast media, was striking for its confrontational style. Arcand clearly perturbed PKP right off the bat by suggesting that Quebecor's debt load had grabbed him by "by the throat." Then the aggressive host observed that the Quebecor president had shown up at the gala for the Gemini awards with Snyder on his arm. A startled Pierre Karl confirmed that, yes, he and Snyder were there together. Arcand observed that there might be a conflict of interest in such a privileged relationship between a broadcast executive, such as Péladeau, and a producer, such as Snyder.

Pierre Karl was clearly working to control his emotions as he dealt with Arcand's impertinent questioning. "We should be very proud of her. She's had enormous success," the Quebecor boss observed. Arcand interrupted, asking what was the nature of his relationship with the sexy talk-show host. "She's my friend," PKP said simply, barely restraining himself. It was an extraordinary event, a talk-show commentator taking on the owner of his own network about his personal life. In addition, Arcand zeroed in on what seemed to be Pierre Karl's fatal flaw: an inability to engage, motivate and keep good people. He said Pierre Karl had a cowboy image, and that he "terrorized" employees. Pierre Karl denied the allegations.

But there are weekly reports of key executive defections from the newly acquired Vidéotron cable company and its subsidiaries. One news story in *The Globe and Mail* indicated that about a dozen former executives and employees at Vidéotron Telecom, the cable company's telephone subsidiary, had sued the company, alleging they were being fired without proper compensation. In another report, Guy Beauchamp, the former president of Vidéotron's cable operation, asserted in a lawsuit that he was dismissed unfairly on the pretext that he had made serious mistakes in his job. The same Guy Beauchamp had been a vital cog in the Vidéotron machine, and had sat in the front row with Pierre Karl at the CRTC hearings ruling on Quebecor's takeover of the cable company. He alleged he was fired shortly after he returned from an investment trip selling a Quebecor bond issue in the United States.

In Canada's small media community, reports of Pierre Karl's lack of people skills gained momentum. The president of one major company told me that Pierre Karl has one great weakness—he doesn't engender loyalty. The executive added that people will always leave when they find themselves considered extraneous to a company and its CEO. Wherever I go, Pierre Karl's enemies and friends say the same thing—often sadly, for they admire Pierre Karl's smartness and his enthusiasm. "He is bright, he is suave, but he lacks people skills," says a former Quebecor executive. "It's a shame. Books will be written about this."

As controversy swirls around Pierre Karl, I meet him late one August afternoon, in his nondescript office in the equally nondescript Vidéotron headquarters on Viger Avenue East, just north of Old Montreal. He has moved out of the Quebecor head office building on nearby rue Saint-Jacques, sending a clear signal that he is focusing on fixing problems at Vidéotron. Pierre Karl's own office is an expression of the belt-tightening mood. He has pointedly rejected the more regal quarters of Vidéotron's former chairman and founder, André Chagnon—it is being occupied by another of Péladeau's senior managers. The boss's quarters contain few trappings of his rank: There is a desk, a small meeting table and, in the corner, a television plays non-stop during the interview, its sound reduced but not entirely eliminated. Still, leadership has its perks. Halfway through the interview in this non-smoking building, Péladeau stops to ask if he can smoke and pulls a fat Cuban cigar out of a box behind his desk.

Pierre Karl seems relieved that Quebecor's latest high-level defection, former chief operating officer Monique Leroux, has actually left to take a better job at the Desjardins credit union movement, and has been kind to Quebecor in her press statements. So, I ask Pierre Karl, how does he deal with this image that he is a heartless employer? He says the image exists only because Quebecor is under the media spotlight all the time. It was the same burden his father had to bear when he had to lay people off. "I remember one famous story written in *L'actualité* ten years ago. The guy wrote that my father fired so many people that he will be able to fill the Forum," at that time the home of the National Hockey League's Montreal Canadiens. "That was ten years ago," he yells. "What can you say against that? That's a nice image—that he fired so many people that he could fill the Forum."

Yes, he says, "we have fired people in the past, we fired people recently and we will probably fire people in the future." It is part of the process of taking over troubled companies and turning them around, which was his practice in France, where he turned around Jean Didier, or in Canada, where he says he must now apply the same scalpel to a bloated, badly managed Vidéotron.

Certainly some high-profile managers have left Quebecor, but the company has a very large management corps. He says the press hasn't paid as much attention to the people who have joined the company, or have been longtime Quebecor loyalists. He points to Pierre Francoeur, the head of Sun Media, "who has been working for the company for twenty years. But that's boring. [Companies] have been bought or merged, and at the end of the day you cannot have two chiefs. When the people who are founders are gone, it is not always easy."

Pierre Karl does have one high-profile defender, and an unlikely one at that: Daniel Lamarre was one of the first defections from Vidéotron. As Quebecor was preparing to take over the Chagnon properties in 2000, he left as president of TVA to take a senior business development role at Cirque du Soleil, the renowned Montreal performance company. He insists he left not because of Pierre Karl but because Quebecor's vision was different from his own. He and the Chagnons had wanted to build TVA as an international player in broadcast and production, but that would not happen soon under Quebecor's Fortress Quebec model.

"I was André Chagnon's guy—André Chagnon was my mentor. I would have died for him. So when the deal happened, then I didn't feel as loyal or as committed because it was a new company," says Lamarre, interviewed in Cirque du Soleil's rambling new headquarters building in a field in northeast Montreal. When Guy Laliberté, the founder of the Cirque, called, he was receptive because his new job would include international business development. Lamarre feels the management turnover at Quebecor/Vidéotron has been "more a myth than reality. It's in the paper all the time—one day someone left and they made a big thing of it." He argues that what people forget is that many Quebecor executives have been with the company a long time. It is also normal when there is a takeover that the people who were there before the change of ownership would start to drift away, just as he did.

Lamarre, a short, compact man in black shirt and slacks and brown suede jacket, says his departure also reflected a change in values. "I found myself very close to the Chagnon's values; I don't find myself as close to the Péladeau values." Chagnon was project-driven, he says, as opposed to money-driven. "When you're the size that Quebecor is now, with the Caisse as shareholders, with the stock market looking over your shoulder every day, you have to think in a different way."

Still, there remains keen concern about whether Pierre Karl can attract the kind of high-powered team that will propel him towards his goals. He seems more and more isolated, trying to put out the fires all by himself. Charlie Cavell seems more distant from his old protégé, preoccupied with his printing operations. Erik Péladeau, the older brother, has taken on more of an advisory role. Erik sits on the boards of all three Quebecor companies—Quebecor, Quebecor World and Quebecor Media—and on various board committees. "I talk with him, not daily, but very often," Pierre Karl says.

Erik had been president of Quebecor's communications division in the mid-1990s, but with the purchase of Sun Media, the family members' role in the newspapers became more that of shareholders, rather than managerial. Erik was comfortable with that transition and moved out of management. "That's his nature; I've been more in operations," Pierre Karl observes. "I went to Europe, cut my teeth in the printing business in the U.S. and then my dad passed away. I was running the U.S. printing operation for a while—I did the Quebecor-World Color transactions."

PKP maintains that the overhaul of Vidéotron has been more dramatic than expected because Quebecor was unprepared for the cable company's lazy and unmotivated monopoly attitude in sales and customer service. "We'd always been in the open market, running companies that were in competition. We had bought companies that were in bad shape but we never bought a company that was a former monopoly. Finding out the attitude of a monopoly is amazing—it's an experience."

The best operators in the cable business, the Shaws, don't have this monopolistic attitude—they have been in other businesses besides cable. PKP says, "They are entrepreneurs, not only cable owners, so they're sharp. Mr. Chagnon and Vidéotron were a little bit the laugh of the industry." The Chagnons let Vidéotron spend a lot of money on new technologies that did not always pan out, Pierre Karl observes.

Vidéotron's sleepy attitude may have worked when there was no other strong competition, he suggests. But now there is a tough, well-financed, rival nipping at its heels, in the form of satellite TV, including Bell Canada's ExpressVu. Pierre Karl says he respects Jean Monty for his success in affecting a culture change at Bell, turning a historical monopoly into an effective selling organization. "He changed it and the boat was bigger than Vidéotron—that was a pretty big boat. It gives me confidence in my capacity to achieve the same objective at Vidéotron, which is a smaller boat. Once again, like convergence, it's not going to happen in a weekend, it's going to take time."

As for André Chagnon, the dignified former Vidéotron chairman doesn't want to get drawn into a debate over Pierre Karl and the cable company. He is now running the Lucie and André Chagnon Foundation, a huge $1.4 billion charitable trust that is dedicated to the prevention of illness and the war against poverty, particularly the ongoing cycle of youth poverty. The entire capital pool of the trust—the largest family foundation in Canada—has been funded by the sale of Vidéotron to Quebecor. "It's a second life for me," Chagnon says. "It's busier and more fun than ever, and I can see this potential. I have seen people crying with joy at something we did for them, and I had never seen that before." Chagnon seems saddened by the events at Vidéotron, but he insists he has put it all in the past. "I cannot pass judgment on what others are doing because I am not there anymore," he says. He seems mystified that Pierre Karl has suggested that there was a monopoly atmosphere at Vidéotron. "He did not buy a monopoly industry—it was not there at the time," Chagnon insists.

At one point, there are reports that Quebecor has been strapped for cash, that it is being forced to extend the terms by which it pays suppliers. For Pierre Karl, this speculation is the work of "Monday morning quarterbacks" who don't bother talking to the company. If Quebecor was strapped for cash, how would it have been able to do one of the largest bond issues in the United States? He lashes out against one report quoting a supplier who said Vidéotron was paying bills on a ninety-day basis, instead of the thirty days he was accustomed to. PK argued that nothing has changed in Vidéotron's payment terms. "You know, I just don't find [it] normal to pay suppliers at thirty days, but then, you know, someone complains." He insists that "there's no fucking news in it but it's on the first page of *The Globe and Mail.*"

Pierre Karl has tremendous resources to influence public opinion in French-speaking Quebec, but he insists that is the furthest thing from his mind. He was able to alleviate some concerns when Quebecor voluntarily submitted its own tough code of conduct to the CRTC, pledging editorial independence of its news organizations in television and newspapers. In fact, reporters from TVA, for example, cannot even talk about their stories to journalists from *Le Journal de Montréal.* This conjures up absurd scenarios—reporters avoiding each other on the street so they won't have to discuss what they're working on. This restriction has dismayed the other convergence players, who worry about the precedent. "I didn't like the artificial framework Quebecor agreed to do, which I think is dumb on their part," Jean Monty said. "They put themselves in a straitjacket that will not work. I don't know why they did that."

But Pierre Karl argues that as much as anything, it reflects a historical precedent. When Quebecor bought the financially troubled TQS television network in 1997, it was a rare Canadian example of a newspaper company buying a television network. At that point, the CRTC discouraged such cross-media ownership, but the regulator waived its opposition to allow the survival of TQS. As part of the quid pro quo, Quebecor was forced to introduce this tough code of conduct. And once it had made this commitment in regard to TQS—which it has since sold—it felt it had to volunteer the same conditions in seeking to acquire TVA.

This almost draconian code would seem to tie Pierre Karl's hands in any plans to create editorial convergence. However, following the Quebecor hearings on the Vidéotron takeover, the CRTC renewed CTV and Global's broadcast licences under much less restrictive conditions—it insisted on separate news structures and careful monitoring for diversity, but left open the potential for co-ordination between print and broadcast journalists. "Now we hope things will change," Pierre Karl says. "Why would there be one rule for Quebec and one rule for Canada?" Quebecor would now expect to be able to relax its restrictive separation of journalists.

Indeed, newsroom convergence would seem to be almost essential for Pierre Karl to achieve his business goals. In contrast to Izzy Asper, Pierre Karl does not see his media as a platform for opinions. In Quebec, if you want viewpoints, you read the highly regarded *Le Devoir* newspaper. The content of Quebecor Media, he says, will be straight news, which can be continually repackaged for its different outlets. "At the end of the day, if the Concorde crashes or Ariel Sharon gets shot—whatever—it is the same news. So why spend five, six or seven times for the same news when you are able are able to pay for it once and repurpose it?" *Le Journal de Montréal*, he points out, is a newspaper that doesn't have opinions. "More and more people don't need to get opinions anymore [from the media]; they have the capacity to have their own opinions. What they want is facts, as many facts as possible, from which they form their own opinions."

Although he was one of the Vidéotron defectors, Daniel Lamarre believes PKP's vision looks solid over the long term. Quebecor is in a controlled environment, well protected by language barriers, and an owner of very strong media properties. "The synergies between newspapers and broadcast are very clear—the match is so natural. If you want to control the province of Quebec, and you have TVA and the *Journal de Montréal*, you're it. In terms of the marketing approach, it's a big, big tool."

The advertising world is itself already converging, he says. "In Toronto now, four or five agencies at most control 80 to 90 percent of all ad dollars spent in Canada. If you want to face that power, you'd better be well equipped with your own bargaining power. That's what Quebecor is building here, that's what Bell is building in the rest of Canada." And it could be argued that is what CanWest is doing, too.

Lamarre believes that if PKP can succeed in Quebec—and that should be evident over the next two to four years—he will be able to do the same thing in English Canada, starting with the Sun chain as a base. (There are others who see the *Sun* papers as orphans in Quebecor and potential candidates for sale to pay down debt.) "I always call the province of Quebec a laboratory. That's why he's got the Caisse's support: the Caisse wanted to protect this market and he has benefited from it. With the support of the Caisse's deep pockets, why not push it out?"

But even though Pierre Karl now oversees one of Canada's communications giants, don't come to him looking for a Technicolor vision of the new media world. Ask him about media convergence and he describes it in simple terms—it's really about industry consolidation; the big are just getting bigger. He is reluctant to roll out a grand vision, even though Quebecor is often called the Quebec version of AOL Time Warner. If that all happens, it would be very nice, he says, but that's not what Quebecor's strategy is about, at its core. He explains it through the analogy of how his famous father built the family's large printing business: "We printed newspapers, then flyers, then magazines, then books. In the beginning, it's all printing, Now, it's all media and it's getting bigger and bigger."

When asked about Quebecor's vision for expanding beyond the province of Quebec, PKP practically squirms: "Vision is a word that makes me uncomfortable. Vision can mean a lot of things, We're more operators, nuts and bolts guys. What's the price of your ink? Why are you spending that amount of money? That's how we've been educated and that's the culture of the company. It's true that's not the BCE approach, and a lot of companies run differently. For them money is not an object, but that is not the culture of our company."

Convergence is largely about efficiencies, he says, in a message that may be directed as much to his bankers and to his investment partner, the Caisse de dépôt, as to this visiting journalist. To make his point, he often drifts back to talking about his training ground in the printing business. In the past, he would buy many printing companies and one of the benefits was that he could then buy materials in bulk for the best deal. He laughs in recalling that when he would buy a company, the top manager might say that his ink cost 20 percent more than what Quebecor paid, but, he would explain, 'My red is really red.'" Pierre Karl becomes animated, his voice rising into mock-conversation sarcasm.

"Oh, I understand, your red is really red. Okay, darling, I understand, so you just change your suppliers and you get 20 percent off your ink price, and at the end of the day, it goes on the bottom line and you have a more efficient way to run a business. And then with savings you generate, you buy other companies."

So Pierre Karl has spent more than $5.4 billion to create a content and cable empire because it is inevitable that the big will get bigger and the opportunity exists to spread costs over different media. "In printing, you have the capacity to get better financing and ink prices because you deal with the same suppliers. You buy your machines cheaper because you are buying more machines. Consolidation brings big savings."

These days, those savings apply particularly well to content, which Quebecor needs not just for television but for the Web site, Canoe, and for all those newspapers. "I need to fill the pipe with content, so instead of buying it, I am generating it. A lot of this content is coming from the media assets on which Quebecor Media is based, so I don't have to pay twice." He uses the example of astrology services, which are a common staple of both newspapers and on-line services. He already has an astrology column in *Le Journal*, so why bother to pay for nineteen more astrology services? Pierre Karl sees no discernible different in astrology gazers—they're providing an equivalent service. "I'm sure they can get really competitive," he jokes. "You can replicate this many times and you get what is called convergence. But it is more like consolidation, managing more efficiently down the road.'"

This obsession with savings may be what bankers long to hear, but detractors say it also betrays what others see as Pierre Karl's lack of vision. "He is not articulating what he wants this company to become," says one well-regarded media analyst, who watches Quebecor closely. Others argue that he is the prisoner of sudden whims, or the next bright manager he meets. He is a compulsive personality who falls in and out of love—with people, ideas and the companies he buys.

For Pierre Karl, the payoff will come in time, but it will not happen tomorrow, and he asks for patience. He recalls a recent conversation with AOL Time Warner's chief operating officer Bob Pittman in New York, when they both agreed they were facing a long process. "These are things that are built day by day, bit by bit." Pierre Karl agrees that it is only a Quebec strategy so far, but after all, his own father started small in Quebec with a weekly newspaper in 1950, long before he founded *Le Journal de Montréal*, and look at what Quebecor is today. And after all, it is his father that this is ultimately all about.

But will Pierre Karl hang in long enough to see the realization of his strategy for Quebec, let alone for the rest of the Canada? He needs a strong economy, more stringent cost-cutting and patient backers if he is to avoid selling off precious assets. In early 2002, Quebecor indicated that it may have to write down Vidéotron's assets by more than $1 billion, according to new accounting rules. It was a sign that the siege was not over for the bright, brash scion of Quebecor.

As our interview ended, Pierre Karl mentioned that he was only a few weeks away from his birthday, on October 16, which was also the anniversary of Marie Antoinette's beheading. It seemed somehow appropriate, I pointed out, because the perception was that heads were rolling at Quebecor, too. Pierre Karl roared with delight at this observation. Life was not so bad that he couldn't enjoy a joke, even at his own expense.

16 CONTENT AND DISCONTENT

DARREN ENTWISTLE AND JEAN MONTY HAD A LOT IN COMMON. Both were native Montrealers, both ran major Canadian phone companies and both had worked for Bell Canada—in fact, Monty led the holding company that controlled Bell Canada. Both were aggressive managers who, frankly, would have liked to eat each other's lunch. Both executives made big bets on the future, buying high-priced assets in the overheated telecommunications market of 2000. Like Monty, Entwistle, the president of Telus, Canada's second-largest telephone company, believed that to survive, any telecom carrier needed access to strong content properties—from news to sports to Internet games to home security systems.

But that's where the similarities ended. Jean Monty believed his company, BCE, had to actually own these content properties, and in 2000 he invested billions in TV channels and a newspaper—in addition to buying a troubled overseas telecommunications carrier called Teleglobe. Darren Entwistle, the thirty-nine-year-old president of Telus, spent billions in buying a national cellphone company, but steered away from owning content. He insisted his company didn't have the competence to manage content well. "Do I think content is important? Absolutely. Does Bell think content is important? Absolutely. It is the manifestation and execution of that belief where we differ," said Entwistle, the hard-nosed president of the telephone company for British Columbia and Alberta. "Jean Monty thinks the best way to execute on that belief is to take an ownership position. Telus thinks the best way to execute on that belief is to strike partnerships and alliances."

The ownership versus alliance debate represents a fundamental split in the Canadian communications industry: Is it better to pay large sums for these key content assets, or contract with partners? It was perhaps natural that Telus ended up on the opposite side of the business debate from BCE. Once close allies in the cozy club of Canadian phone companies, the two had become bitter rivals in the nineties, a result of clashing interests and international entanglements. Telus was one of the fascinating question marks in the great convergence wars. In British Columbia and Alberta, it had a solid business base and a cash flow that would make it a formidable foe. Based in the Vancouver suburb of Burnaby, it was the product of the 1999 merger of Western Canada's two major telephone companies, Alberta Telephone and B.C. Tel. The company served notice from the beginning that it wanted to take on Bell Canada in its own bailiwick of Eastern Canada. Indeed, Telus bought Clearnet Communications of Toronto in 2000 for more than $6 billion, which gave it a national presence in the wireless market. Then it moved into Bell Canada's Ontario and Quebec markets, offering voice and data communications to business customers. For many months, one of the most common sights on Toronto, Ottawa and Montreal streets were crews of workers laying down Telus's urban networks as part of its Eastern offensive. But as it marched into Eastern Canada, its critics said Telus seemed to have left its own Western flank exposed to an counter-attack by BCE, and to some extent Shaw Communications, a strong rival in high-speed Internet services. Also, Telus's expansion created its own headaches, including a debt that approached $9 billion. Entwistle himself was viewed by some observers as vulnerable, as he drastically cut jobs and costs.

The precocious Entwistle had become CEO in mid-2000, replacing George Petty, a U.S.-imported executive who had presided over the merger of the two provincial telephone companies, but then clashed with its board and a major U.S. investor over expansion strategy. He had sought a takeover of Clearnet, was overruled by the board and left the company. Darren Entwistle arrived to accomplish the takeover that Petty had wanted. Only thirty-eight at the time, Entwistle had lived and breathed telecommunications since he was a kid. He had worked for Bell during summers in university, and his father had been a forty-year employee of the telephone giant. He joined Bell after getting his M.B.A., moved into its international subsidiary and eventually ended up with Bell's British partner, Mercury, on a two-year secondment in corporate finance. He then switched over to Mercury's parent, Cable & Wireless, the British telecom company, where he did mergers and acquisitions and rose quickly into senior management, before coming back home to Canada.

Entwistle, reputedly a tough cookie, argued that the main reason his company would not be owning content was that it didn't want to stray beyond its "core competence." One reason was the difference in corporate culture. "Look at how many M&A actions fail and how often culture is at the root of why they fail." Entwistle believed that mixing content with a telephone company would create tremendous strains, particularly in allocating scarce capital during difficult times. If you're down to your last $100 of capital, he asked, do you invest it a new wireless technology or in maintaining your core network, which despite its low margins is still your engine of profitability? Or do you go out and get additional content by buying, for example, Alliance Atlantis, a film producer and TV broadcaster? He questioned whether you can even make good choices, given the breadth of decision making this would require. And once you bought Alliance Atlantis, could you keep the good people essential to creating that valuable content?

During an economic slowdown, it would be hard to tell the people at Bell Canada, which was still BCE's engine of profit, that they should accept more layoffs and more pain to make up for the fact that BCE is going to experience a shortfall on the content side—or in its Teleglobe network operations. "Now, I'd be one pissed-off puppy if I was a Bell Canada saying, 'All right, we're the ones delivering the results—our results are pretty damn good. Teleglobe is doing badly. Content is experiencing all kinds of problems. Why leave it to us to feel all the pain?'" He insisted he was not being critical of BCE, but that when a company stretched itself so widely, it had to expect these tensions. BCE would feel these tensions intensely, and Entwistle's comments proved prescient, even though he was not immune to the second-guessing of telecom strategies.

Entwistle acknowledged that managing alliances is hard, too, maybe as hard as buying TV channels and newspapers. The difference is that with an alliance, you aren't laying out billions of dollars. "If you spend $1 billion, you'd better damn well be sure for the sake of your shareholders you deliver return on that investment. What is your probability of success—20 percent, even one out of ten? Nine times out of ten, you fail. It's easier to extricate yourself or wind up a partnership or an alliance than it is with an equity investment."

Jean Monty, of course, had heard it all before, and he agreed that BCE would have to strike some alliances. But to create products and services for the new media, he felt he had no option but to put his money on the table and buy content players. His future competition would come from those powerful U.S. Internet players, such as AOL and Microsoft, that had in-house content development arms. In the development of new products, he believed there were always tough questions: Who is going to fund this work? Who gets the margin on any sale, or absorbs the loss—or, as they say in business, who has to take the haircut? Who puts the work on his or her balance sheet in terms of development costs? "We said to ourselves, we'll never be able to compete with AOL and Microsoft if they do it internally and we try to do it in partnership with someone else. We'll argue on margin and funding until we're blue in the face and the other guys win the market. So we concluded we had to own."

Peter Nicholson, Monty's strategy lieutenant, argued that without owning the whole process from beginning to end, BCE was doomed to failure, particularly when it was driving an uncertain process towards an equally uncertain outcome. "It was hard to see how you would take a couple of companies, neither of which controls the other, both of which have major preoccupations in their existing businesses, and get them to seriously co-operate—to get them to create something people can't clearly define."

Nicholson's view was that the new company would have to "mix and match skills from across this family in all kinds of ad hoc and exploratory ways." He couldn't imagine going to *The Globe and Mail* as a separately owned company and saying, "Well, can you spare a few bodies to kind of brainstorm with us on Thursday?" That couldn't possibly work, and even less so with an independent CTV, where it would mean tying up expensive production capital and valuable producers. But because BCE owned the whole game, it could set aside $70 million to fund new-media product development, and try to push brainstorming across the system. At least, that was the theory. "The problem in the case of this particular media/Internet convergence is we didn't have a clear picture of what the winning services or formula would be," Nicholson admitted. "Not only did we not have a clear picture, we did not have a fuzzy picture. We knew it was going to be an act of creation."

So there was no proven model for what Monty was doing, but he didn't let that bother him. In his view, there was no other choice. What would have happened if he had not made the big bet on convergence? BCE's wireless and data business would have grown nicely for a while, but after five years, the future would have been uncertain. BCE would likely end up as a small telephone carrier in a small market waiting for the foreign ownership rules to change and to be gobbled up by a big foreign company—"which is not something I like." Monty felt he had developed a strategy that would extend until 2005 and probably much longer. "We might be wrong in this, but if we are right, the horizon is so far ahead that I don't have to worry. I have to worry about the execution, not necessarily whether we have a strategy."

Jean Monty's old partner, Charles Sirois, said BCE faced an immense cultural challenge—of mixing *The Globe and Mail*, for example, with other subsidiaries to create new digital products. For Sirois, the challenge was "like putting a snake and a chihuahua in the same room and saying, 'Make kids.' I don't know if the *Globe* is like a snake and BCE Emergis is like a chihuahua," he said. "But this is exactly what is going on and the one who succeeds in doing that will be the big winner." That puts immense pressure on the man who must engineer this intricate copulation—a television programmer in his mid-forties, with a cool demeanour and flowing white tresses, by the name of Ivan Fecan.

There was no grand view of the outside world from Ivan Fecan's second-storey office in Bell Globemedia's headquarters in a Toronto suburb. The windows were built high on the wall, making it impossible to see anything but blue sky from his desk. Instead, the focus was on the twenty-five or so television images flashing from two banks of monitors on his south wall: displays of CTV, TSN, Discovery and other channels. Another big screen sat beside his desk, tuned this afternoon to reporter Andrew Bell describing the day's tanking stock markets on ROB-TV, the newest in Fecan's growing stable of television properties. It seemed appropriate that the entire design focus was on television, the small moving image. This was, after all, the office of the president of Bell Globemedia, the company that controlled CTV, *The Globe and Mail* and a raft of other media properties. He was, next to Leonard Asper, the most important media executive in the country. "I don't believe in spending a lot on offices," shrugged Fecan, whose cooped-up energy sometimes finds him slouching lopsided in his chair. "I'm pretty comfortable. I've got my monitors, my computers and all of that going."

They made an odd couple, Jean Monty and Ivan Fecan. Monty was the technocrat, a product of a Jesuit college, the University of Western Ontario and the University of Chicago. Fecan was the son of an immigrant single parent, who grew up poor in the Kensington Market area in downtown Toronto, spoke no English until he was five, who dropped out of university and went to work in TV. He was a man with an instinctive gift for programming, whose mentors were an eccentric collection of broadcasting geniuses—Margaret Lyons, the sage dragon lady of CBC radio, Moses Znaimer, the eccentric genius of CITY-TV, and Brandon Tartikoff, the brilliant late entertainment chief of NBC.

A visitor suggested that the banks of television images were a nice design touch for a broadcasting executive, but Fecan was having none of that. This was not just ornamental, he insisted. "It's amazing what you catch out of the corner of your eye." There was no doubt that he was always watching, that this was his life—that he was born to be a television executive. But now he was something more, the manager to carry BCE's dreams into the convergence age. Given his background, it was easy to question whether Fecan had the right stuff. He seemed too much the programmer, the political climber, lacking in the managerial *gravitas* to carry it off. Yet Jean Monty viewed Fecan as part of the package when he bought CTV and combined it with *The Globe and Mail* and Sympatico. "There was no question when we went after CTV that we wanted Ivan to stay from the outset," Monty said. So when BCE teamed up with the Thomson family to merge *The Globe and Mail* and CTV, Monty told the Thomsons, "We've got a good guy. We're not even going to do an analysis of whether he's the only guy; we'll bet on the horse we've got."

The job's importance matched the breadth of BCE's ambition— which was pushing not one but all the various versions of modern-day convergence. It had made a heavy investment in content through the *Globe* and CTV, from which it hoped to develop new information services to send down its connectivity pipes—the Internet, satellite and telecommunications links. That was the vertical model, and BCE was the biggest player in Canada on that side. It was also working on the horizontal model—the attempt to sell cross-media advertising packages—television, print and on-line properties—to big advertisers. That was the same game that CanWest was playing, but BCE's chief strategy officer, Peter Nicholson, saw this as "conventional convergence"—the "low-lying fruit," in his words.

Both companies also intended to "repurpose" digital content, such as news and entertainment, to send across these platforms. And, although this is a ticklish issue in the nation's newsrooms, they would like to have flexible journalists who could report across various media, when it is appropriate. There was also the traditional media cross-promotion—and anyone who read *The Globe and Mail* and saw the vibrant full-colour ads featuring veteran CTV news anchor Lloyd Robertson knew that was happening in spades. When all is said and done, this enhanced ability to promote brands and programming across different media may be the only big tangible win from convergence.

Monty insisted that Fecan was being left to run Globemedia as if it were an independent company, just like all the bosses of his other divisions. Fecan, he said, is "our media executive and he is our convergence initiative, but more on the horizontal side," he says, meaning the different platforms of print, television and the Internet. When the discussion was about the vertical play—integrating content and carriage—every unit leader got involved, including the presidents of Bell Canada and BCE Emergis.

A former senior BCE executive, who knows the company culture, said the danger lay not in giving Fecan too much authority but too little. Fecan had to drive not just the horizontal convergence but also the vertical integration with the pipes. His grasp of content that would sell, that would attract eyeballs and dollars, was what would make or break BCE's experiment. "I think Ivan should be the tail wagging the dog," the executive said. "He should be the one saying, 'Jean, you need to have this kind of high-speed access' or 'Jean, you've got to do this with ExpressVu.'" This executive was worried that the convergence game would be captured by the telecom guys, who take a very incremental approach. "It's all about capital—it's transactional, show-me-the-money," he said. But for convergence to really occur, "you have to step out of that box and say, what kind of things have to exist in order to make this market fly? What kind of customer device has to be in the home? What kind of gateway?" The telecom approach is far too slow. "But if the content guys were driving it, then you'd end up with a bit of a leap in terms of how the market will develop."

When told of this statement, Fecan, who sports a healthy ego, slipped into the teamwork lingo that befits a senior executive in a large corporation. Ideas come from everywhere, including the telecommunications people, he said. He worried that when you say the process has to be driven by this group or that group, you've already lost the game. "Once you say 'content good, techie bad,' I really believe you've lost it already."

For Fecan, the challenge of finding new convergence products was a balancing act between listening to what consumers want, and pushing out products that people haven't even dreamed of but that knock them off their feet when they hit the market. Fecan, a media junkie, was fascinated by a 1938 archival photo that showed CBC news announcers reading their reports over the air from glass booths situated in *The Globe and Mail*'s Toronto newsroom. It was a reminder of how things had come round again—today, the *Globe* newsroom has TV cameras where reporters hold forth on the day's events for CTV and ROB-TV. In many ways, Fecan concluded, convergence is not very new—it is just the technology that keeps changing. He felt the modern-day version was often made by the technicians to look more complicated than it was. History displays plenty of industrial convergence models, where two media have been brought together in new ways—from the clock-radio to television, which merged radio and motion pictures. What's different now is digitization, the revolutionary ability to move images and text around from one medium to another, to create entirely new products, and the vast potential of the Internet as a form of communication. But at this point, there is no certainty about what exactly will be embraced by the consumer. Fecan once joked to a colleague, who had just given an exhaustive analysis of the trials of getting print and broadcast people to work together, that "I know convergence will work, but I just hope it will happen in my lifetime."

Fecan is a complicated character who doesn't fit neatly into categories. Often characterized as vain and achingly ambitious, he has at the same time surrounded himself with strong, smart women, including his mother and his wife, television producer Sandra Faire. His mother, well educated in the Soviet Union, fled to Canada in the 1940s, only to find that she could not find a job commensurate with her education. She ended up cleaning houses in Toronto, and doting on Ivan, the only product of a failed marriage. He grew up cocky, attended Harbord

Collegiate, a training ground for upwardly mobile inner-city immigrant kids, but dropped out of Toronto's York University three years into a film degree and hit the road. At one point, he found himself almost broke in a small Saskatchewan town, where, as he likes to say, the next bus went to Saskatoon and the next train to Prince Albert. The train left first, and he found himself in Prince Albert, knocking on the door of the local TV station. He talked himself into a job as a producer of commercials.

In those days, all the station's commercials were on slides, and Fecan convinced the manager to move to ads with real action because there was more revenue to be made. But the station manager took him aside and said he realized Fecan was from Toronto. "You think you're hot shit," the man said, "but everybody's got something to offer, and the first thing you're going to learn is humility. And you're going to work as part of a team and if I see any attitude, you're out the next day, bang. You learn from everybody, and the second you distance yourself, you're toast."

Fecan learned to fit in, which has become another of his strengths. He moved to the CBC in Toronto, where he helped develop the long-running science radio show *Quirks and Quarks*, under the guidance of Lyons, the smart autocrat who led the public network through a radio revolution. He worked as a news director under Moses Znaimer at CITY-TV and was there in the late 1970s when Alan Waters at CHUM bought the innovative Toronto television station. He watched how Waters gave CITY financial stability but knew enough not to change or undermine the product. He saw parallels to what he has since done at Bell Globemedia, trying to accomplish things without destroying the particular flavours of *The Globe and Mail* and CTV.

By the 1980s, Fecan, the boy wonder of Canadian broadcasting, was a known commodity south of the border. He was lured to NBC by Brandon Tartikoff, a legendary TV programmer who, as head of NBC Entertainment, had helped rescue the network from some of its darkest hours. Fecan, at the tender age of thirty-three, became a producer and Tartikoff's go-between to some of his comedy programs, including *Saturday Night Live,* produced by another expatriate Canadian,

Lorne Michaels. Tartikoff taught Fecan the importance of replenishing a good product or paying the price in squandering a ratings lead. "It's not a monopoly—you've got competitors who are out there waiting for you to make a mistake. And you also have to watch them to capitalize on their mistakes."

Fecan was at NBC when it was taken over by industrial giant General Electric, which tried to bend the television network to its highly disciplined management systems. Some things worked and others didn't, and gradually, General Electric's legendary CEO, Jack Welch, realized that a TV network isn't like any other industrial business. There are, of course, parallels to an industrial conglomerate named BCE taking over CTV, but Fecan insisted, "Jean Monty is a different kind of cat—he is a conglomerate leader at the top of his game."

Through the network battles, Brandon Tartikoff survived, and that was his greatest legacy to Fecan. "Brandon was one of the most ferocious competitors around. It's a mistake to think he was a programmer—my God, the guy was like a driven baseball coach. He just was looking at his operations day and night and looking at his competitors day and night." Clearly, Fecan believed Tartikoff's intensity had rubbed off on him.

As a young broadcasting manager in Chicago, Tartikoff had fallen ill with Hodgkin's disease, which is usually fatal, but after a chemotherapy treatment, the cancer went into remission. This second chance propelled him into a fast-track career, leading him to the senior entertainment at NBC. But he got sick again in the mid-nineties and succumbed to the disease in August, 1997, after Fecan had left NBC to return to Canada. Fecan, who had stayed in touch, wrote a touching tribute in *The Globe and Mail,* describing his mentor as "the greatest television programmer of all time."

Fecan had come back to Canada to run English-language programming at the CBC, and there were victories: he created a development system that produced hit shows at the people's network. He moved up to head of arts and entertainment and to vice-president of English-language TV. But he will forever be linked to the decision to move CBC's nightly news show to nine o'clock from its ten o'clock slot in November, 1992. As viewers tried to accommodate this jarring change, the network got pummelled in the ratings, to the benefit of CTV News, led by the venerable Lloyd Robertson, a former CBC anchorman himself. Fecan's enemies dined out on the humiliation. According to a CanWest executive at the time, his network couldn't believe it when the CBC switched to nine o'clock, "We said, My God, this is like our competitor is committing harakiri." Fecan was derisively nicknamed "Mr. Nine o'clock" by Global managers, even though the idea was initiated by other executives at the network. *The National* was moved back to ten o'clock.

Fecan endured, developing an image as that rare creature—a Canadian broadcasting mogul. Along the way, he developed a friendly relationship with Doug Bassett, who, as the son and heir to John Bassett at Baton Broadcasting, was one of the warring chieftains at the CTV Network. According to *CTV*, Susan Gittins's history of the network, Doug and Susan Bassett met Ivan and Sandra Faire through the owner of a Toronto antique store. "God, darling, he loves old English furniture just like we do," Bassett told his wife as they walked to their car. "He can't be all bad." Fecan later told Gittins that the old English furniture was more Sandra's idea than his. Bassett was building up Baton, in partnership with the Eaton family, as the consolidator of CTV, and lured Fecan away from the CBC with the dream of running his own network. He joined Baton in 1994, and succeeded Bassett as president in late 1996—only the third president of Baton in its forty-year history.

CTV was a mess, as its various factions, including Baton and WIC, were bidding against each other for valuable programming. The focus of the Canadian TV industry's programming efforts are the May shopping trips to the United States, where the Canadians would buy up inventory for the fall seasons. Global had done well, picking up a lot of hit shows. Fecan says this led to the reputation that CTV was bad and Global was good, but the difficulty in landing top shows was a reflection of CTV's splintered forces and lack of concerted buying power. "In the past, when CTV was not a united company, people spent more time bidding against each other in CTV, so CanWest was able to establish six or seven years of real dominance in top-twenty shows," Fecan recalled. That became a major catalyst for the integration of all the CTV stations. "All of the owners looked and said, 'You know what, these guys are eating our lunch.' We recognized at Baton that somebody had to take it over— CanWest was running circles around us because we were bidding against each other."

Since the CTV network had become unified under Fecan, "there are some seasons we do better than CanWest and some seasons they do better than us, but I don't think anyone has a lock on top twenty anymore." Still, one investment analyst suggested that Global's approach to buying U.S. programs seemed more sensible, putting together buying teams of programmers and ad sales people who could develop an integrated approach. Besides, the analyst argued, CTV was run by programmers, and not only that, by programmers who cut their teeth at the public network, CBC.

Fecan, the artful programmer, scoffed at the criticism, pointing out that at that precise moment of the interview, CTV had more top-ten shows than Global. "I don't think Global has any system that we don't have. We do sales analysis, as well, of what we think we will make on a program." However, he argued, Global does have a structural advantage because it has acquired a group of former WIC channels, which, in addition to the Global Network, give CanWest more program capacity than CTV. That gives Global a leg up, he said, in terms of shelf space for U.S. programming. That's important when you realize that about 90 percent of new American programs fail the first year. "To some degree, if you beat those odds consistently, you are doing better than the other guy. But if the other guy has twice the number of lottery tickets, then you really have your job cut out to beat him."

But by the fateful year 2000, outside events had shaken CTV and Fecan. The Eatons, facing the collapse of their department store empire, had sold their CTV controlling interest into the market, as part of a Baton public share offering. The network had become susceptible to takeover. BCE made its $2.3 billion bid in February, 2000, and took CTV into its fold. The bid needed CRTC regulatory approval, which meant public hearings and a long ten-month wait while the network was held in trust. During that time, BCE and CTV could have contact, but BCE could not in any way influence the direction of the business. Fecan did, however, work with Monty on the deal with the Thomson family, which would bring *The Globe and Mail* under BCE's control. Asked if he considered the addition of the *Globe* as a natural fit with CTV, he laughed and said, "You just got to roll with it."

One of the Fecan team's big challenges was to get print people to work in broadcasting and vice versa. It was a tough sell because the two cultures—and newsroom routines—are so different. Part of it was simply snobbery—newspaper people saw themselves as serious journalists, distinct from what they characterized as the blond and lacquer-haired airheads of commercial television news. The television people saw newspaper reporters as plodding and hopelessly set in their ways. Similar divisions existed on the advertising side, since salespeople viewed themselves as specialists in one medium or another. Also, there was concern that the convergence giants would heap huge extra workloads on reporters in order to cut costs, although that was not the case in the early stages—except for journalists who savoured the extra media exposure. Both CanWest and Bell Globemedia responded that their aim was to do more news with expanded resources, but skepticism still abounded.

A critical test of Fecan's vision took place in May, 2001, at CRTC hearings on the renewal of both Global's and CTV's broadcasting licences. The meetings, in Hull, Quebec's cavernous Place de Portage, were pivotal, as the networks' convergence strategies clashed with the CRTC's concerns about maintaining diversity of voices. It marked a tentative move by the CRTC into regulating print media, as newspapers became integrated with their broadcast cousins. There was some concern that this was an unwelcome expansion of government regulation.

Fecan was part of the CTV panel, sitting in the front row alongside Trina McQueen, the respected president of CTV, who like Fecan had once been an executive at the CBC. Throughout the hearings, the message from CTV was clear: the fruits of convergence would be better news and more views, not fewer. There was always the implication that CTV, so crucial to Canadian programming, was now under a stable owner that could provide the necessary resources to carry out its mandates. McQueen joked that if Doug Bassett's definition of a network was a bunch of people quarrelling, CTV was still a bunch of people quarrelling, but creatively and constructively.

Fecan, who is actually quite shy, was at his cool, collected best, seemingly at ease in handling the commissioners' questions. At the breaks he would converse with his wife. The couple together were a compelling sight, flawless in their tailoring, two beautiful fair-haired people amid a sea of shabbily dressed bureaucrats and journalists. At one point, Fecan told the commission he identified strongly with the diversity issue. He never dreamed he could become a vice-president at the CBC, or president of "that WASP bastion Baton," and certainly not the position he currently occupied. He assured the panel that journalistic and editorial independence was paramount at Bell Globemedia. There would be synergies between the *Globe* and CTV newsrooms but they would stop far short of integration. Editors would consult each other, and there would be joint projects, for example, on polling.

Both CTV and Global were opposed to having a code of conduct imposed on them by the CRTC as a condition of licence renewal. In its CRTC hearings, Quebecor had volunteered a very tough newsroom code, in which journalists from their newspapers were forbidden to even communicate with their television counterparts, and vice versa. But Pierre Karl Péladeau operated in the French-language arena, where Quebecor had established overwhelming market dominance. Also, CTV officials argued that diversity among their properties came almost naturally and did not need to be imposed. The *Globe* is a newspaper of opinion; the CTV network does not have opinions. The *Globe* is upmarket and elitist; CTV is populist. Fecan at one time put the distinction this way: The *Globe* is Pusateri's—a reference to an upscale food emporium in Toronto—while CTV is more mainstream, like Loblaw's.

To head off a CRTC-imposed code, over one hectic weekend, Global and CTV drew up a common code of conduct to apply "in the context of commonly owned media." The following Monday, at the hearings, they released copies of this "statement of principles and practices." Both networks pledged to maintain news management structures for television that would be separate from their newspaper operations. The news managers of television operations would not sit on the editorial boards of any newspapers owned by the parent companies. What's more, the two organizations would have a mechanism to deal with any complaints arising from these principles, and would report to the CRTC on an annual basis.

The release of this statement set off a flurry of excitement amid the drone of humdrum testimony. Reporters scrummed the presidents of the two television networks, CTV's McQueen and Global Television's Gerry Noble, in the corridors. Peter Murdoch, a vice-president of the Communications, Energy and Paperworkers Union of Canada, dismissed the code as window dressing. Noble and McQueen, otherwise rivals, stood together, comparing notes and watching Murdoch deliver his sound bites to the scribbling reporters. At least on this issue, Canada's warring private networks could find some common ground.

But the issues would not go away: When you create media conglomerates—even in the interests of building strong Canadian players—do you snuff out diverse voices of comment and opinion? The question applies not just to cross-media ownership but to the concentrated ownership of a single medium, such as newspapers—and the Aspers would wade into that arena as well.

A couple of months later, David Colville, the acting chairman of the CRTC, would meet with a representative of AOL Time Warner, who was fascinated by this uniquely Canadian discussion of how to maintain diverse voices in a converging media. Colville explained to her that in a country the size of Canada, it is a serious issue when the biggest phone company owns the largest private television network and one of the two national newspapers; and when the second largest television network owns the other national newspaper and most of the major regional newspapers. For Colville, this would be a major test for the CRTC in the future: "It is a primary concern of the commission to ensure a diversity of voices."

Like most corporate presentations, it started off with a video full of flashy graphics accompanied by a thumping techno-beat, just the thing to evoke a cutting-edge company. But for the jaded seen-it-all-before types at *The Globe and Mail,* it seemed ludicrous. There were uplifting testimonials by CTV anchor Lloyd Robertson and *Globe* investigative editor Victor Malarek on how they collaborated on a story about Children's Aid Societies. There were sound bites by middle managers who spouted the now tired clichés about how this new media world was going to unfold. It was all about "cross-promotion," "broadband user interface" and "best of breed content." And of course, the new math: "One plus one plus one equals more than three."

The video was the rah-rah kickoff to a crucial event in the career of Ivan Fecan. He had motored downtown from his offices in the northeast Toronto suburb of Agincourt to meet with his new employees at *The Globe and Mail* and talk about Bell Globemedia in its first five months. The *Globe* culture, indeed any newspaper culture, was skeptical of hotshot television programmers-turned-media executives. Also, there had never been a warm relationship between the prickly Fecan and some of the *Globe's* entertainment writers.

Convergence was a hard sell here: Some *Globe* staffers had embraced it, appearing as talking heads on CTV and ROB-TV; others had shunned it or just laughed it off as a passing fancy. There was an entrenched newspaper culture that militated against any cheerleading. It was this cussedness, in fact, that made newspapers so effective and so compellingly readable. And all this was happening in the middle of a newspaper war, and at a time when feelings were raw because of concerns about budget cutting.

Phillip Crawley, the feisty Churchillian publisher of the *Globe*, introduced Fecan, explaining that while his boss is well-known for a glittering TV career, he was once a regular freelance contributor to the defunct *Toronto Telegram*. The *Globe* now occupied what had been the Telegram's building, until it was closed down in 1971 by John Bassett, who also owned CFTO television, which was the foundation of Baton, which took over CTV, which Fecan had been running for the past five years. It's a small world, this Canadian media world.

Fecan garnered favourable reviews for his expressed commitment to the journalistic values of the *Globe*. He explained that the boosterish video had been prepared for a management retreat a few weeks earlier at Toronto's Masonic Temple, a midtown mausoleum best known as the home of the Mike Bullard comedy show. The retreat was interrupted by a power failure that forced its managers out on the street. The event was able to resume under candlelight, which some wags suggested was appropriate: Very little light could ever be shed on the issue of convergence. For Fecan, the power outage was serendipitous: "We kind of got to know each other a little bit better, to try to understand what the opportunities are in the company."

Bell Globemedia, he explained, was a $4 billion company in its initial valuation. "We're about the same size as the CanWest group of companies, and we are about 4 percent roughly of the value of BCE, which gives you a sobering perspective as well." He took the audience through the reasons the company was put together. There was, he said, "the feeling that as isolated islands we're not going to prosper in the environment where our competitors are joining and trying to offer consumers multimedia packages and experiences." Bell Globemedia was well positioned with leading brands and a conservative balance sheet, but he also addressed the one concern on the *Globe* people's minds: He had no desire to take the paper down-market.

He explained that there are plenty of convergence opportunities in ad selling, in back office synergies, and in marshalling increased resources for doing the things that matter most. "But the biggest opportunity is digitization, which is a fancy way of saying what convergence means today." He explained that the new convergence means that "pretty much all the signals are electronic and they're all on Internet protocol of one kind or another, and that means we can move the content around, take a paragraph and move it to a cellphone, or a pager or any different kind of things." And if Bell Globemedia didn't try to exploit this opportunity, it would be an imitator and fall behind.

As an example of convergence, he mentioned that CTV had thirty-five journalists and four television stations in Northern Ontario—"and I believe *The Globe and Mail* has a grand total of zero in Northern Ontario." He suggested that the merger with CTV would mean better access to information on the ground for *The Globe and Mail* than it would otherwise have. It's a sadly ironic remark, given the fast shifting economics of the media business. Six months later, in a cost-cutting measure, CTV would cut back on its Northern Ontario operations, eliminating forty jobs and consolidating its four supper-hour news programs into one regional program based in Sudbury. This would be part of 150 job cuts nationally, none of which, the network said, were attributable to convergence.

On his day at the *Globe,* one of Fecan's biggest tests came from John Doyle, the television critic for the newspaper, who voiced the concern of many in the room that *Globe* reporters would be muzzled in their coverage of CTV, Bell Globemedia and ultimately the parent BCE—that one of the victims of convergence would be the ability to cover your own boss. Subject to editorial policies regarding fairness and accuracy, he says, Fecan said he would defend any columnist writing to express any opinion. "I guess the one thing I ask of the editorial staff is to make it entertaining," he said, and then speaking directly to Doyle, said, "You're very entertaining."

Although he couldn't dispel all the skepticism, Fecan survived his afternoon at *The Globe and Mail.* But other storm clouds were gathering. The September 11, 2001, terrorist attacks in the United States served to deepen an already serious advertising recession. Bell

Globemedia had also introduced a brace of new media services, based on subscriptions, in the fall of 2001. Some of these, such as GlobeinvestorGOLD.com, a personal finance product, seemed to find a market, but a sports service TSNMAX would be a flop. So did people really want to buy sports information that could appear suddenly on their cellphone screen? It was clear that convergence would be a hit-and-miss proposition. What's more, Jean Monty himself came under increased pressure, not so much from his investment in Bell Globemedia, but from an international subsidiary, its e-commerce unit and particularly the ill-fated Teleglobe.

Closer attention was being paid to Michael Sabia, the former civil servant with a biting, ironic sense of humour, who had become president and chief operating officer of BCE, and was Jean Monty's heir apparent. At some point, sooner or later, BCE would probably be his to command, and Monty would step back from his day-to-day duties. Sabia is the son of feminist Laura Sabia, the first president of the National Action Committee on the Status of Women, and can point to a glittering résumé. After economics training at the University of Toronto and Yale University, he had moved to Ottawa, where he rose quickly in the civil service, a path that included taking a key role in pushing through the infamous Goods and Services Tax. He served as deputy secretary of the Privy Council under Paul Tellier, and joined Tellier when he moved across to the Canadian National Railways to oversee its privatization. Sabia described himself as a "shit disturber" who was always asking questions about what was put before him. He joined BCE in 1999, rose to president and was part of the team that developed BCE's convergence strategy, although there are rumours that he was privately skeptical about the need to own all these content assets that would flow through BCE's pipes. It was felt that when he became CEO, the products of Monty's diversification would certainly undergo more rigorous financial scrutiny.

In this atmosphere, rumours were floating that Fecan might be vulnerable in his job. Asked whether he is feeling the personal stress of having so much of BCE's hopes riding on him, he admitted, "Do I worry? Yes. Am I scared? Absolutely. Totally petrified. Am I confident it is going to work brilliantly? At some point, I am. Am I confident we are going to be the ones that get there first? No, but I sure hope we are."

CONCLUSION THE LAST MOGULS

AT 8:45 A.M., JEAN CLAUDE MONTY STRIDES TO THE PODIUM and looks out at the audience of financial analysts assembled for this early-morning briefing in late April, 2002, by the senior executive team of BCE. Monty has just announced that BCE will be cutting loose Teleglobe, its troubled long-haul network subsidiary, from any further long-term funding. The move, which increases the odds of Teleglobe filing for bankruptcy, is humiliating for Monty, who bought full ownership of Teleglobe two years earlier for $7.4 billion as one of the cornerstones of his Internet and connectivity strategy. The last few weeks have been among the toughest in Monty's life, but the chief executive officer of BCE seems to be taking it in stride.

Instead of taking questions from the floor, a sombre Jean Monty, in grey suit, blue shirt and deep wine tie, announces that a new press release has just been issued. With this statement, the air seems to be sucked out of the room—something big is about to happen. Monty promptly announces that he has resigned as chairman and chief executive officer, that he will be replaced by president Michael Sabia as CEO and by board member Richard Currie as chairman. Betraying little emotion, he tells the startled analysts, gathered in a conference room at Toronto's Sheraton Centre, that "it's obvious that BCE has gone through a difficult period with Teleglobe and it is important that we turn the page in all respects."

Without a whimper, with little muss or fuss, one of Canada's most impressive executive careers comes to a screeching halt. Jean Monty, the smart, charismatic CEO of BCE, is the first of the Kings of Convergence to lose his crown. To the end, he is defiant to his critics, who say he has overreached in his ambitious diversification into media and the Internet: "A lot of people said Bell could not grow back in 1998, but it did," he points out. A lot of people said it did not have an Internet strategy, but it does now, he continues. He insists that this growth will continue, as BCE builds on its media and e-commerce strengths.

Jean Monty, normally accommodating with the press, is taking no interviews this day. As he leaves the stage at the end of the briefing, he shakes hands with a reporter, who insists on asking him one question: Did he quit or was he asked to leave? "I resigned," he says with a tight smile, and rushes out the door. "Jean did the right thing," agrees Richard Currie, the new chairman and a retired food-company executive.

The resignation is a thunderbolt that strikes Bay Street, the financial press and the various holdings and tentacles of BCE, one of Canada's largest industrial companies. The immediate reaction is that an era is over, but which era? The convergence era? The Internet era? The era of the superstar CEO? For many journalists writing for the next day's newspapers, the easy conclusion is that the end of Monty's BCE career is a repudiation of media integration. In their view, what follows will be deconvergence, an unbundling of BCE's integrated media and telecommunications complex, and a return to being just a stolid, cash-generating utility. But at the press conference that follows Monty's announcement, Sabia, the new chief executive officer, is quick to confirm that BCE still has a convergence strategy and that Bell Globemedia is still part of it. In fact, amid all the bad news about Teleglobe, BCE's media unit reports marginally improved financial performance in the first quarter of 2002. A day later, Leonard Asper would announce CanWest's financial results for its second quarter and the judgment would be the same—no dramatic breakthroughs on convergence, but no disasters either. At the same time, BCE's new chief, Sabia, does not "own" his company's convergence strategy in the same way that Jean Monty and Leonard Asper did, and will be less reluctant to discard it, if he feels that is the way to go. In the weeks to come, he would talk of returning to the basics of BCE's business.

It was not media convergence that claimed Jean Monty, even though it may yet be one of the casualties of his fall at BCE. His downfall was caused by the same factors that had destroyed many telecommunications careers in the early 2000s—he spent huge amounts on telecom network capacity at the top of the stock market, and just as the vast over-supply of fibre-optic lines in the world was becoming apparent. Teleglobe became part of the flotsam of once high-flying communications carriers who couldn't pay their bills anymore—just like Global Crossing, and 360Networks. Because a determined, single-minded Monty had made the investment, and because he had committed BCE to supporting Teleglobe's debt, he had to take the fall. Although Monty could have stumbled along in his job, making excuses, quitting seemed the honourable thing to do. To some extent, Teleglobe was part of BCE's convergence thrust—it would provide the long-haul pipes, the global connectivity, for its new-media and Internet strategy. But it was also an extension of its core telecommunications business, much more so than *The Globe and Mail* and CTV. Teleglobe was a company that BCE should have bought—but that purchase should not have happened at such an inflated price in the overheated market of early 2000. Monty also relied far too much on the acumen and friendship of Charles Sirois, who was Teleglobe's chairman, CEO and Monty's longtime ally—the two men became estranged because of the deal's outcome. That was the irony of Monty's departure: He always believed that 90 percent of business was execution, but in this case he failed miserably to execute. In the end, Jean Monty, one of Canada's smartest managers, the man who sold Nortel at its peak, looked like nothing more than a twenty-five-year-old dot-com kid, a victim of irrational exuberance and the naïve optimism that characterized the 1999–2000 stock market bubble.

As Jean Monty was falling on his sword, other convergence champions worldwide also seemed to be flirting with self-destruction. Monty's resignation came on the same day that AOL Time Warner—the product of the mega-merger that started the whole craze—announced a loss of US$54 billion, the largest quarterly shortfall in U.S. corporate history, as it continued to write down the value of its big deal in early 2000. It came at a time when the company's brain trust was deeply divided over the future of America Online, the company's slumping Internet service. Also, the affairs of Vivendi had become a French farce, with CEO Jean-Marie Messier coming under fire for dismal financial results, moving his home from Paris to New York, and diminishing the Frenchness of the media company. When Messier fired the head of Canal Plus, the French television network, the TV boss and his employees retaliated by seizing air time on the television network to state their case. Evenutally, Messier would be forced out of his job by angry shareholders, led by Canada's Bronfman family, which had sold Seagram to Vivendi in exchange for a large stake in the French media company.

Pierre Karl Péladeau was still wrestling with a staggering $8 billion debt load, created largely by his investment in cable television and the media, and the Aspers were writing down billboard assets in Australia and trying to unload non-core properties, such as their smaller Canadian papers. Remi Marcoux's GTL Transcontinental picked up some of those papers, signalling its intention to be a buyer of some assets that the Kings of Convergence were now compelled to discard. It seemed that all over the world, the Kings were slipping from their thrones. Rather than becoming William the Conqueror, they seemed like hapless King Canute, unable to turn back the waves of nationalism, dubious investment decisions and disastrous public relations.

In the wake of Jean Monty's resignation, the self-obsessed media world was rife with speculation over the future of the communications conglomerates: Would parts of Bell Globemedia be up for sale, now that a new and perhaps more skeptical management team was running BCE? Would the Thomson family, which still loved the *Globe,* take a bigger stake in Bell Globemedia, with asset prices reduced and Jean Monty gone from the scene? Ken Thomson, as he handed over the chairmanship of Thomson Corporation to his son David, insisted that wasn't contemplated although David acknowledged that it was an option. Would Rogers Communications and CanWest move closer together, along with the Shaws, to create a counterweight to BCE? Torstar's decision not to make a big convergence investment seemed vindicated, but it could still make a purchase or become part of a larger entity. Media observers talked of another round of consolidation with potential ownership changes at Astral, Alliance Atlantis, Craig and, possibly, CHUM, which may yet become part of Corus or Rogers. And Quebecor might have to sell assets to appease its creditors.

Convergence was clearly evolving in ways that seemed startling and chaotic. But should we be surprised? Unpredictability was always the most predictable part of this story. It was inevitable, from the day that Jean Monty launched his lavish $2.3 billion bid for CTV, that some or all of these great experiments in consolidation would end up in de-consolidation, that they would fall apart and re-form in different configurations. Business is always in a state of flux, merging and de-merging. One year, big sprawling companies are the thing—the next, they are breaking themselves up. In ten years, the landscape will likely look much different again.

All this upheaval would come as no surprise to David Colville, the veteran CRTC commissioner who spent a lot of time at various regulatory hearings asking the leaders of the Canadian multi-media empires to explain the benefits of their mergers. All he got was a few references to old ideas—the opportunity to do cross-promotion and maybe sell some advertising packages across several media, including newspapers and television. "But I don't see the business case—I haven't seen it yet," said Colville, a Nova Scotian whose assessments of the media landscape are as stark and true as the paintings of his famous uncle, Alex Colville.

In the CRTC hearings on BCE's purchase of the CTV network, Jean Monty told the commissioners that his company didn't want to be just a carriage player—it wanted to be a "destination company." "It isn't clear to me how the combination of being a carrier and a destination adds value from a business point of view," Colville said in his dry, laconic way. He didn't think it was clear to BCE either. Similarly, when he asked Pierre Karl Péladeau to make the business case for his Vidéotron takeover, the young Quebecor boss said he hadn't figured it out yet. Nobody had figured it out yet.

Some people thought it was unfair of Colville to grill the media barons so intensely on their business plans. After all, it was early in the game. But Colville felt it was important for the CRTC to see the potential benefits of these various versions of convergence. The Commission's challenge was to find a balance between two policy goals: to ensure a diversity of Canadian voices amid cross-media mergers, and to give these media giants the flexibility to try new things. That was difficult, he said, when the companies themselves didn't really know where the benefits were going to arise. How could the CRTC give them the flexibility to experiment if they themselves could not articulate what they hoped to achieve? For Colville, that's what made this moment in history so frustrating and fascinating: So much was riding on the choices, and yet so little was known about the outcome.

Management consultant Jonathan Goodman put it another way: there is a mystery and a reality to media convergence. Goodman, the son of a *Toronto Star* newspaperman and now managing partner for the Monitor Group in Toronto, believes that some of the reality is clear: content can be digitized; future journalists will work across various media; joint ownership of media allows extensive cross-promotion. But much of the mystery still remains: What will consumers buy, and how will advertisers use this new cross-media capability? What will people want to watch, in what form, at what cost and on what devices? The big media deals reflected different approaches to solving the mystery—and different ideas about how it all fits together.

For some players, media convergence had turned into a foolhardy financial adventure; even as a practical business model, it was a work-in-progress. Think of these companies as laboratories: Ted Rogers is working on branding and billing convergence—and, even more radical, sports convergence, based on the shaky foundation of an erratic baseball team. CanWest and Bell Globemedia are trying to educate the advertising world on cross-media buying packages. Bell Globemedia has hired a "convergence journalist" who writes stories for *The Globe and Mail* newspaper while reporting for CTV news at eleven o'clock. Newspaper companies, such as Torstar, CanWest and Quebecor, are trying to adapt to a new media world, as more classified advertising migrates to the

Internet. A new breed of versatile and photogenic multi-media journalists is starting to generate content across a range of print, Internet,
television and radio. The increasing concentration of mainstream
media will generate fiercer debate over how to ensure the diversity of
editorial voices—and the Aspers will continue to make waves, because
they feel they bring a new voice, they have the vehicles and "retreat" is
not part of Izzy Asper's vocabulary. Meanwhile, the industry awaits a
fresh generation of executives who have actually grown up in a world of
convergence. When this group emerges, things will really change.

As Monty's departure underlined, the flurry of media deal making in
2000 was symptomatic of the dot-com and telecom binge of the late
nineties. Every major convergence company would now agree that it paid
too much for the assets it bought, although they all insist they didn't see
any choice: It was a time when the properties were available, and they had
to own them. Indeed, it was a feeding frenzy, but for entrepreneurs like
Izzy Asper and JR Shaw, it is senseless to look back—they are, by nature,
forward-looking optimists. Leave it to analysts and business journalists to
debate whether these bets made any sense. Less fortunate were the
other public shareholders who came along for the roller-coaster ride.

Indeed, the four major family companies—Shaw, Rogers, CanWest
and Quebecor—have the advantage of a longer time horizon than widely
held firms like BCE. Although they are all public companies, each has a
family in charge that is looking beyond the next quarterly earnings
report. Leonard Asper, in particular, believes he has the benefit of a long
time-span to see his multi-media plan bear fruit. "We believed media was
a special business and we could build something that could perpetuate
itself in generations to come," he says. "I've got a twenty- to thirty-year
personal time horizon of running this. It's going to have to be a global
media company and my goal is to be one of the top five. I want to be
sitting on the stage with News Corp and Viacom and those other ones."
The Shaws, too, have more time, with Jim and Heather both in their
early forties. But their business style is more opportunistic, and the
Shaws could be persuaded to cash in early. The future of Rogers

Communications depends on the ability to manage a still troubling debt, and to effect a smooth transition to a new generation of owners and managers. No one will ever be as passionate, visionary or hardworking as Ted Rogers, but there are good people waiting in the wings. As for Pierre Karl Péladeau, who knows? Smart and mercurial, he is the true wild card. He could lose it all or end up owning it all.

Even though family ownership is, by nature, patient money, it is not clear what will happen to these companies as the patriarchs depart from the scene. Will their children be as eager to carry on, particularly as convergence moves on to its next phase—global ownership consolidation? Foreign ownership restrictions are under increasing pressure, from both outside and inside Canada. As foreign buyers are allowed to increase their presence, the first to go will be the Canadian cable and telephone companies, but can the content players be far behind? Foreign companies such as Comcast, Viacom and Disney will become direct owners of Canadian operations, rather than working through proxies. The implications are infinite: BCE could be sold in parts and reduced to a core telephone utility. Indeed, the future shape of BCE was one of Michael Sabia's first challenges as he tried to deal with the potential fate of the 20 percent of Bell Canada held by SBC Communications of Texas. (In the end, he announced that BCE would buy back the SBC stake for $6.3 billion, confirming his commitment to simplifying BCE's structure and business.) The Rogers group may dissolve entirely into cable, wireless and media arms; Shaw and Telus could be sold; and Quebecor/Vidéotron may be dismantled. The winners would be Canadian shareholders, including the children of the favoured families that control many of these companies, and possibly consumers, who may enjoy more choice. The losers will be anyone who cares about Canadian culture and identity. The Kings of Convergence may be the last Canadian moguls, making their way to the exit.

Jean Monty was the first big casualty of Canadian convergence, but he left his mark on the scene. Although his avowed goal was to turn BCE into a growth company, his diversification moves also could be seen as a series of bets on technology and marketplace outcomes. In his view, a company as big and important as BCE had to buy options on the future, most of which would fail, some of which might be so-so, but one or two of which might turn out spectacularly. So that was what BCE Emergis, Teleglobe and Bell Globemedia were all about? "No question, no question," Monty agreed, but he insisted that all his options were interrelated—indeed, convergent. Monty and his team had read the work of a young Toronto consultant, Michael Raynor, who argued that large diversified companies can succeed only by investing in options that reflect a range of possible futures. Raynor, a director with Deloitte Research, said that in a world that is changing quickly, large companies don't have the agility to move in tandem with change—they have to be moving ahead of change. He calls it being strategically flexible—they have to diversify in a way that anticipates change. That could also sum up what CanWest, Rogers, Shaw and Quebecor have done, as well—they have invested in options on an elusive future. Some of the options have been absurdly expensive—take Vidéotron or Teleglobe—imperilling the company's very ability to execute its strategy. Also, any holder of options has to decide when to exercise those options, when to sell them and when to let them expire. Monty failed badly on that score, and the other moguls will have to confront those challenges as well.

Convergence is a story that has run through a few introductory chapters, and has lost and gained a few characters, but the plot has yet to unfold entirely. As it does, it will be shaped by the factors of technology, strategy and ego. That potent mix was present in all my conversations with the titans of Canadian communications—and never more so than with Izzy Asper. Sitting in his home, on his black-and-white sofa, puffing on a Craven A, Izzy Asper admits his guest has a good idea for a book. From a distance, convergence does look like an ego play by people who just want to be big players. But he insists it's more than that—the strategy works on several levels. Forget about the magical New Economy for the moment. When you live in Canada, he says, you face limitations. If you are a public company generating profits and cash, you quickly face the fact that your growth horizons are constrained. "In the media business in Canada, the opportunities for growth are very rare and very limited because of complex regulatory stuff and competition law. There's a CRTC that will change direction under new leadership every few years. And we've been the beneficiary and the victim of CRTC decisions." The result is that when an opportunity for growth comes around, you want to take advantage of it. Call it convergence, if you want, or just plain opportunism.

Izzy Asper, in fact, isn't quite sure what convergence means: "I'm not hip to the thirty-year-olds' conversational lingo and the slogans I hear everywhere, the 'platforms' and 'solutions.'" At the same time, he understands the importance of size and scale: That's when you have two television stations, but you only need one receptionist instead of two. "There are specific efficiencies that convergence can create," he says. Also, when you combine television, radio and print, instead of duplicating your efforts, you can do more—you can actually create more content with the same resources.

Despite all the talk of de-convergence, crushing debt and expired options, it is clear that Izzy and the other moguls can never be entirely satisfied, at least while they are still walking the earth. But where will their ambitions lead them? In the end, they may see no choice but to succumb to the wave of globalization, as their communications empires surrender control to foreign partners or acquisitors. But some Canadian players may yet become the eaters instead of being eaten. That will depend on the political and regulatory climate, and on the drive and ego of the Kings of Convergence and their heirs. Will they be builders in this new global market, or mere caretakers? Says Izzy of his own children: "They don't look like caretakers to me, and I don't want caretakers. If they were, they'd be better off taking their chips, investing them in high-yield debentures and having boats or becoming ballet dancers." The future of convergence Canadian-style ultimately rests with these kinds of choices.

ACKNOWLEDGEMENTS

This book was truly an adventure. There were times when I wondered if it would ever get written—when the events of September 11 pre-empted my first book-writing "vacation" and pulled me back into *The Globe and Mail;* when I had the car accident coming home from a broadcasters' convention in Ottawa; when I found myself in hospital as my deadline loomed. The fact that it is now complete is a tribute to the people who helped me. It is daunting to try to acknowledge them all, but I will name a representative sample.

I must start with Mike Babad and Cathryn Motherwell, my *Report on Business* editors, and *Globe and Mail* publisher Phillip Crawley and former editor-in-chief Richard Addis, who were all extremely support-ive. The book could not have been written without Keith Damsell, the *Report on Business* media reporter and my daily sounding board. There were more targeted contributions from Sean Fine, Jacquie McNish, Bertrand Marotte, Allan Fotheringham, Sarah Scott and many others. Thanks to Dave Pyette for telling me every day, "You're a machine," and to my pod-mates—Marian Stinson, Marina Strauss, Greg Keenan and Bruce Little—for listening. I constantly mined the great reporting of Lawrence Surtees, Eric Reguly and desk neighbour John Partridge. To get my head around the big issues, I called on Richard Siklos, Brenda Dalglish and especially Bob Brehl, whose sound judgment and generous support made a huge contribution.

A lot of other people helped, including Denis Carmel, Jan Innes, Geoffrey Elliott and Bruce Leslie, Luc Lavoie, Diane Nykolyshyn and Peter Biro. I was aided immensely by conversations with Terry Kawaja, Geoffrey Sands, Peter Miller, Jonathan Goodman, Iain Grant, Richard

Stursberg, Thierry Roussin, Kevin Shea, Ron Lloyd, Bud Sherman and by the reports and commentary of Carl Bayard, Ben Dubé, Susan Reid, Stephannie Larocque and Scott Cuthbertson. I was privileged to talk at length to Louis Audet, Geoffrey Beattie, Françoise Bertrand, André Bureau and Ian Greenberg, John Cassaday, André Chagnon, David Colville, Drew Craig, Hugh Dow, Darren Entwistle, Seymour Epstein, David Galloway, Paul Godfrey, Peter Grant, Ed Jarmain, Doug Knight, Daniel Lamarre, Robert Lantos, John MacDonald, Michael MacMillan, Rémi Marcoux, John McLennan, Paul Morton, Peter Nicholson, Janice Platt, Mark Rubinstein, Juris Silkins, Charles Sirois, Allan Slaight, Jay Switzer, Tony Viner, Colin Watson and others too numerous to mention. Then there were the people who spoke off the record or without attribution, or who just met me for a cup of coffee to bounce ideas around. Thank you all very much.

Most of all, I enjoyed broad access to a fascinating group of people, the last great media moguls in Canada. Gail, Leonard, David and Izzy Asper, while they are the *Globe's* rivals in the newspaper wars, were extremely generous with their time, as were Ted Rogers, Phil Lind and John Tory Jr.; and Melinda and Edward Rogers Jr. I appreciate the hours spent talking to JR, Jim, Julie and Heather Shaw; Pierre Karl Péladeau; Ivan Fecan; Jean Monty; and Conrad Black.

My editor, Meg Taylor, was a calming, thoughtful presence; she knew what would soothe my soul in the final weeks—a copy of Lucinda Williams's *Essence.* Thanks to my wise agent, Dean Cooke, and to the intelligent guidance of Maya Mavjee, publisher of Doubleday Canada, and editor John Pearce.

Bea Riddell has been a mentor and a constant reminder of what a journalist should be. Dave Scobie and Ken Taylor are old friends who fed and housed me in Calgary. Liz, Steve, Jane, both Scotts and Doris gave freely of their love and support. Then there are those who give me strength every day—Elaine, Katie, Martha, Mom, Jayne, Gayle and Grant and their family, and, of course, Molly. It's your book too.

INDEX

Abdul, Lorraine, 57
Abitibi-Consolidated Ltd., 167, 288
ADSL (transmission format), 124, 277
advertising
   cross-media packages and, 328
   decline in after Sept. 11, 319
   limited Canadian budgets for, 251
   media and, 250–52
   news media and, 136–37
   television viewer avoidance of, 177
Agnelli family, the, 146
Air Canada Centre, 183
Alberta Telephone, 302
Aldred, Joel, 22
Alliance (films), 73, 222
Alliance Atlantis Communications Ltd., 183,
   209, 214, 219–24, 303, 326
American Telephone & Telegraph, 235
America Online. See also AOL-Time Warner,
   3, 214, 304
   as a company that controls all customer
      relations, 125
   doubtful future of, 326
Ameritech, 29
Amiel, Barbara (Mrs. Conrad Black), 44, 147
Anderson, Harry, 40
AOL-Time Warner, 123, 133, 316
   announces first large loss, 325
   merger of, 3–6, 116, 136
   sports ownerships by, 178
Arcand, Paul, interviews Pierre Karl Péladeau,
   289–90
Archambault (music stores), 169
Argus Corp., 140
Asper, Babs (Izzy's wife), 57, 61
   family life of, 255–56
Asper, David, 1, 55
   as chair of Southam newspapers, 263
   his experience before joining CanWest,
      258–59
   far flung company assignments of, 261
   personality of, 261
   pushes editorial centralization, 265–67
   his relationship to brother Leonard, 255
   as Winnipeg booster, 265
Asper, Gail, 55, 149, 255–56
   the Asper Foundation and, 260
   joins CanWest, 70–71, 257
   personality of, 261
Asper, Izzy (Israel Harold). See also the Asper
   Family, 6, 8, 19, 120, 237–38, 329
   announces purchases from Hollinger, 150, 250

appeals unfavorable CRTC ruling, 78
asserts rights to editorial control, 13
attempts to buy WIC, 78–80
   his concern for son Leonard, 254
   conversation with Ted Rogers, 245
   cross-promotions with Ted Rogers, 185
   decides to bid for all of Global TV, 70–71
   his early interest in communications, 61–62
   family life of, 255–56
   his final words on convergence, 332
   gains control of Global TV, 64
   heart attack of, 69
   his home, 53–54
   interest in the Toronto Star by, 210
   loses control of his distillery, 59
   his love of newspapers, 68, 144
   negotiates with Conrad Black re
      newspapers, 143–49
   his perceived foes, 65–66
   personality of, 54–55, 138, 141–42
   philanthropist, 260
   political career of, 59–60
   political loyalties of, 212
   potential bidder for CTV, 116
   starts new Winnipeg television station,
      62–63
   succession of, 126–27, 249–50, 254,
      261–63
   sues Robert Lantos for libel, 74
   trains in law, 58
Asper, Leon (father of Izzy), 56–58
Asper, Leonard (son of Izzy), 1, 56, 137, 142,
   145, 238, 306, 329
   advertising media and, 250–52
   announces 2002 CanWest financial status, 324
   at Global Television, 260
   his conversation with Ted Rogers, 245
   defends editorial policy of CanWest, 265–66
   his goals for CanWest, 253
   justifies costs of fighting for perceived
      rights, 75–76
   meets with JR Shaw over WIC, 79
   on Quebecor, 169
   his relationship to brother David, 255
   role in WIC division his, 262, 281
   succession and, 249
   his transition to corporate life, 257
   a typical day of, 253–55
Asper, Susan (wife of Leonard), 253
the Asper family. See also individual family
   members and CanWest Global
   Communications, 125, 316

announces intentions for the Southam
media, 150-51
attempt to buy *Winnipeg Free Press*, 138
business expertise of, 136–37
buys Southam papers, 1–2
their continuing interest in TSN, 129
at the CRTC hearings into sale of WIC, 135
decide on CanWest careers, 260
declining Australian assets of, 326
East vs. West rivalry and, 264–65
extent of media ownership by, 3
their interest in dominating advertising
media, 137, 144–45
political views of, 142, 266
pride and the, 268
secret due diligence work done by the, 148
senses of power and powerlessness in, 3
succession within, 9
The Asper Foundation, 55, 260
Asper Jewish Community Campus, 55
The Asper School of Business, 55
Assiniboine Park Winnipeg, 57
Astral Media (Montreal), 209–10, 215–16, 326
history of, 217–18
succession and, 218–19
AT&T (American Telephone & Telegraph),
6, 16, 31, 100
AT&T Canada, 31, 235, 244–45
Atkinson Charitable Foundation, 211
the Atkinson family, 210
Atlantic Satellite (ASN), 116
Atlantis (films), 73
founding of, 220
the Audet family, 38, 210
Audet, Louis, 246
Australia, 67
Asper holdings in, 76–77, 135, 250, 326
Fairfax chain of newspapers in, 141

baseball, as television content, 175
Bassett, Doug, 115, 312
Bassett, John, 115, 312, 318
the Bassett family, 20, 22, 192
Baton Broadcasting, 192–94, 312
BCE (Bell Canada Enterprises). *See also* Bell
ExpressVu; Bell Globemedia, 31, 38, 136,
145, 302
buys CTV, 181
corporate strategy of, 122
creates Bell Globemedia, 122–33
debates best ownership of "content", 123–25
distinguished from Quebecor, 297
hatred of by others, 115
history of, 99–102
importance of its CTV takeover, 118
interest in sports ownerships, 180
as monopoly, 17

partners with Lycos, 125
praised by Jean Monty, 98
printing subsidiary of, 86
its purchase of CTV and *Globe and Mail*,
98, 100
in Quebec, 159
rivals to, 155–57, 185, 187
threatened by Ted Rogers, 118
undervalued book value of, 102
willingness to overpay by, 120–21, 208
its wish to own content, 301
BCE Emergis, 122–23, 305, 308
gambles taken on, 330
B.C. Tel, 302
BCTV (British Columbia TV), 78
Beattie, Geoff, 125, 127, 131
Beaubien, Philippe de Gaspé, 28, 105, 218
Beauchamp, Guy, 290
Bell, Alexander Graham, 99
Bell, Andrew, 306
Bell Canada, 244, 301, 308
hires Monty, 104
its legacy for BCE, 97
Bell Canada Enterprises. *See* BCE
Belleville *Intelligencer* (newspaper), 135
Bell ExpressVu (satellite service), 47, 121,
156, 181, 283, 294, 308
Bell Globemedia, 7, 234, 306, 310, 315,
317, 328
code of conduct for, 316
founding of, 98, 121
gambles taken on, 330
improved 2002 financial performance of, 324
large advertising clients and, 251
rumored division of, 326
status of in 2001, 318
under Ivan Fecan, 308
Bell Mobile, 6–10, 105
the Belzberg family (Vancouver), 28, 105
Benson, Edgar, 58
Berkshire Hathaway Inc., 275
Bernstein, Ruth "Babs." *See* Asper, Babs
Bertelsmann, 5, 123, 182
Big Pipe (Shaws' network service), 276
Bilderberg conference, 146
Black, Conrad, 2–3, 7, 44, 56, 92, 125–26, 237
on the Asper editorial policy, 268
decides to sell his papers, 135–36
his assessment of Quebec's Caisse, 169–70
leaves the Australian market, 140–41
negotiates with Aspers re newspapers, 143–49
personality of, 138–42
his rescue of the London *Daily Telegraph*, 139
respect for, 151
the Blackburn family (London Ont.), 198
Blue Jays. *See* Toronto Blue Jays
Boliska, Al, 226

Bombardier, 88
Book Television, 227
Boyle, Harry, 45
Boys and Girls (television adaptation of), 221
"branding convergence". *See also* convergence,
    184–85
Brascan, 23–24
Bravo! (channel), 227
Brehl, Robert, 80
British Broadcasting Corp., 224
British Telecom, 235
Bronfman brothers, Edward & Peter, 23, 217
Brown, George, 100
Brown, Michael, 127
Brubeck, Dave, 57
Bruner, Al, 62–63
BSkyB (satellite service), 178
Buffett, Warren, 275
Buffy the Vampire Slayer, 176–77
Bullard, Mike, 318
Bureau, André, 218
Bureau, Jean, 219

Cable & Wireless (U.K. telecom), 303
cable television
    business advantages of, 155
    market size of, 157
    and ownership of television channels, 181
Cablecasting Ltd., 44
Cablevision (cable company), 178
Cain, Jackie, 54
Caisse de dépôt et placement du Québec, 82,
    288, 297
    campaigns against Rogers bid for
        Vidéotron, 165–67
    influence of, 169–70
    partners in Maxwell Graphics purchase, 87
    its role in Quebec business, 163–64
Calgary Herald (newspaper), 138
Cambridge Reporter (newspaper), 92
the Campbell family, 210
Campbell's Soup, 192
Canada Consulting Group, 213
Canada Development Corp., 61
Canada.com (internet portal), 138, 143
Canadian Alliance Party, 66
Canadian Cablesystems, 21
    Rogers' purchase of, 23–24, 44
Canadian National Railway, 320
Canadian Pacific, 31
Canadian Radio-television and
    Telecommunications Commission
    (CRTC), 45
    allows Rogers to buy Sportsnet, 183
    approves cable ownership of analog
        channels, 203
    approves WIC dispersals to Aspers and

Shaws, 80, 197
    awards PrideVision must-show status, 274
    changing nature of the, 332
    its concern to maintain diversity of views,
        314–17
    considers CanWest application for Alberta
        television station, 77–78
    considers CTV bid to increase stake in
        Netstar, 116
    considers terms to renew Global TV and
        CTV, 314–17
    considers terms of sale of Vidéotron,
        81–82
    debates cable ownerships of channels, 181,
        191
    delays issuing new television licenses in
        Alberta, 76
    denies Torstar's bid for new television
        station, 207–8
    its difficult balancing act, 327–28
    its hearings for a new Ontario television
        license, 214
    impedes Bell Canada's non-communication
        enterprises, 101
    limits Shaw's sports channel ownerships, 194
    looks for Canadian television content, 72
    Maclean Hunter hearings and the, 38
    makeup and mandate of the, 182
    print media regulation and the, 314
    Quebecor's code of conduct and, 295–96
    relaxes policy limiting local radio market
        control, 197
    resists letting cable owners buy satellite
        too, 47
    seen as impediment to progress, 65
    Unitel hearings and the, 31
Canal Famille (television channel), 216
Canal Plus (television network), 326
Canoe (web portal), 93, 159, 298
    genesis of, 161
    staff morale at, 162
Canoe.qc (French language version of
    Canoe), 163
Cantel Wireless. *See also* Rogers AT&T
    Wireless, 28, 105
    name change of, 185
"Canterbury Tale" (code name), 146
CanWest Capital, 61, 65, 68
CanWest Field (ballpark), 253
CanWest Global Communications. *See also*
    the Asper family (*and its various members*),
    1, 7, 53, 56, 185, 214, 328
    battles for ownership of WIC, 196
    its competition with BCE, 307
    controversy over editorial policy of, 2,
        267–68
    expands abroad, 76–77

future of, 329
large advertising clients and, 251
plans for expansion by, 136
potential bidder for CTV, 116, 129–30
its potential partnerships to counter BCE, 326
profits from dissention at CTV, 193
purchase of newspapers by, 131
risk taking at, 250
its vulnerability to a recession, 252
willingness to overpay by, 208
CanWest Radio NZ, 77
CanWest Ventures, 69
Capital Cable Television, 41
Capital Communications, 167
Case, Steve, 4, 214
Cassaday, John, 45, 117, 182, 282
arranges Nelvana purchase, 199–200
experience of, 192–94
joins Shaw Communications, 194–95
manages Corus from Toronto, 198
needs WIC assets at Shaw Communications, 196–97
views on Nelvana under Corus, 201
wooed by JR Shaw, 189–91
Cavell, Charles, 86–87, 91–93, 159, 293
CBC, criticized by Izzy Asper, 72
CBS television network, 252
cellular phone systems, 28–29
CFCF (Montreal), 192
CFMT (television), 23
CFRA (radio), 229
CFRB ("Canada's First Rogers Batteryless"), 18, 64, 200, 234
CFTO (television), 20, 22, 318
Chabot, Colette, 85
Chagnon, André, 88, 246, 291–94
invites Péladeau to joint business venture, 162
his proceeds from the sale of Vidéotron, 169
his reasons for selling Vidéotron, 157–58
talks with Ted Rogers, 155–57
Chagnon, Claude, 158, 288
the Chagnon family, 288
recommends acceptance of Rogers' bid, 164
Chagnon Foundation. See Lucie and André Chagnon Foundation
Chalmers, Floyd, 32
Chartrand, Luc, 87, 89
Chatelaine (magazine), 33
CHFI (FM radio), 22
Chicago Sun-Times, 136
Chicago Tribune, 5, 253
Chrétien, Jean, 103, 141, 268
conflict of interest allegations against, 2
CHRO (television), 229
CHUM (radio) Ltd., 63, 183, 209–11, 214, 224–30, 310, 326

Cirque du Soleil, 292
CITY-TV, 226–29, 306, 310
creation of, 226
Speaker's Corner and, 227
CKND (Winnipeg television station), 63, 144
Clark, Joe, 20
Classic Communications, 38
Clearnet Communications, 302
CMT (Country Music Television), 197
Cockwell, Jack, 23
Cogeco (cable company), 38, 155, 210
Vidéotrons's future and, 288
Collège Jean-de-Brébeuf, 84
Colson, Dan, 143
Colville, Alex, 51, 327
Colville, David, 202, 316
his views about convergence, 327
ComboBox (BCEs multi-media delivery device), 98
Comcast, 238, 243, 330
Comedy Network, 116
companies, family owned, 329
conflict management, the key to, 193
consolidation. See convergence
"content" (media)
as assets, 4–5
different forms of corporate access to the, 301–2
who should best own it, 123–24
convergence. See also "branding convergence"; media, Canadian holdings before convergence, 3
AOL-Time Warner as impetus for, 4–6
billing and, 328
in Canadian media, 7–11
creation of pay incentives to facilitate, 186
current prospects of, 329–32
distinguished from cross-promotion, 185
efficiencies and, 297–98
fear as one motivation for, 11
impacts of, 5–8
limited justifications for, 327
reversing of, 244
rumored end of, 324
sports and, 328
versus outsourcing, 10
as zeitgeist, 136
Conway, Geoffrey, 38
Conway, Julia. See Royer, Julia Conway
"core competence", 303
corporate alliances, difficulty of maintaining, 304
corporate culture, merger failures and, 303
Corus Entertainment, 7, 45, 51, 117, 129–30, 182, 274, 326
acquisition spree of, 199
criticism of WTN purchase by, 203
experiences harder times, 202

possible takeover of Astral Media by, 219
split off from Shaw Communications, 198
Craig, Drew (son of Stuart), 77–78, 226–27, 262
Craig, Johnny, 61
Craig, Stuart, 61–62, 76–78
Craig Broadcast Systems, 207–8, 210, 214, 227, 326
Crawley, Phillip, 318
cross-media, 150, 252, 295, 307
mergers, 118, 209, 328
ownership, 7, 22, 118, 316
cross-promotions, 4, 18, 169, 175, 180, 187, 208, 213–14, 307, 317, 327–28
distinguished from convergence, 185
Crown Trust, 140
CTV, 7–8, 131, 136, 159, 212, 295, 309–12, 327
Cassaday as president of, 189
code of conduct for, 316
"content" and, 115–16
Globe and Mail staff on, 317, 328
morale at, 192–94
new shareholders' agreement at, 193
purchased by BCE, 111
purchases TSN, 175
rivalry with Global TV, 312–13
seen as impediment to Asper success, 65, 72–73
severely pares staff in Northern Ontario, 319
specialty channels of, 250
under BCE, 305–7, 312–14
CTV (book), 312
CTV Sportsnet, 175
CUC Broadcasting Ltd., 37–38
cultural sovereignty, Canadian obsessions with, 202
Currie, Richard, becomes Chairman of BCE, 323–24
Cyr, Ray, 101, 104–5, 107, 110

Danby, Ken, 51
D'Avella, Michael, 46–47
Davey Commission (on mass media concentration), 3
Davis, Murdoch, 265
Davis, William, 240
debt (corporate), convergence and, 135
de Grandpré, Jean, 99, 101, 104, 107
Delgado, Carlos, 179
Deloitte Research, 331
Deneuve, Catherine, 289
Desbiens, Michel, 288
Desmarais, Paul, 84, 218
the Desmarais family, 159
Didier, Jean, 90, 291
Diefenbaker, John, 20, 240

digitization, advantages of, 319
Diller, Barry, 173
DiMaggio, Joe, 200
Dion, Céline, 289
Discovery Channel, 116
Disney, 5, 330
its difficulties after purchase of ABC, 201
sports ownerships by, 178
Domi, Tie, 180
Donahue (forestry corp.), 86
sale of, 167, 288
Dougherty, Kevin, 83
Dow, Hugh, 251
Doyle, John, 319
Drive-In Classics (television), 227
Duplessis, Maurice, 139

the Eaton family, 20, 22, 192, 312–13
"ebitda" accounting, 47–48
editorial diversity, debate over. *See also* CanWest, 251–52, 328
The Edmonton Journal (newspaper), 138, 265
Eldredge, Todd, 189
Electrohome, 192
Elliot, Randy, 43, 273, 276
Emerson, Garfield, 32, 241, 244
Entwistle, Darren, 277
corporate philosophy of, 301–2
early experience of, 302–3
Epstein, Seymour, 62–65, 68, 264
bids against Asper for communications assets, 69
ESPN (sports channel), 74–75
Estevez, Emilio, 178
Evans, Mark, 124
Excel Communications, 106
Excite@Home, 16, 160, 243
bankruptcy of, 276
ExpressVu. *See* Bell ExpressVu

Fafard, Joe, 51, 280
Faire, Sandra, 238, 309, 312, 315
Falcon Lake, 54, 145, 148
The Family Channel, 197, 216
Famous Players, 21
Fashion Television, 227
Fecan, Ivan, 115, 117, 159, 184, 194, 234
his accomplishments at CTV, 312
BCE's expectations of, 307–8
at the CBC, 311–12
challenges faced by, 306–9
early experience of, 309–12
kept on after BCE purchases CTV, 121, 129–30
maintains CTV's hands off in Netstar sale, 76
meets with *Globe and Mail* staff, 317–19

merging CTV and Bell Globemedia, 314–17
personality of, 306, 309
recent mood of, 320–21
film production, drawbacks of, 223
The Financial Post, 32–33, 83, 92
Fireworks (production unit), 252
First Choice (pay-TV), 217
Fisher, Larry, 259
Fisher, Roger, 193
FM radio, emergence of, 22
foreign media ownerships
effects of relaxed rules concerning, 330
lobbying for relaxed limitations on, 9, 244
significance of, 166
"Fortress Quebec", Quebecor's model of, 292
Fotheringham, Allan, 92
FP Publications, 3, 68, 144
Francis, Bob, 26
Francoeur, Pierre, 291
Fraser, Matthew, 19
freedom of the press, 1
Friends of Canadian Broadcasting, 72

Galloway, David, 151, 208
his vision for the *Toronto Star*, 212–15
Gates, Bill, 235, 239
GCT Transcontinental, 86
General Electric, 311
General Foods, 192
Gittins, Susan, 312
Global Crossing, 325
Global TV (network), 1, 6, 54, 69, 135, 159, 193, 295
court ordered auction of, 70
programming by, 67–68
its rivalry with CTV, 312–13
Global TV (station), 62–65
The Globe and Mail (newspaper), 6–8, 68, 290, 311, 328
Asper tax column in, 144
breaks story of BCE purchase, 131
its circulation war with the *National Post*, 147
as a "content" source, 119
not for sale by the Thompsons, 142
purchase of, 111, 121
ROB-TV and, 196
staff of hear Ivan Fecan's pep talk, 317–19
under BCE, 305–10
GlobeandMail.com, 132
GlobeInvestor.com, 132
GlobeinvestorGOLD.com, 320
Godfrey, Paul, 92, 174, 176
his dilemmas as Blue Jay president, 180–81
Goodman, Jonathan, 328
Goods and Services Tax, 320
Gore, Albert, 199
Graham, David, 36, 44

Graham, John Webb, 19, 231
Greenberg, Harold, 216–18
Greenberg, Ian, 215–19, 223, 228
Greenberg, Stephen, 219
the Greenberg family, 210, 217–19
Griffiths, Emily (widow of Frank), 78–79
Griffiths, Frank, 75, 78
the Griffiths family, 193
Gross, Paul, 222
Groupe Vidéotron Ltée. See Vidéotron
GST. *See* Goods and Services Tax
GTC Transcontinental (publishing), 210
Guelph *Mercury* (newspaper), 92, 209

Halifax *Daily News*, 2, 267
The Hamilton Spectator (newspaper), 92, 209
Harbord Collegiate (Toronto), 309–10
Harlequin Enterprises, 209, 213
Harrington, Richard, 127, 131
Harris, Mike, 231
Headline Sports, denied to Shaws by CRTC, 194
Hervet, Isabelle. *See* Péladeau, Isabelle (wife of Pierre Karl)
Hicks, Tom, 179
Hindmarsh, Harry, 211
the Hindmarsh family, 210
Hirsh, Michael, 199–200
Hollinger Inc, 131, 135
sells to CanWest, 150
HomeStar, 46
Hometown Television, CRTC hearings and, 214–15
Honderich, John, 210, 212
the Honderich family, 210
Horn, Alan, 184, 241
Hubbard, Gardiner Green, 100
the Hunter family, 32

Imagineering, 62
Imperial Oil, 18
index, puzzling self-reference to, 340
In Praise of Older Women (film), 222
Interbrew (Belgium), 174, 232
the Internet, potential of, 309
Internet telephony, 157, 246
Ireland, Asper holdings in, 135
the Ivey family (London, Ont.), 63
IWC Co., 63–65

Jarmain, Ed, 20–21
The Jazz Singer (film), 56
Jeffrey family, 40–41
Jerusalem Post, 136
Jolley, David, 213
Jonas, Don, 255
Jones, Khari, 255

Jordan, Michael, 178
journalism, personalization in, 17

Kawaja, Terry, 5–6
KCND (North Dakota television station),
    62–63
Kimber, Stephen, 2, 267
"Kings" of Canadian media, interpersonal
    relations among, 8
Kissinger, Henry, 146
Kitchener-Waterloo Record (newspaper), 92, 209
Klutz (books), 199
Korthals, Robin, 48
Kral, Roy, 54
Kwan, Michelle, 189

Lake of the Woods, 148
Laliberté, Guy, 292
Lamarre, Daniel, 158–59, 292, 296
Lantos, Robert, 73–75, 222–23
The Last Wedding (film), 215
Le Devoir (newspaper), 296
Le Journal de Montréal (newspaper), 84, 89,
    295–96, 299
Le Journal de Rosemont (newspaper), 84
Leroux, Monique, 291
Levin, Gerald, 165
Liberty Media Co., 46
    inspiration for forming Corus, 199
Lind, Phil, 23, 29–30, 44, 171, 232–33, 247
London Daily Telegraph, 136
Lord Martonmere, 22
The Lord of the Rings (film), 220
Lord Thomson (of Fleet), Kenneth. See also the
    Thomson family, 68, 125–26, 128, 142
    sells Globe and Mail, 131–32
    succession of, 243
Los Angeles Times, 253
Luce, Henry, 4
Lucie and André Chagnon Foundation, 294
Lycos, partners with BCE, 125
Lyons, Margaret, 306, 310
Lyric Theater, 57

M2 Universal Communications Management,
    251
Macdonald, John, 109
the Maclean family, 32
Maclean Hunter, 30, 32, 192
Maclean's (magazine), 32
MacMillan, Michael, 73, 274
    his early days at Atlantis, 220–22
    his management at Alliance-Atlantis, 222–24
Madigan, John, 146
Maguire, John, 149
Malarkey Marty, 21
Malone, John, 46, 199, 285

Manchester United (football team), 178
Maple Leaf Sports & Entertainment Ltd., 183
Marcoux, Rémi, 86, 210, 326
Martin, Paul, 266
Maxwell, Robert, 86, 165
    death of, 87
McGovern, Gordon, 192
MCI (phone company), 109
McLean, Seaton, 220, 223
McLennan, John, 109
McNish, Jacquie, 128
McQueen, Trina, 314, 316
media. See also convergence; cross-media;
    film; foreign media ownerships; news-
    papers; television
    Canadian holdings before convergence, 10
    as a commodity, 9
The Media Moguls (television show), 237
Memotec, 106
Memphremagog (lake), 105
Men With Brooms (film), 222
Mercury (U.K.), 235
Merrill Lynch Royal Securities Ltd., 104
Messier, Jean-Marie, hard times and, 326
Messier, Mark, 249
Metroland (newspaper chain), 209
Metronet, 235–36
Michaels, Lorne, 311
Microcell, 106–7
Microsoft, 235, 245, 304
Milgaard, David, 258–60
Milgaard, Joyce, 258
Milken, Michael, 28
Mill, John Stuart, 142
Miller, Gail, 258
Mills, Russell, 268–69
Moffat Communications, 203, 272, 281
    the Moffat family (Winnipeg), 63
Mohammed, Nadir, 241
MOJO Radio, 200
Monarch Life Assurance, 68
Monitor Group (Toronto), 328
monopolies
    attitudes within, 293
    dislike of, 16
Montreal Expos (baseball team), 179
Montreal Gazette (newspaper), 138
    staff's objection to editorial control of, 2
Monty, Jean Claude, 6, 8, 17, 210, 237, 246,
    294, 311
    announces end of BCE funding for
        Teleglobe, 323
    background of, 102–5
    bids for CTV, 115
    bids for Teleglobe, 121
    concerned about his reputation, 97–99
    concerned over Rogers' sports strategy, 183

corporate philosophy of, 98–99, 119,
    301–2, 304–5
creates Bell Globemedia, 121–33
criticism of, 320
customer satisfaction and, 98, 108
decides to buy media content, 111
decides to spin off Nortel, 109–10
as different from other convergence
    seekers, 118
golfer, 103
his interest in Hollinger properties, 145
mistakes made by, 325
perceived lack of public appreciation for, 97
personality of, 103, 119–20, 306
his plans to expand Sympatico's subscriber
    base, 277
resignation of, 10, 323–24
as rival of Rogers and Asper, 185
saves Nortel, 108–9
tarnished by Teleglobe's problems, 107
Monty, Jocelyne (wife of Jean), 103–4, 238
Monty, Rodolphe (brother of Jean), 104
Morrison, Ian, 72–73
Morse, Justice Peter, 69–70
Morton, Paul, 62, 65, 68–69, 264
Movie Max, 197
The Movie Network, 216
Moviepix, 216
MTV, 252
MuchLoud, 227
MuchMoreMusic, 227
MuchMusic, 43, 227
Muchnik, Paul, 257
MuchVibe, 227
multiple ownership, complications deriving
    from, 211
Murdoch, Peter, 316
Murdoch, Rupert, 5
    sports ownerships by, 178

Nadeau, Michel, 164
The National Defence College (Kingston), 104
National Geographic, 224
National Post (newspaper), 2, 7–8, 92,
    138–39, 143, 209
    its circulation war with the *Globe*, 147
NBC (television), 310–11
Nelson, Jungle Jay, 226
Nelvana (animation). *See also* Cassaday, John,
    199–201
Netstar (company), 74–76, 116
Network TEN (Australia), 77
News Corporation, 5, 123, 178, 252, 329
Newsnet, 116
newspapers
    business complexity of, 148–49
    disadvantages of owning, 275

local importance of, 137
New Zealand, 15, 261
    Asper holdings in, 76–77, 135
Nexxia, 123
Nicholson, Peter, 122, 129, 132–33, 304–5, 307
Nickelodeon, 252
Noble, Gerry, 316
Nortel, 100, 118–19
    its independence from BCE, 109
    sales made to rivals of owner Bell Canada,
        102
Northern Telecom, 100–102

The Olden Days Coat (television adaptation), 221
Onex, 68
Ontario Power Generation, 38
Orchestre Métropolitan du Grand Montréal, 83
Osborne, Ron, 32–33, 44, 109
    his career after Maclean Hunter, 38
    negotiates sale of Maclean Hunter, 35–38
The Ottawa Citizen (newspaper), 138,
    268–69
Outdoor Life Network, 116
ownership, multiple. *See* multiple ownership

Paramount Pictures, 252
Parizeau, Jacques, 166
Parrish, Wayne, 161
Paterson, Michael, 256
pay-for-view television, 179, 184, 216–17
Pay Per View Sports, 116
Peddie, Richard, 183–84
Péladeau, Anne-Marie (sister of Pierre Karl
    and Erik), 94
Péladeau, Erik (brother of Pierre Karl), 85,
    87, 239
Péladeau, Isabelle (sister of Pierre Karl), 89
Péladeau, Isabelle (wife of Pierre Karl), 94,
    289
Péladeau, Marie (daughter of Pierre Karl), 94
Péladeau, Pierre (father of Pierre Karl), 9
    business dealings of, 87–90
    death of, 91
    legacy of, 83
Péladeau, Pierre Karl, 6–8, 315, 329–30
    attempts to reform Vidéotron, 293
    his bid for Vidéotron, 87, 95
    cannot yet justify convergence moves, 327
    Canoe management by, 161–62
    in conflict with sister Anne-Marie, 94
    considers partners for Canoe, 159–60, 163
    controversy surrounding, 287–92
    exposed to a high tech world, 160
    hard times and, 326
    justifies Caisse's intervention, 167
    life of, 82–87
    personality of, 81–83, 93–95

potential bidder for CTV, 117
at Quebecor in Europe, 90
Quebecor's future and, 295–99
his relationship with his father, 88–91
rises to CEO of Quebecor, 92–93
his separation from Isabelle, 289
Vidéotron purchase by, 131, 156
The Peterborough Examiner (newspaper), 135
Petty, George, 302
Pittman, Bob, 299
Pitts, Katie, 176–77
Platt, Janice, 220–22
Pokemon, 200
Pratt, Mary, 51
Premier Cablesystems, 24
Prichard, Robert, 207–8, 213–15
PrideVision (television channel), 274
Purdy, David, 239

"Quebec Inc." *See also* "Fortress Quebec",
    88, 105, 117
Quebecor, 88, 156, 161, 326, 328
    AGM of, 287
    buys Maxwell Graphics, 87
    buys Sun Media, 91–93
    code of conduct for the CRTC and, 315
    cuts made at Canoe by, 162
    its debt load from Vidéotron purchase,
        168
    develops bid for Vidéotron, 165–66
    founding of, 84
    future of, 295, 329–30
    needs for growth at, 159–61
    the questioned assets of, 299
    sells Donahue, 167
    succession within, 9
Quebecor Media, 168, 298
Quebecor Multimedia, 160
Quebecor Printing, initial public offering of, 87
Quebecor-World Color, 93, 293
Quirks and Quarks (radio program), 310

Racicot, Michel, 102, 104
radio. *See* FM radio; Rogers Majestic; *and
    individual radio stations*
Radio Canada, 159
Radler, David, 138–39, 147, 151
Raynor, Michael, 331
Reguly, Eric, 131
Reimer, Jan, 49
Replay (video recorder), 176
Richard Ivey School of Business, 282
RNETS. *See* Rogers Network Services
Roberts, Brian, 238, 242
the Roberts family (Philadelphia), 238
Robertson, Lloyd, 308, 311, 317
ROB-TV (financial channel), 128, 306, 309

Globe and Mail staff on, 317
Rodriguez, Alex, 179
Rogers, Chloe, 243
Rogers, Edward Jr. (son of Ted), 23, 238–39,
    241–42, 245
Rogers, Edward Sr. (father of Ted), 18–19
Rogers, Lisa (daughter of Ted), 23, 239
Rogers, Loretta Anne Robinson (wife of Ted),
    22–23, 231, 237–38
Rogers, Martha (daughter of Ted), 23, 239
Rogers, Melinda (daughter of Ted), 18, 23,
    160, 238–39, 241–43
Rogers, Samuel (great-grandfather of Ted), 18
Rogers, Ted. *See also* Rogers Communications,
    6, 8, 44, 106, 125, 328
    asserts Cablevision's right to own television
        channel, 182
    bids for Maclean Hunter, 32–33, 35–38
    bids for Vidéotron, 7, 82, 95
    cellular telephony and, 28–29
    childhood of, 18–20
    his close links to At Home Co. and
        AT&T, 276
    convergence and, 183–87
    corporate goals of, 187
    his corporate philosophy, 28–31, 44
    decline in health of, 231–34
    declines early satellite options, 47
    dislike of BCE by, 118
    his dominance in Ontario markets, 272
    endurance of, 156
    enters Cable market, 20–22
    enters cell phone business, 105
    fêted, 231
    gives up on Vidéotron, 168
    his hopes for owning local telephone
        services, 246
    his interest in CHUM, 225
    his interest in health care, 244–45
    his limits for media convergence, 186–87
    management style of, 25–31, 191–92
    his payment for Sportsnet, 130
    personality of, 17–19, 173–75, 236–37
    political loyalties of, 212
    potential bidder for CTV, 117
    proceeds received from lost purchase of
        Vidéotron, 169
    profit levels of his companies, 25
    relationship to Jim Shaw of, 278–81
    regrets of, 247–48
    sports media sought by, 175–77
    succession and, 126–27, 238–44
    talks with André Chagnon, 155–57
    talks with the Shaw family, 156
    Toronto Blue Jays purchase by, 174
    Tory party affiliation and, 20
    turns his finances around, 234–36

unpopularity of, 15–17, 43
his wish to sell Sun Media, 91
Rogers, Velma (mother of Ted), 18–19
Rogers AT&T Wireless, 105, 235, 241
  branding and, 185
Rogers Cable, 244
Rogers Communications. *See also* Rogers,
  Ted, 214, 241, 272
  bids for Vidéotron, 164
  debt load of, 232
  founding of, 22–23
  future of, 329–30
  gets new Toronto television station, 207
  justifies its bid for Vidéotron, 170
  merger rumors about, 210
  potential partnerships to counter BCE, 326
  succession in, 9, 238–44
  turnover at, 232–33
  its unfortunate investment in Unitel, 232
  Vidéotron's future and, 288
Rogers Majestic (radios), 18, 234
Rogers Media, 200, 236, 262
Rogers Network Services, 235
Roth, John, 108–10
Roy, Francois, 163
Royer, Julia Conway, 38
Rubinstein, Mark, 228
Rugrats, 200
Ryerson University, 232

Sabia, Laura, 320
Sabia, Michael, 122, 320, 323–24
Sakus, Gedas, 108
Salisbury House (hamburger chain), 71
Salomon Smith Barney (bankers), 5
Salter Street Films, 224
satellite television
  future of, 293–94
  in Quebec, 157
Saturday Night Live (television show), 310
Savage, Graham, 25, 28, 233
Schreyer, Ed, 60
Schwartz, Gerald, 58, 61, 65, 140
  his interest in the *Toronto Star*, 212
  leaves CanWest, 68
Scott, Sheridan, 122
Scraire, Jean-Claude, 164
Seagram, 5, 59
Serendipity Point Films, 222
SexTV, 227
Shaw, Brad (son of JR), 39, 50
Shaw, Carol (wife of JR), 40, 42
Shaw, Francis (father of JR), 39–40
Shaw, Heather (daughter of JR), 6, 39, 238,
  275, 329
  assigned to chair YTV, 50–51
  changed business focus of, 196

Corus acquisitions and, 200
her experience prior to Corus, 282–83
made chairman at Corus, 198
no aspirations to be CEO by, 282
succession by, 190–91
her view of the future, 284–85
Shaw, James Jr. *See* Shaw, Jim
Shaw, James Sr. *See* Shaw, "JR"
Shaw, Jim (James Jr.). *See also* Shaw
  Communications, 6, 33, 36, 39, 41, 43,
  238, 242, 329
  assigned to run the cable empire, 50
  changed business focus of, 196–97
  description of, 271
  dominance in Vancouver market due to, 272
  his early years as CEO, 271–72
  his experience prior to becoming CEO,
    277–79
  his knowledge of Ted Rogers, 27–28
  management style of, 273–75
  meets with Aspers over WIC, 79
  Moffat negotiations and the, 281–82
  personality of, 195, 272–74, 278–81,
    283–85
  relationship to Ted Rogers of, 278–81
  his thoughts about the future of CHUM,
    230
  succession by, 190–91, 195
  WIC negotiations and, 272, 281
Shaw, "JR" (James Sr.). *See also* Shaw
  Communications, 6, 33, 238, 329
  bids for Maclean Hunter, 35–38
  buys CUC media, 38
  childhood of, 39–40
  his corporate philosophy, 44, 46, 49
  his first Corus AGM, 198
  his first interest in cable television, 40–41
  offers Jim his first promotion, 278
  personality of, 39–40, 42–45, 195
  his pleasure at successes at Corus, 204
  succession to, 285
  woos John Cassaday, 189–91, 194
Shaw, Julie (daughter of JR), 39, 50
Shaw, Les (older brother of JR), 40–43
  JR's relationship to, 190
Shaw Communications, 190, 302
  acquires media assets, 48
  founding of, 41–42
  future of, 329–30
  growth of, 43–51
  moves to Calgary, 49–51
  museum, 51
  its potential partnerships to counter BCE, 326
  is split in two, 196
  succession at, 194
Shawcor, 42
the Shaw family. *See also individual family*

members, 6, 8, 125, 219
the Asper's experience with, 140
attempts to buy WIC, 78–80
barters for part of WIC assets, 135
decides to split Shaw Communications in two, 196
potential bidder for CTV, 116
succession within, 9
western base of, 17
wish to own more specialty channels, 182
Shaw Industries, 42
Shaw Ventures, problems at, 275
Sherman, Bud, 60, 77
the Sifton family newspapers, 139
Sirois, Charles, 105–7, 120, 305, 325
Slaight, Allan, 63–65, 153, 250, 264, 272
the Slaight family, 200
Snyder, Julie, 289
Soros, George, 146
Southam newspaper chain, 1–3, 136, 139, 152
Spar Aerospace, 233
sports, as a business, 184
sports-media convergence models, 179
Sportsnet, 116, 130, 156
bought by Rogers Communications, 183
Standard Broadcasting Co., 64, 153, 200, 272
Star! (channel), 227
StarChoice Communications (satellite service), 46–47, 186, 279
Stavro, Steve, 180
St. Catharines *Standard* (newspaper), 135
the Steinberg family, 217
Steinbrenner, George, 179
Stern, Paul, 108
Stojko, Elvis, 189
Strike, Tom, 145
Strom, Harry, 41
Stursberg, Richard, 132
Suncor, 285
Sun Media (chain of newspapers). *See also individual city papers*, 33, 68, 144, 174, 212
former parent of Canoe, 159–60
for sale by Rogers, 91
Sunshine (film), 222
Superchannel, 197
Surtees, Lawrence, 100
Sussman, Peter, 223
Sward Jim, 173
Sweeney, Bruce, 215
The Sweet Hereafter (film), 222
Switzer, Jay, 229–30
Switzer, Phyllis, 226, 229
Sympatico (internet service provider), 7, 98, 124, 131
expansion plans for, 277

Sympatico-Lycos, 121, 125
synergy, limits to, 201

T3 (New Zealand television), 76
Taillefer, Alexandre, 160
Talbot, Jean-Guy, 163–64
Talk TV, 116
Tanenbaum, Larry, 180
Tartikoff, Brandon, 306, 310–11
Telebec, 104
Tele-Communications Inc. (TCI), 46, 199
Teleglobe, 106–7, 121, 301, 303, 320
its BCE funding cut off, 323
the causes of its demise, 325
gambles taken on, 330
Telemedia (Montreal), 200, 218
telephone businesses, some advantages of, 155–56
Telesystem, 105
Teletoon, 194
television. *See also* cable; pay-for-view; satellite television
specialty channels and, 137
Tellier, Paul, 320
Telus, 8–9, 185, 244
affected by Shaw, 277
early history of, 302
future of, 330
its potential partnership with Shaw, 125
its wish to leave content management to others, 301
Teoli, Ida, 122
the Thall family, 210
This Hour Has 22 Minutes (television series), 224
Thomson, David, 126, 131, 243
Thomson, Kenneth. *See* Lord Thomson (of Fleet), Kenneth
Thomson, Peter, 131
Thomson, Richard (Dick), 24, 48, 243
Thomson, Roy, 126, 243
Thomson Corp., 125–28, 131, 136, 138, 142, 144
business philosophy of, 126
the Thomson family. *See also* Lord Thomson, 7, 20, 121, 125, 307, 326
their interest in sports ownerships, 180
newspapers and, 136, 139
360Networks, 275, 325
TiVo (video recorder), 176
Toronto Blue Jays (baseball team), 7, 175, 232
broadcast rights and, 180–81
business value of, 179–80
Toronto-Dominion Bank, 24, 32, 48, 61
directors of, 155
Toronto International Film Festival, 215
The Toronto Star (newspaper), 92, 207–9

The Toronto Sun (newspaper), 91
Toronto Telegram (newspaper), 318
Torstar, 8, 92–93, 145, 159, 328
    dissention among the owners of, 211
    future of, 326
    history of, 211
    reported to be bidding for CHUM, 225
    its situation after Y2K, 207–10
Tory (political party), 20
Tory, Jim, 20
Tory, John Jr., 15–16, 20, 173, 177, 236–37,
    243–44, 281
    early experience of, 240
    future of, 240–41
Tory, John Sr., 127, 142, 160, 169, 231
Tory Tory Deslauriers & Binnington (law
    firm), 20–21
TQS (television network), 295
Traders (television series), 74
Treehouse TV, 194, 197
Tribune Co. (of Chicago), 5, 145–46, 178, 253
Trout, Kenny, 106
TSN (Total Sports Network), 74, 116,
    180–81, 306
    purchased by CTV, 175
TSNMAX, failure of, 320
TV3 Ireland, 77
TVA (Quebec television network), 82, 158, 295

Unitel, 30–31
Universal (film) Studios, 5
University of Manitoba, 55
University of Toronto, 232
University of Western Ontario, 190–91

Vancouver *Sun* (newspaper), 138
Vaughan, Sarah, 57
Viacom, 5, 182, 329–30
    as Asper role model, 252
Vidéotron, 7, 88, 117, 155
    contest for ownership of, 81–82
    lawsuit over the sale of, 164, 166–67
    Péladeau's assessment of, 163
    reasons for a sale of, 157–58
    Roger's unsuccessful bid for, 232, 236
    uncertain future of, 287–88

Viewer's Choice, 197, 216
Viner, Peter, 262
Viner, Tony, 160, 176, 236–37, 239, 262
Vivendi Universal, 5, 123

Walt Disney Co. *See* Disney
Warner Communications. *See also* AOL-Time
    Warner, 4
Waters, Allan, 63, 211, 224–30, 310
Waters, Jim, 225, 229
Waters, Ron, 225, 229
the Waters family (Toronto), 209, 225
Watson, Colin, 29, 44, 232–33, 239
Watson, Thomas, 99
Weaver, John, 288
Welch, Jack, 311
Wells, Jennifer, 22
WIC, Western International
    Communications, 192, 312
    CanWest acquistions of, 150
    CRTC hearings on sale of, 135
    division of assets of, 117, 140, 262
    the battle over, 196
    sale of, 78–80
    unavailable to Izzy Asper, 75
Wilson, Lynton ("Red"), 109–10
Winnipeg Blue Bombers (football team), 254
Winnipeg Free Press, 68, 136
Winnipeg Goldeyes (baseball team), 253
Wintermans, Jos, 235
Wolch, Hersh, 258
Women's Television Network. *See* WTN
Woodbridge (holding company), 125, 131
World Color Press, 93, 159
World Trade Organization, 9
WTV (Women's Television Network), 130,
    203, 279
Wylie, Andrée, 81

YTV (Youth television), 38, 190–91, 197

Zerbisias, Antonia, 207–8
Zevert, Cecilia, 56
Znaimer, Moses, 43, 226, 306, 310